Merely Being There Is Not Enough
Women's Roles in Autobiographical Texts by Female Beat Writers

Heike Mlakar

DISSERTATION.COM

Boca Raton

Merely Being There Is Not Enough:
Women's Roles in Autobiographical Texts by Female Beat Writers

Copyright © 2007 Heike Mlakar
All rights reserved. No part of this book may be reproduced or transmitted in any form or by any means, electronic or mechanical, including photocopying, recording, or by any information storage and retrieval system, without written permission from the publisher.

Dissertation.com
Boca Raton, Florida
USA • 2008

ISBN-10: 1-59942-656-0
ISBN-13: 978-1-59942-656-3

MERELY BEING THERE IS NOT ENOUGH

MERELY BEING THERE IS NOT ENOUGH

Women's Roles in
Autobiographical Texts by
Female Beat Writers

Heike Mlakar

Contents

1 Introduction	1
2 Historical Background	4
2.1 Economic Boom and Social Repression	4
2.2 Truman, McCarthy, and the Cold War	7
3 Women in the 1950s	10
3.1 Enforcement of Gender Roles	10
3.2 Bad Girls	13
4 Women Beats' Life Writing: The Memoir Genre	17
5 Sexual Identity: Notions of Sexuality in Beat Times	28
6 Diane di Prima's *Memoirs of a Beatnik*	34
6.1 Shocking Details	36
6.1.1 The Aftermath of the Previous Night	36
6.1.2 More than just Friends?	38
6.1.3 City Spring and Country Summer	41
6.1.4 Luke	43
6.2 Real or Made up Orgasms? Reality Versus Fiction	45

6.3 Towards a Categorization of Memoirs	51
6.4 Diane di Prima – A Female Neal Cassady?	59
7 Joyce Johnson and Hettie Jones: Confide in me!	**64**
7.1 Joyce Johnson's *Minor Characters*	65
7.1.1 A Side Glance: Elise Cowen (1933-1962)	67
7.1.2 Distorted Memory and Fluid Time	70
7.1.3 The Kerouac – Johnson Connection	80
7.1.4 The Process of Writing a Memoir	83
7.2 Hettie Jones' *How I Became Hettie Jones*	84
7.2.1 The Joneses' Search for Identity	84
7.2.2 Setting up Scenes	89
7.2.3 Jones' Coming-of-Age	95
7.2.4 Past Places in How I Became Hettie Jones	104
7.3 Reader Identification with *Minor Characters* and *How I Became Hettie Jones*	110
7.4 Categorizing Johnson's and Jones' Memoirs	116

8 Brenda Frazer's *For Love of Ray*	125
8.1 Frazer's Forced Textual Self	128
8.2 The Outlaw Prostitute	132
8.3 Baby Rach	143
8.4 Racism in *For Love of Ray*: Frazer's Kerouacian 'Romantic Primitivism'	148
8.5. Narrative Devices, Language, and Categorization	153
8.6 Drugs, Sex, and the Bremsers' Spiritual Love	162
9 Conclusion	170
Works Cited	I

1 Introduction

Are there not some private matters which should better be left private? And what about the innocent victims who find themselves dragged into somebody else's life writing, being presented in a way that is by no means flattering? "As the power of the voice alone has dwindled, a mass culture has emerged, on a plane unparalleled in history, urging Everywoman and Everyman to tell The Story of My Life," Vivian Gornick criticizes the contemporary boom of self-revelation (Pinsker: 2003: 313). Some critics go as far as to call the explosion of intimate, highly confessional women's memoirs an intellectual fraud, symbolizing our cultural decline, as many female memoirists belong to the "poor me school" of the battered, abused, and infuriated victims. Even feminist critic Carolyn Heilbrun wishes the masses of intimate publications would stop. Fifteen years after her groundbreaking *Writing a Woman's Life* (1988), she avows: "Pushed to the wall with a gun to my head, I would have to admit that I wish the flood [of women's memoirs] would abate. Women, so long silenced, now seemingly speak in chorus" (312).

Yet, does memoir really give narcissism a bad name, as many literary critics suggest? How, then, can I convince the reader of this dissertation that the Beat memoirs of Diane di Prima, Joyce Johnson, Hettie Jones, and Brenda Frazer are not just sentimental, confessional 'memoir bizz'? "The trick is to embrace history, not oneself," Sidonie Smith discloses the secret (1998: 33). Yet, what is wrong with embracing oneself? Diane di Prima, Joyce Johnson, Hettie Jones, and Brenda Frazer are four female Beat writers of America's rigid 1950s and 1960s who manage to skillfully embrace both, their personal stories *and* history. In di Prima's *Memoirs of a Beatnik* (1969), Johnson's *Minor Characters* (1983), Jones' *How I Became Hettie Jones* (1990), and Frazer's *For Love of Ray* (1971), all four women of the Beat Generation present themselves as autonomous female writers who dare to write about themselves in the first place. Yet, alluding to Smith, all four female writers of the Beat Generation also participate in an important form of collective memorialization. Their memoirs provide building blocks to a more fully shared national narrative. The memoir boom we are facing nowadays should therefore not only be understood as a proliferation of self-serving representations of individualistic memory, but as a stimulus to keep cultural memory alive.

While literary criticism has so far generated masses of publications on the works of Jack Kerouac, Allen Ginsberg, William Burroughs, Michael McClure, Gary Snyder, and other male Beats, studies of women Beat writers are infrequent. Until recently, the few bibliographies of works by female Beat writers have been incomplete or inaccurate. Beat scholar Ann Charters was the first critic who included some of the most well-known texts by female Beats into her 1992 Beat anthology *The Portable Beat Reader*. The only two anthologies assembling women Beats' biographies and extracts from their works are Brenda Knight's *Women of the Beat Generation: The Writers, Artists, and Muses at the Heart of a Revolution* (1996) and Richard Peabody's *A Different Beat: Writings by Women of*

Introduction

the Beat Generation (1997). Even though some articles about Beat women have been published during the last years, most of them focus on women's biographical roles as wives and lovers of the male icons. Detailed textual analyses of their works, however, are rare. More recent works of feminist literary criticism include Ronna C. Johnson and Nancy M. Grace's *Girls Who Wore Black: Women Writing the Beat Generation* (2002), and Larissa Bendel's *The Requirements of our Life is the Form of our Art: Autobiographik von Frauen der Beat Generation* (2005).

Acknowledging female Beats is significant for various reasons: Female writers of the Beat Generation have often found themselves positioned as women, but not read as writers. Indeed, the Beat movement of the 1950s is notable for a considerable number of women writers who were part of the scene but have been dismissed or overlooked, even as they wrote both privately and publicly. Even though female Beats produced a larger and more coherent body of work than apparent, many texts are out of print and have disappeared from the literary scene. Prominent examples for this unavailability are Joyce Johnson's *Come and Join the Dance* (1962), or Brenda Frazer's *Troia: Mexican Memoirs* (1969). Other works, like Edie Parker Kerouac's memoir *You'll be Okay* (1986) have not yet been published. Beat's masculinist insistence on individual truth paradoxically included feminism in its reach, inconsistently nurturing female dissidents and artists who were mostly invisible exemplars of the Beat movement. In the literary canon, however, women Beats have been omitted and excluded. By including the many disavowed Beat texts into literary criticism, female Beats and their oeuvre step out of the shadow of male dependency.

This dissertation assesses female Beats' use of the memoir genre to invent themselves as beat subjects, focusing on the way everyday life effected their writing. The paper theorizes the memoirs of di Prima, Johnson, Jones and Frazer, and their contributions to the Beat movement, addressing their refusal to be silenced by assumptions about their fitness as subjects and authors of Beat writing, and about their literary strategies; it explores how all four broke the 'Code of Cool' that confined their sex to the status of the silent bohemian 'chick'. Furthermore, *Memoirs of a Beatnik*, *Minor Characters*, *How I Became Hettie Jones*, and *For Love of Ray* will be analyzed according to various autobiographical subcategories.

To make women Beat writers visible and to categorize their memoirs, this study engages in the paradoxical task of defining a category of Beat writing when, in a fundamental way, it is the nature of Beat writing and its rebellious aesthetics to refuse labels. Many women of the Beat movement engaged in other schools or writing scenes, such as the New York School, Black Mountain, or San Francisco Renaissance, simultaneous to their participation in the Beat movement. Several female Beat writers have rejected the Beat category or resist the label of Beat writers. Their diffidence about a movement whose male adherents often ignored women's writing and excluded them as viable literary innovators on the basis of their sex is understandable. Moreover, it is "uncool" for female Beats to show loyalty: It is quintessentially beat to refuse identification with the movement and generation. Nevertheless, it is the function of literary critics to make sense of literature's evolutions and developments by recognizing and defining schools, movements, and writers' aesthetic tendencies. Particularly concerning the recovery of overlooked and negated writers, grouping the Beat movement's female memoirists respects their visibility as artists and makes their literary expressions legible.

Women Beats unsettle the categories of Beat writing and culture. Thus, a revision and reexamination of Beat history is required to understand the movement's literary expression. The four Beat memoirs at hand portray realities which are not evident in the works of their male contemporaries. They give an enormous insight into American culture of the 1950s and 1960s, a culture which tends to forget about these women, mistakenly painting them as mere helpmates and muses to the men bringing a new literary world into being. Having been dismissed for so long, this work contributes to make the prolific literary productions of female Beat writers visible.

2 Historical Background

2.1 Economic Boom and Social Repression

It is generally accepted that the late 1940s and 1950s were a time of both spreading consumerism as well as social and political repression in the United States. "Rarely has a society experienced such rapid or dramatic change as that which occurred in America after 1945," historian William Chafe points out (1986: 111). Despite illusory assumptions of stability and calm, the 1950s were "more a time of transition than of stolidity" (144). The Cold War, McCarthyism, and an incredible postwar economic boom marked this era which was probably the most oppressive in modern U.S. history. The fifties are characterized by changes from production to consumption, from saving to spending, from city to suburb, from blue to white-collar jobs, and from an adult to a youth culture. Advertising and the mass media, militarism, information technology, automobiles, education, and mobility are appreciated as central elements of American society nowadays. In the 1950s, however, "Radio had been replaced by television with its potential to condition us all into more efficient and insatiable consumers"; and after the Second World War, "seven million men had returned to make babies and build supermarkets, malls and four-lane highways all over the country," as John Tytell points out (1986: 47). In the postwar years, the shift from entrepreneurial to bureaucratic organizations was obvious, and consumerism based on affluence rather than lack had outrun the established social and cultural order. Middle class nuclear families were in confusion about how to raise their children now that consumerism and the decline of conservative religious thoughts were obvious in all parts of society.

During this time, the buzz word for American culture quickly became 'family'. Family life became the ultimate symbol of security for Americans tired of depression and war. During the 1950s, men and women were able to realize their 1940s dreams, namely to live a life of luxury. The first step was to move from the cramped neighborhoods of the city, where families often roomed together in close proximity to each other, into suburbs. Homes were sold to eager buyers with the emphasis that "the most important room in any home is the family room" (Ehrenhalt: 1995: 194). Suburbia soon became a synonym for "togetherness," where men, women, and children shared common experiences and grew together as a secure family. Once achieved, this was important for further attainments of the postwar 1940s dream. For those U.S. citizens who bought houses outside the city centers, namely the white middle class, suburbia offered the economic security of owning a home, the emotional security of marriage, and long-lasting security of raising children. Possessing a house was something this generation's parents were not likely to have had. Suburban life was finally made complete by establishing the breadwinner/homemaker roles for men and women. As the quality of life continued to increase constantly, U.S. culture sent a message to the world: Never before in history had so many people been so affluent.

While some public critics were suspicious of the ongoing changes, most Americans were proud that the U.S. were the most prosperous and successful country in the world, a nation where every citizen could live a wealthy life. This new wealth included having a beautiful house in the city's suburbia, one or two flashy cars, a good white-collar job for the males, and domesticated full-time wives and mothers who sacrificially loved their families. Consumer goods and free time activities played a crucial role. However, being white was the precondition to reach these goals. One report written at the end of the 1950s expressed the fifties-lifestyle this way:

> In one brief 10-year period, America's face was remade. Vast suburban areas sprang up to receive millions of Americans pressing out from the cities. Ribbons of superhighways were laid across the country. A huge expansion of air facilities helped tie the nation into a compact unity [...]. Whole regions changed their complexion. Deserts were turned into boom areas. Power was harnessed on a stupendous scale to ease the burden of work. Nearly 30 million added people were provided for, and on a steadily rising standard of living. A car was put in every garage, two in many. TV sets came into almost every home. There was chicken, packaged and frozen, for every pot, with more to spare. (Satin. *The 1950s:* 16)

Despite the exaggeration of Satin's position, America's affluence was based on the immense increase in economic investments that had been triggered by the Second World War. Statistics from the postwar years on homes, household appliances, automobiles, TV sets, highways, and shopping centers, or on teenage spending on entertainment, cosmetics, and clothes clearly show America's economic growth. The gross national product climbed by 250 percent between 1945 and 1960; between 1947 and 1960, the average real income for American workers increased as much as it had from 1900 to 1950. At the end of the 1950s, 60 percent of all U.S. citizens were house owners, 75 percent of families had a car, 87 percent a TV set, and 75 percent owned a washing machine (cf. Breines 1992: 3f.).

Suburbia was made perfect by new household appliances that facilitated being a housewife. The dependence upon new fridges, washing machines, or stoves, as well as the social pressure to resemble other suburbanites, was a major factor in the increase of American consumerism. Consumerism led to a double effect in the lives of suburbanites: Families spent more time and money shopping, which brought newer and better products on the market. Therefore, larger houses to store the family's purchases in were required. Due to the fact that "Americans became far more mobile than ever before" (Satin: 1960: 19), cars became the most important investment next to homes. With the invention and purchase of new household appliances, the image of the housewife was strongly improved. Washing machines, sewing machines, improved stoves, and refrigerators were considered "labor saving appliances that made it possible for housewives to be leisured and glamorous, not household drudges" (May: 1994: 73). How well a woman kept her household became a criterion for her success as a wife and mother and the "career" it represented.

After World War II, the G.I. bill for veterans made low interest loans possible for millions of soldiers coming home from the frontline. This also promoted the building boom, as the demand for home ownership skyrocketed. The bill also provided educational assistance for college attendance and other trainings. In the postwar years, millions of ex-soldiers went to college (cf. Eisler 1986: 15f.). In 1956, the number of white-collar jobs outnumbered blue-collar jobs for the first time in U.S. history, and America officially became a postindustrial or service economy with a new managerial class. For millions of working class people, however, like the millions of colored people who had migrated from the south to the urban north and west in search of better lives, this shift to a service economy was not yet obvious.[1] Despite the Holocaust, the threat of the atomic bomb, and McCarthyism, it seemed that Americans felt safe and happy. For most of them, Auschwitz and Hiroshima did not foreshadow the end of Western hegemony. However, the war, Holocaust, and the dropping of the atomic bomb on Hiroshima and Nagasaki fostered people's nihilistic and alienated attitudes, which were manifested in existentialism and the Theater of the Absurd. In 1959, Norman Mailer stated that Americans would probably never be able to fully comprehend the "psychic" destruction the concentration camps and atomic bomb had caused, subjecting them to the "intolerable anxiety" that life and death are meaningless. In Mailer's view, the results are cruel: "We might be doomed to die as a cipher in some vast statistical operation in which our teeth would be counted, and our hair would be saved, but our death itself would be unknown, unhonored, and unremarked" (1959: 242).

The fear of the bomb and the anti-communist propaganda made people nervous. School air-raid drills, hiding under the school desk, name tags in case of incineration, and fallout shelters were on the agenda in the 1950s. Sociologist Wini Breines writes about the public controversy to deny a neighbor access into one's shelter or not in case of an emergency. Some American males pointed out that "it would be just to defend their nuclear families with guns, forbidding others to enter, presumably because supplies and/or air were not endless" (1992: 7).

American popular culture after the Second World War was deeply conservative. While Europe and Japan disappeared as enemies, a new hostility towards Russia emerged, and preventing communist activity was the primary national aim during the gloomiest years of the Cold War, from the late 1940s until the mid-1950s. The U.S. government mobilized alliances all over the world to fight both the real and imagined USSR expansionism. At home, politicians competed with each other to show their dedication to the cause of the "Free World". These years are often referred to as "McCarthyism" to describe the political situation of the era, but these containment policies were far more than a phenomenon associated with Joseph McCarthy, Junior Senator from Wisconsin.

The official culture that emerged in the 1950s was deeply conservative, and American politicians powerfully declared that the U.S. would continue their economic boom. America had been the only Western nation whose infrastructure remained intact during the war. Popular culture and the media, in general, consequently emphasized the enemy within, conveying the feeling that people had to watch out. The cultural attack on communism had a deep impact on American society, beyond political

---

[1] For a closer analysis of the working class in this period, see W. Chafe, *The Unfinished Journey*, 111-117, M. Jezer, *The Dark Ages: Life in the United States, 1945-1960*, Chapter 5, and G. Lipsitz, *Class and Culture in Cold War America*.

results. The repression of American culture finally resulted in increasing intolerance and the pressure to conform.

2.2 Truman, McCarthy, and the Cold War

After the dropping of atomic bombs on Hiroshima and Nagasaki, and the construction of an 'iron curtain' between Soviet-controlled Eastern Europe and Western Europe, the Cold War between the capitalist and communist countries escalated. American policy makers agreed that the Soviet Union was frantically trying to support and establish communist regimes all around the world. In a speech to Congress in 1947, President Truman demanded funds to combat communist uprisings in Turkey and Greece, where the communists had triggered a civil war. This announcement became generally known as the 'Truman Doctrine' and can be seen as the beginning of the Cold War. Truman's policy of containment aimed to prevent communist expansion anywhere in the world. The U.S. feared that one state after another would fall under Soviet influence in a domino effect. This led to America's direct participation in conflicts and wars all over the world (cf. Mauk 2002: 162f.). The Truman administration followed a strict anti-Soviet policy, launched the Marshall plan to rebuild a capitalist society in Western Europe, and secured economic and political control in Latin America. As a result, from 1945 until 1973 the income of an average American family was doubled because of the flourishing economy during the time of the Cold War. The Truman Doctrine was the basis for an incredible economic boom that was followed by a huge increase in U.S. productions and exports. In March 1945, Undersecretary of State William C. Clayton had reported to Congress "We've got to export three times as much as we exported just before the war if we want to keep our industry running at somewhere near capacity" (Wittner: 1974: 7). More intense than the Roosevelt administration and the policy of the 'New Deal,' Truman focused on economic expansionism. He was aware that America's affluence was depending on the nation's hegemony in connection with worldwide markets. His policies fostered the capitalist "free enterprise," which stood in stark contrast to the communist "planned economy".

Truman's containment politics became the cornerstone of American foreign policy throughout the Cold War. America's strict anti-Soviet policy, the Marshall Plan to rebuild and stabilize capitalism in western Europe, and investments in Latin America and the Middle East lead to prosperity and increased consumerism. However, the postwar years were also characterized by a return to conservative social and political codes and to strictly enforced gender roles. While America's consumer culture blossomed, political repression rose as "the FBI used illegal wire taps and created the Security Index, a list of millions of citizens who might require detention in the event of a national emergency" (Fordham: 1998: 60). As Arnold A. Offner points out, "the 1950s were mean, Cold War and conformist; the promotion of the American Way [...] was an endless flood of propaganda via black-and-white television and *Time* and *Life* magazines" (2002: 51). The National Security Act of

1947 centralized control over all parts of the military in a new Department of Defense and at the same time created the Central Intelligence Agency (CIA) and the National Security Council (NSC). The Act gave increased power to the President, facilitating invading countries without declaring war. The United States were in a state of permanent military preparedness.

The imminent fear of communism, which finally led to increased political repression during the 1940s and 1950s, is generally known as McCarthyism, the era of Senator Joseph McCarthy. Even though McCarthy gained notoriety at the height of the anti-communist aggression of the time, his career lasted only four years, from 1950 to 1954. The fight against left-wing tendencies began as early as 1946 (or even 1939) and extended into the 1960s. The most spectacular incidents of these years – the Hollywood blacklists[2], the Hiss and Rosenberg cases[3], FBI Director J. Edgar Hoover's anti-communist obsessions – are important to explain the special role of American ideology during that time. McCarthy intended to demonize and scapegoat alleged communists, but also homosexuals. His strategy was effective, and consequently, avowed communists were harassed, insulted, and their careers destroyed. Due to the time's anti-communist and homophobic rhetoric, a whole nation was intimidated and terrorized.

Joseph McCarthy, who was the icon of this era, was a skilled demagogue whose wildly irresponsible affronts against communists brought him the public attention he wanted. Thousands of alleged communists lost their jobs, were put on the FBI watchlist, were denied their passports, and oppressed by sanctions during that period. A whole nation was alert because of concerns about domestic communism. The violation of civil liberties that occurred during McCarthyism could not have been carried out, however, without the support of the nation's political and social elites. Since the end of the war, the U.S. administration saw the Soviet Union as a colonialist enemy committed to an agenda of worldwide expansion which could only be stopped by America. The Greek Civil War in 1947, the communist coup in Czechoslovakia, the blockade of Berlin in 1948, the communist takeover in China, the Soviet detonation of an atomic bomb in 1949, and finally the outbreak of the Korean War in 1950 – these were all indicators that Stalin intended to gradually spread communism all over the world. What changed the fear of communism into a national mania was not the likelihood of an attack, but the anti-communist propaganda of the U.S. government. After all, communist parties were far more successful all over Europe, and here, they were free of accusation and repression. The United States as a nation would probably not have declared the containment of communism the main priority had Washington not led the way. What followed were grave violations of civil liberties that characterized the McCarthy era. Newspapers, magazines, TV, or the radio were the government's allies, largely because they willingly accepted messages that came from Washington (cf. Schrecker 1994: 6f.).

---

[2] In Hollywood, but also in all national TV channels, people who were dismissed by one network or studio were also banned by others. The same was the case for actors.

[3] Alger Hiss, a New Deal government official, was convicted by a Federal Court in 1950 of having given classified documents to the Soviets. Rosenberg was electrocuted in 1953, mainly because he would not confess that he was a Soviet spy. Until today, it remains unclear whether he was a Soviet agent or not.

From one day to the other, Americans who turned against the government were considered criminal. The Anti-Communist Loyalty security program for government employees was initiated in March 1947. FBI Director J. Edgar Hoover and his associates were keenly prosecuting "non-patriots". Since declaring one's political views could arouse suspicion, many people avoided to lay open their attitudes in public. Instead, to the despair of intellectuals, middle-class Americans found it was safer to conform to the norm. Both students and professors tried not to attract attention or trigger any controversies.

In some respects, the rebel subculture of the 1950s, whether beatniks or hipsters, were the symptoms of this cultural crisis in America. McCarthyism successfully destroyed the American Left and traditional working-class communities. Some of the disaffiliated young people, alienated from conservative postwar culture, reacted to consumerism and political repression by enjoying exhibitionist and promiscuous lifestyles. Disillusioned by Tennessee Williams, Elvis Presley, and *I love Lucy*, the Beats escaped into an urban subculture that permitted anonymity and companionship as well as several alternatives to the nuclear family. In his investigations about the 1960s Greenwich Village Beats, sociologist Ned Polsky found out that the typical male beatnik, unlike the ordinary working man/husband/father, avoids work as a "matter of conviction," being convinced that "voluntary poverty is an intellectual gain" (1967: 159). For most Beats, poverty was something completely new, insofar as two thirds of them came from middle or upper class families, as Polski suggests: "They totally 'resign' from society in so far this is possible, not at least from its politics, and reject extreme political sects with no less vigor than they reject major parties" (162). In contrast to the normative white middle class American man, the beatnik sees himself as a victim of society and popular culture, or as John Clellon Holmes puts it: "To be beat is to be at the bottom of your personality, looking up" (1967: 123).

3 Women in the 1950s

3.1 Enforcement of Gender Roles

Until recently, feminist critics and historians, in general, have paid less attention to the years from 1945 to 1960 than they did to the years before and after. Women of the postwar era, it seems, were less fascinating than women workers during World War II, or second wave activists of the late 1960s. Many people still see the postwar years as a romantic, allegedly simpler, happier, and more prosperous time, representing family togetherness, domestic life, and white middle-class housewives who stayed at home to rear children and clean the house. This stereotype has been nurtured until today in reruns of situation comedies, in popular movies, and in TV series.

Many critics of the postwar years have stated that this "placid" time was particularly restricting for women. It is generally agreed that during the 1950s and early 1960s, image makers, politicians, and public figures supported shared dreams of servile wives, making homes for their husbands and children. Men, in contrast, were told to represent strength and masculinity. Freed from depression and war, they were supposed to live out their individualism at women's expense. The new moral codes for women were arbitrary and abnormal, not caused by tradition. While soldiers coming home from the war started new civilian lives under peacetime economy, the media, church, media experts, psychiatrists, and others made clear that real American women were dependent and docile. Being economically, intellectually, or sexually independent was often considered as deviant and abnormal.

In the two decades following the Second World War, women were ordered to accept the cultural emphasis on domesticity and femininity as a woman's proper role. Marriage and motherhood presented the most important aims in the late 1940s and 1950s. Women had to cope with the same oppressive forces inflicted on the society at large. Gender roles became more narrowly defined and, in fact, even more repressive than before and during the war. Michael Davidson points out the nature of this repression with "its subordination of women to housekeeping and childrearing roles, when, only a few years earlier, they had entered the marketplace in unprecedented numbers as part of the war effort" (1989: 176).

In the postwar years, men had returned from overseas to discover their wives, mothers, and sisters had effectively taken over their jobs and thus, their place at home. The message conveyed to women was that "they would best serve the needs of the returning soldiers by becoming their wives and mothers of their children, rather than by competing with them for jobs and training programs" (May: 1994: 60). It is crucial to remember that these men returning from war were determined to lead different lives than their fathers did. For U.S. women, the end of the war brought nearly as many changes as war time itself. As men returned to their jobs, or to college by way of the G.I. Bill, women returned to their domestic roles at home. During the war, the nation had praised female workers for their support, and they were called, in the words of a contemporary, "noble, impeccable, shining" (Banner: 1984: 212). But within half a year, many opinion makers let these women down, criticizing them for having worked during the war and thus having destroyed the American nuclear family. The criticism was devastating and resembled the anti-suffrage rhetoric early in the century. The antifeminist stance of the 1920s and 1930s had been widespread, but the antifeminism of the postwar 1940s and 1950s was much stronger: Women were accused of being bad mothers and wives, because they had left home for work.

Like many other "experts" of the time, Agnes Meyer strongly argued against women in the workforce. She wrote: "What modern woman has to recapture is the wisdom that just being a woman is her central task and greatest honor [...]. Women must boldly announce that no job is more exciting, more necessary, or more rewarding than that of housewife and mother" (May: 1994: 54.) However, despite the containment of women, some were unwilling to quit their working careers to return home. Those who continued their jobs had to face a number of obstacles, like lack of childcare and problems in maintaining a home, children, and a husband. These were all responsibilities of a woman, even if she worked the same number of hours as her husband. The media was influential to propagate women's return to their suburban homes until "their primary childrearing duties were over" (56).

After the war, the phrase 'Nuclear Family' turned up as one of the keywords of the time. In U.S. popular culture, the new focus on normative gender roles could be seen in all parts of daily life. In newspapers and magazines, on the radio and billboards, *Rosie the Riveter*[4] was replaced by the homemaker as the national feminine model. Most fictional texts in women's magazines were about heroic housewives, whereas non-fiction articles almost exclusively dealt with housework, preparing meals, and child care. Emphasizing the general position that women are most successful as beautiful wives or sirens, female film stars of the 1950s were either sweet, innocent, and characterless, like Doris Day, or, like Marilyn Monroe, innocent and sexually aggressive. By the mid-1950s, television was beginning to indoctrinate innumerous American homes. On TV, women were either presented as sex objects or happy housewives. The focus on containment and domesticity was also shown in popular shows like *I love Lucy* and *Father knows best* (cf. Harvey 1993: 89ff.). Fashion conveyed the same female images. During the war, women's dress style was masculine: skirts were narrow; suits were popular; padded shoulders were in vogue. In 1947, however, French designer Christian Dior presented the "new look" on the catwalks, and instead of masculinity, femininity was now the buzzword. His models wore long, full skirts and had wasp waists. In the early 1950s, the new "baby doll" look became the ideal for many women. Not since the Victorian era had women's fashion been so confining.

---

[4] Rosie the Riveter is a fictional character who was created in order to encourage women to join the workforce when factories urgently needed workers during World War II. Before, women mostly fulfilled roles as housewives or held low paid jobs. When many U.S. men went off to war, they left jobs in production, factories, and many other positions that needed to be filled. Women often seized the opportunity to gain independence and took over men's jobs.

Public opinion makers named marriage and having a secure family life as the major aims for young people in the 1950s. Even many college-educated women left their colleges to found a family. Betty Friedan estimates that by the mid-1950s, 60 percent of female undergraduates were dropping out of college to marry. Women were influenced by movies, TV, and popular magazines, which glorified romantic love and marriage. For many young people, early marriage meant escaping from restraints imposed on them by parents and the establishment (cf. Friedan 1970: 45f.).

The wish to marry and create a stable life around a romanticized image of family life was reinforced by other factors. The fear that the birth of fewer children would weaken the U.S. prompted scientists to propagate large families. The superficially tranquil postwar decade had its own tensions and pressures. The United States were involved in a number of worldwide wars and aimed to defeat communism. Recurring cycles of inflation and depression cast a shadow over the new wealth. Home was therefore welcome as a safe refuge.

Despite the rising marriage numbers, the 1950s were a time of sexual repression, and any public talk about sex was taboo. John Tytell points out that this was an era "when masturbation was seen as a cause of insanity and premarital sex was immoral, when half of American women were married by the age of nineteen, oral sex was considered sheer perversion, and adultery and homosexuality were regarded as criminal acts" (1999: 53). In the conservative and sinister 1950s, there were, however, thousands of teenagers who turned against these sexual restrictions. Yet, even males could not publicly write about sexual matters without being persecuted. In those years, novels by Henry Miller or the uncensored *Lady Chatterley's Lover* had to be smuggled into the country illegally. Even though Jack Kerouac had tried to publish *On the Road* in 1950, no editor had dared to publish the work until 1957.

Sex other than marital was shameful. Angrily, many women remember the stiff sexual moral of the 1950s. Teenage girls were in constant fear of "going all the way," or worse, appearing to have, as public opinion was obsessed with female virginity until marriage. Nowadays, critics see a connection between the 1950s fear of the atomic bomb and the anxiety about sexual chaos. Together with female sexuality and communism, homosexuality also posed a threat to U.S. society, leading to a policy of containment for all three scares. Sexual deviation was presented as a major threat for the nuclear family. Due to the fact that women had to conform to society, career choices were limited. Elaine Tyler May, who analyzed U.S. family life during the Cold War, links the containment of communism to the containment of women in the postwar domestic ideal. In the middle of Cold War anxiety, "the family seemed to offer a psychological fortress" (1988: 113) against both internal and external dangers.

Yet, not every American woman adapted herself to the prescribed gender roles of the time. In the years following the war, many American women were not white, middle class, married, and suburban as illustrated in the media; and many white, middle class, married females were neither wholly domesticated nor servile. In the postwar years, not every woman embraced the prevalent cultural focus on family life, femininity, marriage, and motherhood as her primary tasks. As a reaction to the predominant conservative views, a barely visible cultural subculture formed by some white, middle-class women emerged in American cities. Dismissing the dominant mindsets, they chose to imitate male versions showing their discontent.

3.2 Bad Girls

Even though many 1950s women conformed to the "placid 1950s"[5], not all fit the prevailing female stereotype. In 1956, Paul Goodman published *Growing Up Absurd: The Problems of Youth in the Organized Society*, a study on youth culture in the 1950s. At the beginning of his work, he depicts the difficulties teenagers have to face: "We see groups of boys and young men disaffected from the dominant society. The young men are angry and Beat. The boys are Juvenile Delinquents" (1960: 11). To be angry, a beatnik, and a juvenile delinquent were major social categorizations after the emergence of the new hipster subculture. Goodman states that mostly young males suffer from disaffection and disillusionment. Youth problems "belong primarily, in our society, to the boys: how to be useful and make something of oneself. A girl does not have to, she is not expected to 'make something' of herself". Moreover, "her career does not have to be self-justifying, for she will have children, which is absolutely self-justifying, like any other natural or creative act […] our 'youth troubles' are boys' troubles" (13). "Deviants" like beatniks, hipsters, juvenile delinquents, homosexuals, and even communists were seldom female according to public opinion: Females did not necessarily have to make something of them due to the fact that they would soon be good mothers and wives.

Some young women in the 1950s, however, embraced a bohemian lifestyle and found inspiration by provoking sexual mores. It could be argued that these maladjusted women laid the groundwork for the women's liberation movement of the late 1960s and 1970s. Often, they were protofeminists or forerunners of the social movements of the 1960s, positioning themselves as civil rights workers, campus activists, and women's rights feminists.

Due to the fact that the Beat subculture was predominantly male, mostly working class, and overly masculine, sexist, and chauvinist, the process of many Beat girls' identification was very complex. White, mostly middle-class girls who rejected dominant values of the time had few options, and therefore often copied and adapted typically male behavior patterns of revolt and discontent (cf. Breines 1992: 45ff.). Many young girls were attracted to "cool" beatniks and movie stars like James Dean and Marlon Brando in roles of alienation and disrespect for the establishment. Some of them tried to avoid what was expected of them – a life in a city's suburb as a wife and mother – and rejecting these life plans was often connected with an ambivalent attitude about their mothers. Very often, the life plan for young women was unacceptable for them, because societal expectations and

---

5 Joseph Satin titled his 1960 book *The 1950s: America's Placid Decade*. He alludes to the general perception of the 1950s as a time of harmony, family togetherness, and wealth.

those of their parents did not match with their own aspirations. Together with their male counterparts, they rebelled against the bourgeois mindset which included narrow domestic gender expectations. Girls were yearning to be as free as male Beats, leaving behind domestic strains and the women they were supposed to become. Frequently, they were craving to be taken seriously or give meaning to their lives, and 'authentic', 'genuine', and 'real' were prevalent buzz words. However, the 1950s did not offer them a sense of being real. For them, being patronized, virginal, and female did not match with the desire to be significant. When works like *On the Road* were published, many girls were extremely influenced by Kerouac's road trips and wished for similar adventures. Jan Clausen, for example, grew up in Southern California. Aged 16, she read *On the Road* for the first time and immediately realized the "moral and intellectual intensity" of the work:

> Emerging from a childhood of many advantages, I was bitter, suddenly, against my parents, on account of certain experiences withheld from me: Smith Act trials overhanging my formative years; alcohol binges; steamy dramas of marital infidelity; the benny-popping, reefer puffing role models they might have been, tearing back and forth across the continent with infant me asleep in the back seat [...]. My background had been deficient. (Breines. "The Other Fifties": 391)

Yearning to copy Beat men's lifestyles, many young female Beats moved to New York City to indulge in jazz, poetry, shared apartments, and countless afternoon café sessions, because only in Greenwich Village or, to a lesser extent, in North Beach/San Francisco, one could be a real Beat. Ronald Sukenick describes the young girls in the Village as a "grungy purity [...] in its deliberate isolation from the world of Uptown". These female beatniks were "confronted with the promised land of previously repressed impulses, a risky new underground landscape to explore consisting of everything deemed unreal by the dominant culture, which amounts to almost everything" (Breines: 1994: 393).

When girls came to the Village from the Upper West Side, like Joyce Johnson, or from Long Island, like Hettie Jones, they often started to wear typical Beat downtown outfits: black tights from Goldin Dance Supply on Eighth Street, belts with brass spiral fasteners, sandals that laced up the ankle, and dangling beaten-copper earrings. To understand the radical nature of such an outfit, one must remember that the dress code for working women required nylons and high-necked dresses, even in summer. Lionel Trilling's wife Diana did not like the look of the Beat girls – "So many blackest black stockings," she sniffed after seeing them at a 1959 Columbia reading by Allen Ginsberg, Gregory Corso, and Peter Orlovsky (Jones: 1997: 129). In a 1999 interview, Hettie Jones complains about the discomfort of traditional 1950s women's clothes. Taking off one's girdle was a radical move, "without feeling blistered all the time" (Grace: 2004: 160). Wearing pants was also unusual for women. At Jones' College in the fifties, young women had to wear garage mechanic uniforms, "monkey suits," in order to climb all the ladders on the stage. Every decent woman was supposed to wear high heels to work. When Jones first came to New York City, she threw them in the sewer. Instead of high heels, she was wearing weird, red old lady's shoes she got in the orthopedic shoe store. Of the shoes, Jones says: "They were weird! But they were comfortable". Furthermore she adds, "to stop carrying that little pocket book – the kind that came back into style not too long ago" was a radical move: "But instead to wear a shoulder bag and to have your hands free. And what you needed was a big bag anyway if you weren't going to go home at night, you know!" (161).

In general, 1950s' "bad girls" wore black – black leather jackets, boots, and stockings. In comparison to innocent suburban teens, they were represented as darker. For the adult culture of the time, the dualism of light and dark played a crucial role. Maladjusted white teens chose the threatening darkness including African American jazz and blues, while the "good," approved teen culture was light and white. It was a white time in the U.S.: Success was represented in white terms on TV, in advertisements, and other forms of popular culture. Therefore, it is not surprising that beatniks, hipsters, and other outcasts of society felt "black" and were imagined to be dark. Due to the fact that the rest of the society was – superficially – white, the Beats wore black.[6] Hipsters wore black turtleneck shirts, black stockings, or black sunglasses. "I dumped out my inheritance of pastel colors and princes and collected a new bag of black sweaters, jeans, psychopaths and beat fantasy," Sheila Rowbotham recalls (Breines: 1994: 397). Another adolescent says, "I just wanted to be a beatnik. I quit wearing pink and orange and always wore darker colors. I was one of the first people in Charleston to get dark stockings. I was in a shop once and a girl goes, 'Look, Mommy, that lady has white arms with black legs'" (397). Erasing one's difference, assimilating, was a sign of Americanness, and difference was supposed to be invisible in postwar America. The U.S. presented in popular movies, television, and magazines were white. Black people were practically invisible in the mass media, and if they appeared, their portrayal was often racist. Wearing dark or having dark skin signified difference in postwar society. It also meant being unable to attain prevailing values and standards of attractiveness, being an outsider. The good taste and decorum excluded those who did not conform, as they threatened middle-class orderliness.

For WASPs, even Jews were considered dark. "As an outsider Jew I could have tried for white, aspired to the liberal intellectual, potentially conservative Western tradition. But I never was drawn to that history, and with so little specific to call my own I felt free to choose," Hettie Jones explains (1997: 14). She tells how black and white were blurring divisions for her, because Jews were different. Not feeling American, her outsider status and her love of music, especially jazz, indicated that she had more in common with African American people than with mainstream Americans. Combinations of working-class, lower-middle-class, or immigrant backgrounds, as well as lesbianism cast some women aside to societal margins and bohemia. Being attracted to blackness/darkness – symbolized for many girls by beatnik clothes, romances with male outcasts, the love of rock'n'roll, and interest in black culture – many teenage girls were pulled away from their families.

---

[6] In 2002, Ronna C. Johnson and Nancy M. Grace published *Girls who Wore Black*, a collection of scholarly essays on several women writers of the Beat Generation. See Johnson, Ronna C. and Nancy M. Grace (2002). *Girls who Wore Black. Women Writing the Beat Generation*. New Brunswick: Rutgers.

Many of these women became writers and artists, but being excluded from U.S. society, they were not even always welcome among their male counterparts. Even tough they shared the same lifestyle and often started relationships with other hipsters, female bohemians mostly stayed among themselves in expressing their artistic impulses. Women copied the male 'Rule of Cool,' but the Beat "boy gang" – termed by Ginsberg – did not offer an enlightened or empowering vision of women. Seen from this perspective, female Beats did not only have to counter the prevailing conservative gender roles imposed on them by dominant culture, but by joining male Beats, they were often also confronted with sexist attitudes. Many works by male Beats clearly show that they "relegated women to the role of sexual surrogate, muse or mum; it did not raise them to a position of artistic equality" (Davidson: 1989: 175). At the same time, women of the Beat Generation had to define themselves within this available network, because no other social security was available for them. These bohemian women had no "supportive environment of either an underground salon network or a feminist movement" (174). Contrary to that, male Beats were masters of bonding, being involved in homosocialities of male friendship and love, while females had to face the situation that they were excluded from the "Beat Brotherhood". It is crucial to point out that the Beat subcultural revolt was primarily based on men, beginning with small alternative cliques up to the Beat Generation's melting with the Hippie Movement in the late 1960s. Cultural critics agree that Beats' male-centeredness was a successful strategy to rebel against the pressures of conventional family life and consumer culture. Ginsberg's, Kerouac's, Burroughs', Snyder's, or Holmes' lives and writing began to focus not only on a counterculture promising a non-mainstream future, but a counterculture based on the ideal of the "boy gang". Both the U.S. media and male Beats presented female Beats in a pejorative way. In his study about how the media perceived the Beats in the 1950s and 1960s, Steven Watson found out that the general impression was that the male Beats' "favourite activities were smoking reefers, playing bongo drums, and chanting poetry with a cool jazz backup," while the female Beats' "favourite activities were drinking espresso, attending poetry readings, and dating black jazz musicians" (1998: 258-259). Mirroring the prevailing clichés of the time, the media saw Beat men as active while women mostly observed the scene and were given attention only in relation to men.

Yet, women were not passive or totally absent: They were there at a crucial moment in history, observing the subcultural scene as wives, lovers, friends, financial supporters, and drinking mates. What is more, many of them wrote down their experiences, depicting the Beat Generation from an extraordinary, female perspective. Particularly the numerous autobiographical texts written by female Beats are important social documents of the time, because women were often "the most observant and sober witnesses" (Knight: 1996: xi). The following chapter aims to analyze the strongest autobiographical subgenre used by female Beats – the memoir form.

4   Women Beats' Life Writing: The Memoir Genre

> [...] the memoir, which has become an accepted, high genre, is one of immense possibilities, the way you work with cross-genres and documentation. [...] And then, memoir can be so imaginative. There are so many of these smarmy memoirs, but writing a memoir isn't therapy. Yes, it does help you to tell these stories, but it's not a self-help reality. So that should be distinguished. (Anne Waldman in Grace. *Breaking the Rule of Cool:* 269)
>
> Well, life is made up of stories. And it's all autobiographical narrative. In the last few years, I've been trying to figure out where the narrative is going.
> (Joanne Kyger in Grace. *Breaking the Rule of Cool:* 148)

While male Beat authors have continually been in control of the public's interest and readership, most discussions of these icons – Kerouac, Ginsberg, and Burroughs – leave out a number of female contemporaries who were just as much part of the Beat literary movement as their male counterparts. Yet, they have not been absent. Even though resisting categorization, the rather small group of female Beat authors can be subdivided into three major groups. First generation Beat writers – male and female – were born in the 1910s and 1920s. Among the first women Beats are Madeline Gleason (1903-1979), Helen Adam (1909-1992), Sheri Martinelli (1918-1996), ruth weiss (1928-), Carolyn Cassady (1923-), and Carol Bergé (1928-). These writers were contemporaries with Kerouac (1922-1969), Ginsberg (1926-1997), and Burroughs (1914-1997). The largest group, however, occurred in the movement's second generation. The female writers, born in the 1930s, were mostly influenced by seminal works of Kerouac, Ginsberg, and Burroughs. The male writers of this second generation were Philip Whalen (1923-2003), Lew Welch (1926-1971), Ted Joans (1928-2003), Gary Snyder (1930-), Gregory Corso (1930-2000), Michael McClure (1932-), and LeRoi Jones/Amiri Baraka (1934-). The women writers, a decade or more younger than the first generation Beats, often had to face male prejudice against their capacities as writers. Female writers of the second generation include Joanna McClure (1930-), Lenore Kandel (1932-), Elise Cowen (1933-1962), Diane di Prima (1934-), Hettie Jones (1934-), Joanne Kyger (1934-), Joyce Johnson (1935-), Ann Charters (1935-), and Brenda Frazer/Bonnie Bremser (1939-). This generation also includes Beat scholar Ann Charters, who wrote important literary histories – notably her groundbreaking 1973 biography of Kerouac, with which she began building a canon of Beat writing. She was the first to institutionalize women writers in the Beat canon when she edited *The Beats: Literary Bohemians in Postwar America* (1983), where she included seven women. The work of second generation female Beats is marked by a radical critique of traditional literary genres and forms that have been based on women's subordination to men. The transition from Beat to the hippie counterculture in the 1960s was encompassed by Beat's second and third generation. While the civil rights movement had a direct influence on counterculture activism, the Beats provided the hippie community with a dissenting style of conduct. The third generation of women Beats was born during World War II, endured the fifties, and came of age in the sixties. While the second generation of women Beats anticipated the second wave women's movement of the late

1960s and early 1970s, the third generation clarifies the Beat movement's continuity with the hippie counterculture and progressive activist movements. In contrast to first and second generation Beats, they are a gender-mixed group including Ed Sanders (1939-), Bob Dylan (1941-), Lou Reed (1944-), Pattie Smith (1946-), Lester Bangs (1948-1982), or Laurie Anderson (1950-). The most famous female third generation Beat writers are Janine Pommy Vega (1942-) and Anne Waldman (1945-), who identified with sixties and seventies countercultures. Both male and female artists supported a spiritual and political common cause.

In the literary canon, women Beats have been omitted and excluded. Bringing their writing to the surface is significant for several reasons: On the one hand, female Beat writers have written themselves into postwar literature by providing the public with a number of memoirs, poems, and other texts, some of which are early protofeminist documents giving insight into a countercultural revolution. On the other hand, female Beat authors have produced a huge body of works, which is currently not available, because many texts are out of print or unavailable. Out of print, for example, are Brenda Frazer's *Troia: Mexican Memoirs* (1969) and the British version *For Love of Ray* (1971), Joyce Johnson's *Come and Join the Dance* (1962), Lenore Kandel's *The Love Book* (1966), Janine Pommy Vega's *Poems to Fernando* (1968), and ruth weiss' *DESERT JOURNAL* (1977). Due to the fact that many texts have vanished from the market, some of these authors have disappeared with their oeuvre. Other works, like Elise Cowen's surviving poems, have not yet been published, because the owner of her private collection is still unknown. After her suicide, Cowen's parents had destroyed most of her poems. In other cases, female Beat authors often never got the chance to publish their works, such as Hettie Jones' early poetry. Another prominent victim of suppressed female Beat writing is Kerouac's ex-wife Edie Parker Kerouac, who wrote a memoir which has been totally overlooked by literary critics. Excerpts from her memoir *You'll Be Okay* (1987) have been published in Arthur and Kid Knight's *Kerouac and the Beats: A Primary Sourcebook*, and in Richard Peabody's *A Different Beat: Writings by Women of the Beat Generation*, but the text as a whole is still unpublished.[7] Another difficulty to track down female Beat literature is that some works are unrecoverable, because they were printed by small presses which got lost. Literary critics are therefore challenged to locate dispersed, uncollected, and often even unpublished texts. Literature by female Beats seems to present itself as incoherent and intransparent, but at a closer look, female Beat writing creates a meaningful whole. A serious discussion about the Beat canon is therefore only possible when including the many unacknowledged texts by women Beats.

Female Beat artists were a marginalized group within an already marginalized bohemia. Generally, these disillusioned, furious, versatile, and non-conformist women were quite similar to their male

---

[7] According to WorldCat, the world's largest bibliographic database, only five libraries worldwide own works written by Edie Kerouac Parker. The library which owns the manuscript of her unpublished memoir *You'll Be Okay* is Wilson Library/University of North Carolina. See Parker Kerouac, Edie (1987). *You'll Be Okay* [holograph manuscript]. Draft of Parker's unpublished memoirs. Edie Parker-Henri Cru Papers, Beat Literature Collection. Wilson Library, Rare Book Collections, CB#3930, University of North Carolina at Chapel Hill.

counterparts, but such nonconformity was particularly difficult for females. To be unmarried, an artist, to raise biracial children, and to embrace a male version of discontent was doubly shocking for a woman, as social disrespect was enormous. Author Gregory Corso hits the point: "In the fifties if you were male you could be a rebel, but if you were female your families had you locked up. There were cases, I knew them. Someday someone will write about them" (Peabody: 1997: 46). Many young female authors ignored the established expectations to find a suitable husband and create a homestead. Coming from upper middle-class families quite often, they fled their parents' homes in the country or suburbs to attend colleges in the cities and live in their own apartment or one-room 'pads'. Joan Vollmer, wife of William Burroughs, left her home in Albany, New York, and the safe, dull, and uninspiring life she had led, for Barnard College. Edie Parker, Kerouac's first wife, left her hometown Grosse Pointe to find new challenges at Columbia University. Joyce Johnson, Kerouac's girlfriend, escaped Barnard College, because she felt she was merely living out her mother's dreams (cf. Peabody 1997: xiiif.). In *Minor Characters*, Joyce Johnson writes about the adventurous new hopes and expectations once they broke out of their family boredom:

> Naturally, we fell in love with men who were rebels. We fell very quickly, believing they would take us along on their journeys and adventures. We did not expect to be rebels all by ourselves; we did not count on loneliness. Once we had found our male counterparts, we had too much blind faith to challenge the old male/female rules. We were very strong and we were in over our heads. But we knew we had done something brave, practically historic. We were the first ones who had dared to leave home. (Johnson. *Minor Characters*: 17)

Their new unrestrained lifestyle and the seductions of city life often led to deeper troubles: Abortions, drug addictions, humiliations, and poverty were common experiences among Beat women. Finding themselves entrapped in misery and financial plight, they were often forced into typically 'square'[8], conservative role models, becoming submissive wives, muses, cleaning and laundry women for the male rebel artists who were breaking ground for a new countercultural movement.

Due to the fact that the Beat Generation emerged as a reaction to the predominant U.S. culture of the 1950s, it is crucial to consider the moral, political, and historical changes of the time. Most female Beat writers affiliated themselves to the males to protest against the restrictive gender roles of the 1950s. Being "Beat" was far more promising than getting new household appliances. Looking forward to fighting alongside the males, women soon had to realize that they were excluded from Beat experience. Even within the literary circle, most women did not have literary success and remained unrecognized. Often, they were pushed back into the despised roles of being wives and mothers, because the morale of the fifties could not be totally neglected. Decades before, women's networking

---

[8] A 'square' is a conformist, an organized person, or a solid citizen. The term has been used from the 1940s onward by the emerging non-conformist subculture. According to Beat writer Gregory Corso, "A square is some guy who forces himself arbitrarily into a square auto-life mold" (Charters: 1992: 184).

was an important means for artistic gratification, as salons offered some space for creative impulses, but in the 1950s, there were only few options for women artists to interconnect.

Beat men mostly did not recognize women's artistic achievements. Accusing female Beats that they were not as talented as men, Allen Ginsberg shocked many critics by saying that he is not to blame for "the lack of outstanding genius in the women we knew" (Peabody: 1997: 1). The tacit young women in black were nearly invisible, a fact which is also demonstrated by Lucien Carr's pejorative nicknames for poet Elise Cowen, giving her names like "Elipse"[9] or "Eclipse" (Johnson: 1999: 130). Donald Allen's *New American Poetry* (1960), which had an immense impact on the literary criticism of the time, highlights many common aspects between Black Mountain, San Francisco Renaissance, Beat, and The New York School. Yet, among all poets, he only mentions four women poets who are noteworthy for him: Helen Adam, Madeline Gleason, Barbara Guest, and Denise Levertov. Gleason (1903-1979) and Adam (1909-1992), who totally manipulated the traditional ballad form, are Beat writing's intellectual predecessors. Both are founding mothers of the San Francisco Renaissance and wrote during the movement's so-called first generation. Other remarkable female poets, like ruth weiss, however, have been totally disregarded.

For decades, critics have neglected the literary potential of female Beat authors, particularly the women poets who were masters of radical experimentation and innovation. Many works are shockingly confessional and intimate. Similar to poets like John Berryman, Robert Lowell, or Anne Sexton, they depict unflattering accounts of illness, madness and suicide, sexual orgies, abortions, homelessness, alcoholism, and depression. What is also typical for female Beat writings is worrying about race, gender, and the establishment which is pervaded by sexism and oppression of women. Traditional myths about female silence are rewritten, resisting their objectification as mere "chicks" or "ellipses". By building up a considerable and multifaceted body of works, female Beats finally become visible by bringing various Beat perspectives to the surface.

Even though female Beats wrote poetry, prose texts, fictional and non-fictional accounts, poet Ann Waldman calls the memoir the strongest literary genre by female Beat authors (cf. Knight 1996: xi). Their memoirs are so numerous that they can clearly be considered a subgenre of Beat literature. Even though many authors wrote fictional prose and poems in the 1950s, 1960s, and 1970s, they have turned to autobiographical forms during the last twenty-five years. The first published memoirs of women Beats are Diane di Prima's *Memoirs of a Beatnik* (1969) and Brenda Frazer's *Troia: Mexican Memoirs* (1969). Joyce Johnson's *Minor Characters*, whose first edition is subtitled *The Romantic Odyssey of a Woman in the Beat Generation*, followed in 1983. Carolyn Cassady, Neal Cassady's wife and Jack Kerouac's lover, wrote a memoir about her time with Cassady, Kerouac, and Ginsberg, called

---

[9] In collaboration with Lucien Carr, Allen Ginsberg wrote a note on Elise Cowen in *City Lights Journal* two years after her suicide. Their voices alternate from line to line: "How old was dear old Elipse when she went her merry/ way? I wish people I didn't like did that instead/ of her. I feel more loyalty than love for Elipse./ The poems, they're awkward. But it's a special kind/of awkward that comes when someone is direct and/ (if there is an honest) honest. And the beauty of/the written lines that she could see and I could/see, but neither of us could see in her" (Johnson: 1999: 259).

Off the Road: My Years with Cassady, Kerouac, and Ginsberg (1990); in the same year, Hettie Jones wrote *How I Became Hettie Jones*. Edie Parker Kerouac described her times with Kerouac in yet unpublished memoirs; Kerouac's second wife, Joan Haverty, called her memoir *Nobody's Wife* (2001).

During the last twenty years, making the private public has been a strong tendency in literary publishing. The public's probing curiosity in biographies and autobiographies is responsible for having given female Beat writers the literary discourse they have deserved for so long. Women Beats have altered the memoir genre and Beat discourse by inserting their own female subjectivity. Obviously, writing a memoir is popular among female Beats because the borders of the genre are not that strictly defined – in comparison to the classical autobiography. Through interspersing letters, photos, or diary entries centering on their dissatisfaction, Beat literature, in general, is reconstructed in the long run. In their memoirs, Beat women take over positions as both subjects and objects. As memoirists, their narrative discourse offers women the function as Beat subjects, but they are still colonized objects when examining the general norms of the Beat Generation. All memoirs of women Beats have in common that they are bringing back domestic discourses into Beat literature which have been totally refused by men. In *How I Became Hettie Jones*, Jones, for example, names her chapters after the apartments she and her family occupied. Home, meaning motherhood and children, plays a crucial role in most autobiographical texts by females, while Kerouac and others just romanticized and misinterpreted the concept of home. For him, family represented the short-lived moments of connection and tenderness, while family for female Beats is about concrete necessities and practical meanings. Brenda Frazer's *Troia: Mexican Memoirs/For Love of Ray* centers around caring for her husband and child; even Diane di Prima, who detests domesticity and a conventional lifestyle, employs a domestic discourse in *Memoirs of a Beatnik:* She describes her hipster pads in great detail. Even though female Beats rebelled against the establishment, all of these memoirs show that they were not totally anti-domestic, as their writing focuses on everyday details, the household, family, and child care. Paradoxically, their literature derives from the domestic, and does not only resist it.

By using the memoir genre to transform literary narratives of the Beat Generation, women Beats have told subjective tales of their own. They might have chosen this particular genre in order to tell stories which cannot be replaced or written by fictional prose narratives of male Beats, because the autobiographical genre in its pure form has never been used by male Beat writers. The memoir form is also an option to escape censorship. It enables women to write stories outside the male canon of Beat literature, without necessarily conforming to norms created by their male counterparts.

During the last centuries, autobiographies have been written in great numbers, but only recently, literary critics have tried to apply a feminist approach to the genre. Seen from a historical perspective, most autobiographies are stories about the lives of "great men". Classical autobiographies almost exclusively focused on public male figures and were always written by men. Up to the 1970s, literary criticism has primarily treated men's life writings, and little work was done on theorizing women's autobiographies. In Estelle Jelinek's words, most scholars have seen women's lives as too "insignificant" (1980: 4) to analyze them in more detail. However, autobiographical writing by women has been rediscovered especially during the last twenty-five years. Feminist critics like Susan Stanford Friedman, Domna C. Stanton, Rita Felski, Shari Benstock, Estelle Jelinek, or Sidonie Smith were successful in bringing autobiographical women's writing from the shadow into the light.

Literary critics agree that autobiography as a form was invented by Saint Augustine at the end of the fourth century. In his *Confessiones,* self-analysis is valued not for its own sake, but it is important to show the fallibility of humanity. Through his work, he tries to fortify his ideas that divine knowledge is the supreme authority and out of the individual's grasp. The first modern example of autobiography as a declaration of individualism and self-knowledge, however, is *Confessions* written by Jean Jacques Rousseau in the 1760s. This work brought the breakthrough in establishing autobiography as a modern genre. Being among the first authors who write primarily about themselves, he states: "My purpose is to display to my kind a portrait in every way true to nature, and the man I shall portray will be myself" (1953: 13). Protestantism played a crucial role to open the ways for the self-consciousness necessary for writing an autobiography. The prospering of Pietism in Germany and Puritanism in England during the seventeenth century was responsible for the fact that more and more people were now interested in self-scrutiny and spiritual introspection. Following that development, diaries became a new literary genre: Intimate thoughts or details from everyday life were at the center of autobiographical writings and examined for their moral and spiritual meaning (cf. Felski 1989: 87f.).

Literary critics first started to analyze autobiographies as a distinct genre in the 1930s. Yet, at that time, the textual content of the work and moral considerations about its author were in the foreground. Numerous autobiographical works were published in the post-World War I period, but with the exception of Gertrude Stein's *Autobiography of Alice B. Toklas* (1933), female writers have been mostly ignored. Influenced by second wave feminism starting during the early 1960s, feminist literary criticism in general has gained influence.

Literary critics assume that the interest in autobiographical writing has increased since the 1970s because of the fact that biographical writing started to decline in the decades before. Women have written autobiographies for many centuries. But why, then, did feminist autobiographical criticism start barely 25 years ago?

Women's autobiographical writing was frowned upon and seldom taken seriously as a distinct field of study before the end of the 1970s. Their works were deemed too simple, uninteresting, and superficial for literary criticism, academic dissertations, or the literary canon. Women's autobiographies were generally devalued as too unreliable for a critical examination, since their life stories were presented as inaccurate and untruthful in the majority of cases. Up to Estelle Jelinek's groundbreaking *Women's Autobiography* (1980), only few critics – most importantly Georg Misch, Georges Gusdorf, or William Spengemann – had immersed themselves in autobiographical criticism, but they, once more, focused on the lives of great male heroes in history. They analyzed the works of Augustine, Rousseau,

Franklin, Goethe, Carlyle, or Henry Adams, whose successful careers secured their position as cultural capital.[10]

Both within and outside the academic discourse, the status of autobiographical writing has changed drastically since the beginning of the 1980s. In the 21st century, women's autobiography has become a favored study field to debate feminist, postcolonial, and postmodern issues. Autobiography as a genre has also become significant in structuralist and poststructuralist theories, because the blurring between truth and fiction is particularly obvious in life writing. Autobiographical writing challenged the idea about whether somebody's life could be represented objectively or not. Furthermore, critics were interested in how the force of language would prevent attempts of reference and telling the truth. Similarly to second wave feminism, which was helpful to change and revolutionize literary and social theories, women's autobiographical criticism has been influential in rethinking women's issues. Many female autobiographers have used the genre to write themselves into history and into societal significance. Through the impact of women's autobiographical criticism, previously unrecognized subjects were made visible.

Several aspects have been crucial to trigger academic interest in women's autobiography, which has finally led to an enormous selling boom. First, many universities have developed specific gender or ethnic studies programs, which increased the demand for texts that refer to various experiences and topics. Second, many publishing companies have realized that they can make huge profits by publishing women's intimate and confessional life stories. Third and probably most importantly, identifying with the memoirist has led to the effect that women reading other women's autobiographies see them as reflections of their own voiceless aspirations.

While autobiographical criticism has become a generally acknowledged field of research nowadays, feminist critics combated the prevailing rejection of women's writing evident in the scholarly and public mind throughout the 1980s.

The two earliest collections of women's autobiographical writing were pioneering a new development to build up a distinct women's autobiographies canon: In 1979, Mary G. Mason and Carol Hurd Green published a collection of texts written by British and American female autobiographers called *Journeys: Autobiographical Writings by Women*. Even more groundbreaking was the first real women's autobiographies anthology published in 1980: *Women's Autobiography: Essays in Criticism*, edited by Estelle C. Jelinek, was a breakthrough for feminist criticism. She includes fourteen essays

---

[10] The following three works provide a male-centered perspective of the history of autobiography. See Gusdorf, Georges (1980). „Conditions and Limits of Autobiography". In: *Autobiography: Theoretical and Critical Essays*. Ed. James Olney. Princeton: Princeton UP. 28-48. Misch, Georg (1950). *History of Autobiography*. London: Routledge and Kegan Paul. Spengemann, William C. (1980). *The Forms of Autobiography: Episodes in the History of a Literary Genre*. New Haven: Yale UP.

Georges Gusdorf's "Conditions and Limits of Autobiography," first published in French in 1956, sees autobiography as an "art" and "representative" of the best minds of its time, because it "recomposes and interprets a life in its totality" (1980: 38). Similar to Georg Misch's *History of Autobiography*, Gusdorf writes that autobiography is clearly white, male, and Western, "the artist and the model coincide, the historian tackles himself as object. He considers himself a great person" (1950: 31).

analyzing white twentieth-century Anglo-American autobiographers. She clearly distinguishes women's and men's autobiographies: While men often put their professional, successful careers into the foreground, women are more personal and modest about their lives. Staying in the background of the text, they include their social contacts, close friends, children, lovers, or relatives in their writings, while men "idealize their lives or cast them into heroic molds to project their universal import" (1980: 14-15). Contrary to that, women's major goal seems to be a general agreement and understanding for their decisions from the side of their mostly female readership. Considering temporality, Jelinek devises the theory that men's life writing is always a coherent whole characterized by linearity, harmony, and orderliness (cf. 16). Women's writings, however, are generally full of irregularities. Women's lives and texts represent a "disconnected, fragmentary pattern of diffusion and diversity," because "the multidimensionality of women's socially conditioned roles seems to have established a pattern of diffusion and diversity when they write" (17). Women's fragmented, incomplete, elliptical and disconnected texts are not surprising for Jelinek: According to her, women's every day lives are unlinear, diffuse, and diverse, and so their writings are "analogous to the fragmentary, interrupted and formless nature of their lives" (19). Jelinek's work was groundbreaking, because her publication launched several other studies of feminist criticism throughout the 1980s.

Other important feminist critics who followed Jelinek's path are Nancy K. Miller[11] and Domna C. Stanton[12], who were influenced by the equality and difference debate of second wave feminism, but also by French feminism and French literary criticism. In her article "Toward a Dialectics of Difference," Miller propagates a gendered reading in general, but also of autobiography as a genre. She wants both the critic and "normal" reader to "read for difference," in a "diacritical gesture," and argues for reading as "a movement of oscillation which locates difference in the negotiation between writer and reader" (1980: 260).

During the late 1980s, debates changed into another direction. Women's gendered identity was no longer the main subject of feminist criticism, but instead, women's texts, history, and cultural production gained influence, as female autobiographical authorization had been refused for hundreds of years. Critics like Sidonie Smith or Rita Felski attracted attention by showing how patriarchy has fictionalized 'woman' as a concept. Following postcolonial and postmodern writing, many literary critics have started to analyze women as doubly or multiply colonized subjects. Since the late 1980s, works which investigate emergent literatures coming from marginal areas in Africa, Asia, America, or

---

[11] For more information on Miller's theories, see Miller, Nancy K. (2000). "But Enough About me, What do you Think of my Memoir?" *The Yale Journal of Criticism* 13.2: 421-436. In this article, she analyzes the importance of female identification and disidentification when reading autobiographical works. See also her 1994 article "Representing Others: Gender and the Subjects of Autobiography". *differences* 6: 1-27. and her famous 1980 article "Toward a Dialectics of Difference". In: *Women and Language in Literature and Society*. Ed. Sally McConnell-Ginet, Ruth Borker, and Nelly Furman. New York: Praeger. 258-273.

[12] See Stanton, Domna C., ed. (1984). *The Female Autograph*. New York: New York Literary Forum. Through including women's texts from all over the world, Stanton wants to eliminate historical, political, and literary boundaries.

Australia have been published.[13] These new theories have triggered new points of discussion and subjectivities for women. Postmodernist theories have also created new analytical tools for autobiographical criticism, like, for example, Leigh Gilmore's term 'autobiographics'[14] or Jeanne Perreault's 'autography'[15]. Both terms include new approaches which try to destroy the traditional genre of 'autobiography' and find new definitions for 'woman' as the writing subject. Influenced by third wave feminism and postmodernist ideas, the current criticism of women's autobiography has led to a more global attempt to increase the position of women's autobiographical criticism.

Beginning at the end of the 1990s until now, some critics have tried to develop more globalized theories of women's writing. They include Native American, Egyptian, Québecois, or U.S. Latina women's autobiographies. For the first time, African American and Asian American autobiographies have found their way into the dominant canon. The study of ethnic women's autobiographies has become an extensive area in feminist criticism during the last years. Since the Bill Clinton era, the culture of personal exposure has exploded all over the Western world. Making the private public is still booming and has displaced the novel as the master narrative of American literature, even though the culture of self-revelation and confessional writing is not something new in our times.

Recent arguments concerning feminist autobiographical criticism have centered around the following aspects: One problem when analyzing women's autobiographies has been the so-called 'maleness of language'. According to Carolyn Heilbrun, women have only male language available to create their stories. "Through working within male discourse, we work ceaselessly to deconstruct it: to write what cannot be written" (1989: 40-41). Other issues which have turned up in feminist criticism are the construction of women as autobiographical subjects. Over the decades, one of the main problems for female autobiographers "has been 'the difficulty of saying 'I'," as Linda Anderson points out in *Women and Autobiography in the Twentieth Century* (1997: 2). It seems that women are often too intimidated to use autobiography as a genre due to general attitudes about their role in society. Another aspect in the current debate is the problem of differentiating truth from fiction, which is often difficult to distinguish for the reader. Memory can be tricky, vague, and selective, but the female autobiographer is also able to inhabit a space in which the writing subject can create herself over and over again. What Jelinek calls the "autobiographical fallacy of self-revelation" (1980: 10) includes the writer's panic to lay bare grievous, hurtful, embarrassing, or intimate memories. Other views dominating the current debate concern the form and nature of autobiographical texts. According to critic June Purvis, there are two different possibilities to examine autobiographical texts. She considers

---

[13] Two 1990s works give insight into women's autobiographical writing in many remote regions of the world: *De/Colonizing the Subject: The Politics of Gender in Women's Autobiography* was published by Sidonie Smith and Julia Watson in 1992. Also stimulating for international and indigenous feminist movements was the 1993 collection by Francoise Lionnet and Ronnie Scharfman called *Post/Colonial Conditions: Exiles, Migrations, and Nomadisms*.
[14] For more information, see Gilmore, Leigh (1994). *Autobiographics: A Feminist Theory of Women's Self/Representation*. Ithaca: Cornell University Press.
[15] See Perreault, Jeanne (1995). *Writing Selves: Contemporary Feminist Autography*. Minneapolis: University of Minnesota Press.

the autobiographer either as a witness or a representative. Her "descriptive analysis" can be applied when the writer is seen as a witness who provides important information about people, places, and events. Her "perspective analysis" focuses on the writer as a representative who reveals the perspectives of certain social groups (1994: 181ff.).

In the following parts of this dissertation, four Beat memoirs – Diane di Prima's *Memoirs of a Beatnik* (1969), Joyce Johnson's *Minor Characters* (1983), Hettie Jones' *How I Became Hettie Jones* (1990), and Brenda Frazer's *For Love of Ray* (1971) – will be categorized and analyzed in detail. When categorizing these four memoirs, various autobiographical theories which have emerged since the 1980s can be applied. All four works share the following common characteristics: First, all four memoirs are highly confessional and seem to confirm the trend of personal exposure until everything is laid bare. Second, all four writers are forerunners of second wave feminism which developed during the 1960s, because they clearly defy the proposed gender roles of the time. Third, all four works confirm Estelle Jelinek's categories of typical women's autobiographies: The four female Beats do not put their professional careers as writers into the foreground, but they rather depict the lives of their close Beat friends, husbands, and lovers. All mentioned texts are disconnected, fragmented, diffuse, incomplete, and highly unlinear, which is typical for women's writing. Forth, and most importantly, all four works are memoirs. According to Carolyn Heilbrun, autobiographies are about successful careers in the public sphere, whereas a memoir has a narrower, more intimate focus on the memoirists own memories, feelings, and emotions. A memoir is a subgenre of autobiography. It aims to emphasize meaningful, crucial moments in the past – often including a contemplation of the meaning of that event at the time of writing – instead of focusing on a long period of time. Often, the memoirist describes memories to consequently show why they are significant. Generally, memoirs are shorter than traditional autobiographical works (cf. Pinsker 2003: 312f.). Memoirs are generally considered to be more unstructured, fragmented, and incomplete than autobiographical works. The reconstruction of scenes is often more emotional and personal than in autobiographies. Moreover, scenes or a series of events which are lodged in memory are depicted rather than facts about a person's life. Furthermore, critics point out the fictional nature of many memoirs. "Disagreeable facts are sometimes glossed over or repressed […]" (Cuddon 1991: 89).

In Chapters 6, 7, and 8, the four memoirs at hand will be categorized according to various autobiographical theories and subgenres. My hypothetical considerations include the following questions: To which extent are the four memoirs confessional, protofeminist, pornographic/erotic, or semi-autobiographical? Can the category 'coming-of-age-memoir' also be applied to some of the works? Were the books written for therapeutic purposes, and do they therefore represent 'therapeutic memoirs'? Do the four Beat memoirs try to imitate the typically male Beat quest narrative or road tale? These crucial questions concerning characterizing female Beats' memoirs will finally open the gate to new conclusive arguments and results.

In order to understand the cultural history of the 1950s more fully, sexual identity in Beat times will be more closely examined, as sexual matters influenced the building of personal identities for a whole generation of young U.S. teenagers. Heterosexuality, including the complex dating system of the 1950s, was the indispensable norm. A number of young male and female Beats, however, were considered sexual "deviants" by 'square' U.S. society, as they often embraced a bisexual or homosexual lifestyle, which – together with communism – was seen as a major threat to the nation. They endorsed gay rights as a part of their revolt against the hypocritical moral standards of the conservative U.S. popular culture.

5 Sexual Identity: Notions of Sexuality in Beat Times

For centuries, sex has played an important role in bohemianism: Changing partners frequently was the bohemian's most dramatic display of freedom from conventional moral standards. The typical 1950s bohemians denied the common idea that sex was only permitted in marriage, and then only for the sake of creating a family. Bourgeois marriage and conventional family norms were rejected, while eroticism was often the main source of inspiration for works of art[16].

"In the 1950s, sex – if you achieved it – was a serious and anxious act. For all the 'bottled eagerness' of which Holmes wrote, even the beds of the liberated were troubled. The new self-consciousness about coming or not coming – making it a man's duty and triumph that both should come, and a woman's shame if she didn't – brought dread to the question 'Did you?' (1999: 89). Joyce Johnson quite accurately describes the 1950s anxiety about sexual experience. "Real life was sexual" (30), she believed, and sex became a primary arena for development in four women associated with the Beats: Diane di Prima, Joyce Johnson, Hettie Jones, and Brenda Frazer. For Diane di Prima that revolt meant pursuing affairs with both men and women and writing explicit, joyful erotica; for Joyce Johnson, it meant losing her virginity before marrying and getting an illegal abortion in Canarsie; for Hettie Jones, it meant marrying an African-American man, bearing two interracial children, and proudly raising them; for Brenda Frazer, it meant trying to be an equal member in the male-dominated Beat circle and living an outlaw life in Mexico. To call them 'feminist' would be anachronistic, but – with the exception of Brenda Frazer, who was clearly a victim of male exploitation – they did conduct lives that were not subservient to their men, and they looked to other women for support and identity. However, these four women writers of the Beat Generation were clearly forerunners of second wave feminism and later on frequently took part actively in women's issues during the 1970s and later decades.

Throughout the 1950s, sex was a huge issue throughout the United States, as it was *the* topic on TV, in advertising, and magazines.

> When I was about nineteen, pureness was the great issue. Instead of the world being divided up into Catholics and Protestants or Republicans and Democrats or white men and black men or even men and women, I saw the world divided into people who had slept with somebody and people who hadn't, and this seemed the only really significant difference between one person and another. (Plath. *The Bell Jar*: 34)

The social and economic changes of the time weakened many young people's family ties and allowed room for investigating sexual matters. New professional and educational careers were now made possible by capitalism, and consumerism celebrated youth and appearance, focusing on a new

---

[16] For a closer discussion of eroticism used as a main source in art, see Wilson, Elizabeth (1991). "Bohemian Love". *Theory, Culture & Society* 15.3: 37-57.

openness concerning sexual opportunities. Teenage girls were encouraged to become consumers through the promotion of sex and glamor[17] (cf. Jezer 1982: 247ff.). Even the music of the 1950s, rock and roll, was full of sexual connotations. As Michel Foucault sees it, sexual freedom had increased for decades. Sexual exploration and talking about sex had become a way of seeing, articulating, or encountering oneself. For postwar teenagers, building a sexual identity was the basis to find a personal identity. The postwar boom of encountering sex in every magazine and movie, promoted by so called "experts," therapists, counselors, and teachers, produced a new sexual personality, the 'teenager' (cf. Foucault 1980: 243ff.). Sex was no longer hidden and private, but something to be discussed in public. Magazine articles, polls, and literature provided a national frame of reference against which to measure oneself. Teenagers' lives were no longer mainly influenced by family life, but by society at large.

However, the growing public significance of sex in the teenage culture and the sexualization of popular culture did not lead to more liberal attitudes, but finally caused narrow-minded suppressive sexual norms. As sociologist Barbara Ehrenreich points out: "It seems that half the time of our adolescent girls is spent trying to meet their new responsibilities to be sexy, glamorous and attractive, while the other half is spent meeting their old responsibility to be virtuous by holding off the advances which testify to their success" (1986: 21). Girls were encouraged to explore sexual life, but lost their respectability if they did so. Non-marital female sexuality was linked to political threats: Panic due to both communism, or the 'Red Menace', and female sexuality which would finally destroy the nuclear family caused a policy of containment for both societal threats. The sexual rules devised almost always by men were riddles for many teenagers, because their conflicting messages concerning sexual freedom were strictly puritanist. Teenagers of the 1950s were trapped in the middle of a deeply contradictory society which was full of double morals for young people (cf. D'Emilio 1988: 280f.).

Many recollections from the 1950s suggest that much more sexual activity was going on than most adolescents confessed: "Everybody was doing it […]. But it was the Big Lie that nobody was," says an interviewed person in Benita Eisler's *Private Lives: Men and Women of the Fifties*. She found out: "Of all the secrets of coming of age in the fifties, sex was the darkest and dirtiest. As sexual beings, people became underground men and women. For some, leading a double life was no metaphor" (1986: 127). Adding the aspect of "darkness" to the 1950s secret of sex also connected the sexual anxiety to colored people, jazz, and rhythm and blues. Therefore, darkness and sex, sometimes disguised as rock and roll, were a danger for white girls' innocence.

---

[17] In *The Dark Ages: Life in the United States, 1945-1960*, author Mary Jezer includes a statistic about movie advertisements that clearly shows that the use of sex appeal in pre-war ads was never more than 50 percent, while in 1951, 70 percent of all movie ads emphasized sex (1982: 247). Also see Diane Barthel, *Putting on Appearances: Gender and Advertising*, 115f., for an analysis of 1950s sexual anxiety and its connection to capitalism.

Many autobiographical texts written in the 1950s uncover experiences with sexual intercourse. Very often, the female main protagonists who have pre-marital sex have to lie about it.[18] Even though feminine sexual disappointment does not distinguish this generation from earlier ones, exaggerated expectations do. In many works of the time, sex is often presented as disappointing. In Sylvia Plath's semi-autobiographical novel *The Bell Jar*, for example, Esther is warned not to have sex with Irwin. Unimpressed, she is lying in the bed hemorrhaging: "I lay rapt and naked, on Irwin's blanket, waiting for the miraculous change to make itself felt. But all I felt was a sharp, startling bad pain. 'It hurts,' I said. 'Is it supposed to hurt?'" (1999: 187). Irwin takes a shower while Esther bleeds more and more. She finally leaves his apartment, still hemorrhaging, and ends up in a hospital emergency room.

In Joyce Johnson's memoir *Minor Characters*, her first sexual intercourse with a boy named Alex is similarly unpleasant. While having sex, she ponders over Lorca's play *Blood Wedding* she has just read, because there, "the bloodstained sheets hung out the window for all the village to see". Suddenly, "He shuddered against me and cried out a little and it was over. Lying there, I was troubled by an entirely new question: Was this all there was?" (1999: 85). Feminist Betty Friedan (1921-2006) calls this discontent the "problem that has no name," because many 1950s housewives suffered from disillusionment and dreary perspectives. For many women, life was depressing, contrasting the glorified expectations created by the narrow focus on intercourse and its glorified romanticization on TV and in magazines. Depicting the years of her youth, Joyce Johnson connects the meaning of sex to being a rebellious Beat. Sex "was a forbidden castle" (30), and the word could not even be pronounced in public. "Going all the way" was a huge issue, being mystified, extremely dangerous, and often frustrating. Johnson's puzzled reaction can also be seen as a rejection of the female passivity so admired by men, and of the prevailing gender roles which scorned women's immorality if they crossed the line. The rejection of being sexually passive was an influential factor which finally led towards more liberal constructions of femininity during second wave feminism.

During the postwar years, teenage sexual etiquette followed a certain sequence: Asking someone out, dating, and going steady were important steps to establish a sexual system which tried to contain and punish female spontaneity, but also guaranteed that teenage girls observed the rules which led to marriage. The dating system of the 1950s was elaborate and fortified the premarital sexual taboo.

> If, for instance, you were dating a number of men, you might kiss them goodnight on the second or third date with perfect propriety. If you were going fairly steady with someone, you could certainly neck, and might pet above the waist on the outside, if you had not been affiliated long; above the waist on the inside if it looked as though a pin were imminent. Once pinned, girls ceased to talk about what they did, but it was tacitly acknowledged that the field broadened considerably. If a girl was pinned and planned to marry after graduation, it was a forgone conclusion that she had probably gone all the way but it was not discussed in late-night behavioral seminars in the sorority houses. (Siddons. *Heartbreak Hotel*: 87)

---

[18] See, for example, Lisa Alther's *Kinflicks*, Sylvia Plath's *The Bell Jar*, and Alix Kates Shulman's *Memoirs of an Ex-Prom Queen* for fifties-teenagers' experimentation with sexual intercourse.

Society's obsession with being virginal had ambivalent effects: On the one hand, magazines and television were full of sex issues, but on the other hand, punishment and ostracism followed if girls broke the sexual mores. Generally, it was assumed that women were less sexual than men. Therefore, fifties' marriage counselors and advisors constantly reminded girls that men had animalistic urges. Many "experts" advised austereness before marrying and a long courtship, which should distract male sexual urges (cf. Breines 1992: 113).

Historians found out that a peer-controlled dating system had developed since the 1920s. In the postwar years, this system had been expanded: "Going steady became the linchpin of the whole system of developing adolescent heterosexual relationships in the 1950s" (Modell: 1993: 189). During the postwar years, the dating and going steady-system[19] had lowered the marriage age enormously. It seems that young people were directly progressing from dating to marriage, and going steady predicted immediate marriage. Therefore, the specific dating system after the war led to early marriage among America's youth. Before the war, teenagers were often involved in many and varied dates, but after the war, going steady became a symbol of being popular. Similar to the adult world which felt menaced by national threats, young people were also in need of security, it seemed. Teenagers found their security in the steady partner, while adults turned to domesticity and the nuclear family. Already in the first high school year, millions of students were introduced to the supposed advantages of monogamy. One girl recalls, "You latched onto a boyfriend and started to go steady in ninth grade. It was the security thing" (Eisler: 1986: 107).

It can be argued that there are two major reasons for the drastic decline concerning the marriage age during America's 1950s. First, the increasing gap between youth and adult culture represented an unfamiliar, even frightening independence for teenagers; having a steady partner and marrying young were ways to find security. Second, early marriage was propagated as a way out of the ambivalent sexual messages teenagers had to face. Through marrying, females were allowed to embrace sexual activity without having to fear disrespect from society. In *Heartbreak Hotel*, for example, Maggie's boyfriend tries to convince her to get married, because her unwillingness concerning sexual matters has made him sexually frustrated: "We'd have a place, an apartment, the old man would pay for it and for us to finish school. And we'd be – together all the time. We are going to after graduation anyway, you knew that. I just don't think I can wait any longer" (Siddons: 1993: 199f.).

Within the mainstream teenage world of the 1950s and 1960s, necking and petting were widely accepted within the context of the American dating system. While sexual intercourse for teenagers was dangerous, bad for the reputation, and sinful according to America's puritan society, necking was different, because it was considered harmless. Many statistics about sexual behavior patterns suggest that although sexual activity became more widespread in the postwar era, the dramatic sexual changes

---

[19] For more information on the complicated dating system of the 1950s, see Bailey, Beth (1988). *From Front Porch to Back Seat: Courtship in the Twentieth Century.* Baltimore: Johns Hopkins University Press. The author offers a unique perspective on youth culture and modern courtship during the 20th century.

had already occurred at the end of the 19th century, when premarital intercourse increased. Already in the 1920s and 1930s, teenage sex had significantly risen (cf. Rothman 1984: 50ff.). Beth Bailey suggests that the meaning of necking and petting "lay in their naming, in their rise to conventionality, and in their symbolic importance to youth. Sex was accepted by youth, male and female. Necking and petting were public conventions, expected in any romantic relationship between a boy and a girl" (1988: 80). Sociologists refer to the fact that the taboo was on sexual intercourse, but not on precoital sexual activity. For girls, this meant that they could engage in premarital sexual activity without being stigmatized by society and they could stay "technical virgins".

Even though male teenagers wanted to pursue sex further than girls, as surveys show, boys scorned females who were sexually uninhibited or gave too much of themselves. Generally, males were more conservative than females. Ehrmann's extensive 1950s student survey discovered that "the degree of physical activity actually experienced or considered permissible is among males *inversely* related and among females *directly* related to the intensity of familiarity and affection in the male-female relation" (Ehrmann: 1959: 274). Being intensely in love therefore meant a decrease in premarital sex among males and an increase among females. Girls were often more emotionally involved, while boys preferred to have intercourse with someone they did not care for or would not marry.

In many sexual depictions of the 1950s, whether Beat or not, males were mostly represented as active, while females were supposed to be passive. The fear that men might lose control is critical when analyzing the gender narrative of the 1950s. Young men were gravely influenced by ideas about uncontrolled female sexuality and sexual chaos, which were crucial issues in the fifties. Both anxiety due to personal/sexual uncertainties and political threats, namely fear of communism, created ideologies of containment for women and political enemies.

Being virginal and pure is a major theme in women's literature during that time: Esther, Sylvia Plath's heroine in *The Bell Jar*, "saves" herself for her later husband, and her boyfriend leaves the impression of doing the same. When Esther finds out that he is no longer a virgin, she confesses that it is not the idea of Buddy sleeping with someone else that hurts her deeply: "What I couldn't stand was Buddy's pretending I was so sexy and he was so pure, when all of the time he'd been having an affair with that tarty waitress and must have felt like laughing in my face" (57). Esther decides to "go all the way" herself in order to be on one level with her unfaithful future husband. She feels betrayed, because she had tried to keep both Buddy and herself pure for each other, but he has broken his promise by having sex with a "bad girl," unsurprisingly working-class. Esther and Buddy are good examples for the ambivalent sexual standards of the 1950s: Buddy would, actually, not be laughing in her face, because he wanted to marry a virginal woman. He would have had trouble if Esther "had gone all the way" with him before marriage.

Beth Bailey's analyses of the postwar dating system found out that U.S. teenagers found public validation of popularity, belonging, and success through having a steady boy or girlfriend. Moreover, she points out that dating was a competition based on notions of scarcity and abundance: Dating and going steady "valued the scarce resource over the plentiful one, and both located power in the control of scarce resources" (1988: 55). Within this system, females were responsible for sex, blamed for transgressions, and more valued the chaster they were. Teenage girls who went too far were called "cheap": Their market value was low and they were clearly being stigmatized. To avoid being considered cheap, females tried to keep their virtue through "scarcity": "Courtship […] was construed and understood in models and metaphors of modern industrial capitalism" (5).

In the prevalent conservative culture, gender anxieties and the insecurities of the Cold War could be linked to women's containment within domestic boundaries; through domestication, females would establish a perfect world for their men and children. When losing their chastity, however, they would pose a threat to patriarchal society.

Even though U.S. society in the postwar years was superficially chaste and heterosexual, a growing homosexual and bisexual community gained confidence. Especially among the Beat subculture, homoerotic or homosexual relationships were offering an alternative model to the nuclear family. Particularly the members of the Beat Generation often indulged in homosexual or homoerotic affairs. A complex pattern of sexual relations often emerged among the males. Kerouac, Ginsberg, Burroughs, and the Beat "saint" Neal Cassady, for example, were all close friends, but also more than that: Ginsberg and Cassady had been lovers; Kerouac and Ginsberg had been short-term lovers; nearly all of them were more or less in love with Cassady. Like the males were exploring tangled and shifting homosocialities, many female Beats also showed bisexual or homosexual tendencies. Homoerotic matters are therefore an important issue for analyzing autobiographical writings of the female Beats. While authors like Diane di Prima were openly bisexual, Joyce Johnson, Hettie Jones, and Brenda Frazer, in contrast, were not involved in homoerotic or homosexual liaisons. All three writers are determinedly heterosexual, and their memoirs circle around the lives of male icons like Jack Kerouac, LeRoi Jones, and poet Ray Bremser. When focusing on tangling homosexual relations among female Beats, Diane di Prima's erotic or even pornographic *Memoirs of a Beatnik* is particularly interesting. Not only is di Prima defying the typical heterosexual marriage dictate, but she also violates several other cultural taboos, which will be closely looked at in the next chapters.

6 Diane di Prima's *Memoirs of a Beatnik*

Diane di Prima's erotic text *Memoirs of a Beatnik* (1969) is generally often disregarded as "for hire" pornography. Being a young Italian American woman, she violates the cultural taboo of explicitly describing sex with various partners, both male and female, seeking to sexually liberate herself. Di Prima explores sex and sexuality, and follows the typical male cultural myth of a Beat life which promotes sexual excess as a major theme. Her experiments with sex clearly show her belief in free love. Typically for pornographic literature, her minimal story line is frequently interrupted by long sex scenes. Many passages involve heterosexual sex, including an orgy with Kerouac, Ginsberg, and Peter Orlovsky. Yet, she also includes lesbian sex with her friend Tomi, and group sex with her female college roommates. Di Prima is shockingly frank: Most sex scenes are consensual, but the memoir also presents rape and incest.

Di Prima's memoir is playful concerning both the form and content of life writing. She skillfully merges truth and fact, and challenges the author–reader relationship due to the fact that affective bonds cannot be established. *Memoirs of a Beatnik* has more in common with Brenda Frazer's *For Love of Ray* than with *Minor Characters* or *How I Became Hettie Jones*. Both di Prima and Frazer seem to deny reader identification, both repeatedly slip from history into fiction, and both construct fictive/autobiographical characters which imitate typically male versions of Beat writing.[20] As the title implies, *Memoirs* is a risqué text which suggests female life writing. This is true in some respects. Di Prima places her narrator in a verifiable historic setting, depicting her memories of the Village in the 1950s, her pads, the prevailing Beat 'Rule of Cool' pattern of behavior, and the Beat community which invented new forms of literature, art, and music. In comparison to Johnson and Jones' life writings, however, di Prima is not interested in accounting for the 1950s as a historical time or social movement. Therefore, her writing allows her to be more fictive, imaginative, and playful.

In an afterword titled "Writing Memoirs" appended to the 1988 edition of the book, di Prima points out that she decided to write her erotic autobiography to support the extended hippie household she established in San Francisco after leaving New York in the summer of 1968 – a fourteen-room household composed of children, her own and other people's, Zen practitioners like herself, White and Black Panthers, Diggers, rock bands, and other sixties visionaries. To create the feeling of the period, she would play Bird, Clifford Brown, or Miles Davis' "Walking" as she wrote. Under the spell of their cool jazz, "tiny perfect memories of long-forgotten rooms, and scenes, and folks would take me over," she writes (193).

Di Prima openly confesses she made up many of the sexual events in *Memoirs of a Beatnik*. Waiting for a federal grant she had been awarded for her poetry, but had not yet received, di Prima accepted

---

[20] In Jack Kerouac's Duluoz Legend, he fuses poetry and prose, truth and fiction. Similarly, Ginsberg connects life writing and poetry in many of his works, same as Burroughs, who creates a fact/fiction correspondence with Ginsberg in his *The Yage Letters*.

Olympia Press publisher Maurice Girodias' offer to write an erotic book for him.[21] In *Memoirs*, she explains that she had met Girodias in New York, and he had asked her to write sex scenes of "innocuous novels he had purchased as skeleton plots to which the prurient interest had to be added, like oregano to tomato sauce" (191)[22]. Thinking back to the months she wrote *Memoirs of a Beatnik*, she describes her writing process as a time during which she would get up at 4:00 a.m., sit in Zen meditation for an hour, and then go from breakfast to typewriter where she spent the morning composing erotic scenes of her Beat days in the Village. She writes: "Gobs of words would go off to New York whenever the rent was due, come back with 'MORE SEX' scrawled across the top page in Maurice's inimitable hand, and I would dream up odd angles of bodies or weird combinations of humans and cram them in and send it off again" (193).

Di Prima wrote pornographically in order to support her alternative Beat community financially. However, the scenes she produced were not always sufficiently pornographic according to the standards of the genre. Di Prima, who actually experienced many adventures she depicts, often also used her friends' bodies to determine whether particular orgiastic configurations are physically possible or not: "Sometimes," she writes, "I'd wander the house looking for folks to check things out with: 'Lie down,' I'd say, 'I want to see if this is possible.' And they would, clothed, and we would find out, in a friendly disinterested way, if a particular contortion was viable, and stand up again, completely not turned on, and go about our business" (193). *Memoirs* was the only work di Prima wrote in order to earn money, she claims today. Publishing the book was also profitable for Olympia Press. In a 2004 interview, di Prima recollects the time she wrote the book:

> *Memoirs* was the only thing I ever wrote for money and it's earning money to this day. I used personal recollections describing the streets and had a ball doing it. That's all true, but all the sex I made up because they kept sending me back the manuscript saying, "More sex! More sex!" and I would write more sex. It was good money for the time and that is why I did it. I was supporting a commune of grown ups and children and nobody was working.[23]

---

[21] During the 1950s, the first generation of American female erotic writers turned up on the literary scene. Referring to di Prima's *Memoirs*, Michael Perkins comments that "autobiography provided the new Olympia [Press] writers with a framework more conducive to reflection and the analysis of the erotic life than previous writers who had carefully separated themselves from their published fantasies. This first generation of American erotic writers was less afraid of being caught posturing naked before its mirrors" (1976: 95). Analyzing female life writings, Perkins compares di Prima's text about a sexually independent woman to Harriet Daimler's semi-autobiographical novel *The Woman Thing* (1958) and to Mary Sativa's *Acid Temple Ball* (1969), which depicts the hippie drug culture in the Village in the 1960s. Like di Prima, some women waited a decade or two to publish erotic autobiographies covering the period of the 1950s. For example, British expatriate writer Anne Cumming published the first volume of her erotic autobiography, titled *The Love Habit: The Sexual Odyssey of an Older Woman*, in 1978. In 1991, she published *The Love Quest*, a chronicle of her travels and love affairs from 1952 to 1965 (cf. McCormick 1992: 131).
[22] Di Prima contributed to the following two Olympia Press novels: *Love on a Trampoline* by Sarah Darrich (1968) and *Of Sheep and Girls* by Robert M. Duffy (1968).
[23] See Morrisey, Brian. "An Interview with Diane di Prima". *POESY – An Anthology*. April 21, 2006. http://www.poesy.org/interviews.html

Seen from this particular background, *Memoirs* is read from a different perspective. Di Prima's story is split into two parts: on the one hand, her text represents fictive erotica, but on the other hand, she authentically represents New York during the Beat era. Through writing inventive erotica, di Prima departs from the fidelity that is a precondition for the prevalent author/reader contract in life writing. The fictive parts of her memoir clearly overpower the non-fictive scenes of the Village in the 1950s. Both parts, however, establish a narrative whole which refuses formalist constraints, and which confuses reader expectations concerning autobiography.

6.1 Shocking Details

6.1.1 The Aftermath of the Previous Night

Memoirs begins in 1953, the year when the author, born in Brooklyn, left Swarthmore College to find out what real life was about. The book's opening scene[24] details the reactions of the 18-year-old female bohemian poet as she wakes up in an unfamiliar loft in the West Village and remembers the lovemaking of the night before, during which she technically lost her virginity. Expressing a carefree commitment to female sexual activity she shows throughout *Memoirs*, di Prima describes herself lying in bed, contemplating her body after the incidents of the previous night. Uninhibitedly, she writes that the muscles of her thighs feel sore, and when she passes her hand over them, she feels the graininess of dried sperm that has stuck to her legs here and there. In a gesture of self-awareness, she slides her hands between her legs, feeling the lips of her vagina: "The skin was raw as I slipped my fingers inside, exploring gently," she explicitly describes the scene. She goes on,

> He certainly was a big one, I thought. A big one for the first one, that was good. A shiver of pleasure passed over me as I explored the familiar ground and goose bumps started up on my arms. Now, I thought with a little grin of cynical pleasure, I certainly won't have any more trouble using Tampax. *(Memoirs:* 4-5)

In this first scene, di Prima builds up the parameters of her sexual identity – parameters to which she remains true throughout the story. Seeing herself as an independent person interested in sexual adventure, the persona she presents avoids attachment, refuses victimization, and absolutely resists confinement to traditional gender roles. She is a young woman who embraces the advantages and sensations sexual experience can offer rather than adapting herself to traditional "good girl" behavior. Even though di Prima as the narrator loses her virginity in the opening scene, she is not sexually inexperienced. The memoir also includes poetic descriptions of sexual affairs with young women her age, as well as with some Beat males, to whom she did not feel like offering her virginity, however.

---

[24] For a close analysis of di Prima's explicit, joyful erotic writing in *Memoirs of a Beatnik*, see Moke, Susan (1998). "Desires of their own: Twentieth-Century Women Novelists and Images of the Erotic". *Dissertation* Indiana University. 136ff.

Throughout the book, di Prima delights in her sexuality which is a natural part of her life. For example, the morning scene of licking the blood of her pierced maidenhead off from Ivan's penis and then "swallowing" her "childhood" (22) hardly approximates the fear about defloration most female authors would probably have included in such a scene. Some readers might be astonished about the fact that the typical 1950s teenage anxiety concerning sexual matters is completely absent in *Memoirs*. Her defloration by a man she has just met is a personal and sexual development, not a step backwards. While caressing herself, the narrator begins to awaken Ivan, whom she had met the night before in a gay club. Kissing each vertebra of his spine, she knows that at any moment she "could initiate the dance that would satisfy [her] own desire and bring delight to the creature beside [her]" (5). In the middle of this bawdy depiction, di Prima pulls the reader back into the realm of nonfiction. Several times in the book, she interrupts the dominant fictitious forms of erotic writing by juxtaposing nonfiction prose forms. These truthful intersections imply the veracity of the text. Di Prima's textual subversions are clearly shown in the following scene. She discontinues the sexual description of lying in bed with Ivan by inserting two paragraphs, which slightly change the role of the narrative voice. "There are as many kisses as there are people on the earth, as there are permutations and combinations of those people," (5) the narrator explains, supporting her opinion with the description of various types. "There are many, many other major types of kisses – at least twelve come to my mind offhand. List your favorites below," (6) she demands of the reader. This is followed by a blank space which can be used to create one's own list. This particular interactive form of reader participation is, for example, typical of women's magazines, trying to give advice to the mostly single, young, female audience by extended questionnaires. Di Prima's paragraphs, however, clearly make fun of the mass culture form of memoir. Yet, her textual subversions do not only entertain the reader, but also have didactic purposes, which is shown in several passages throughout the memoir.

After having described the varied kinds of kisses lovers can share, the scene again turns to fiction: The first person narrator and Ivan are kissing each other, exploring each other's mouths and bodies, attempting to feel what it is like to be inside the other's skin. She tongues the length of his body and "his full, round balls," until, she writes, "my own desire became more urgent". She goes on, "[I] straddled him so that my moist hole was just above his rod. I lowered myself onto it, guiding it to the proper place, and squirming down over it to take it into my still tight opening. But there was more. I had not taken the huge tool in fully". The two separate slightly so that she can raise one leg up over his shoulder: "His hands on my backwise drew me closer and closer – he was in, up to the hilt". Furthermore, she writes, "At last I gave way, my entire body filled with pleasure, and felt the flood of delight sweep through my flesh as his warm come filled my cunt to overflowing, and with a shuddering shout he collapsed upon me" (9).

In this scene, the ambivalence between the intimate tenderness these first-time lovers create with one another and the pornographic language di Prima uses in order to describe their love act can clearly be seen. Words and phrases such as "rod," "hole," "huge tool," or "in up to the hilt" show di Prima's attempt to accommodate her vocabulary to the pornographic genre in which she writes. Furthermore, she builds up exchangeable roles: Both Ivan and Diane are active and passive. The following passages even more insistently show di Prima's talent to shift between these roles.

When Ivan departs for work, the female narrator stays in his loft drinking coffee, listening to Bach on the phonograph, and reading Federico Garcia Lorca's "Elegy for Ignacio Sánchez Mejias". Pondering over the events of the previous night when she had met Ivan in the Swing Rendezvous, a Mafia-run gay bar on MacDougal Street, where she had gone with her best friend and sometimes lover Susan O'Reilly, her dreaminess is abruptly ended when Ivan's male friend of the night before who had taken O'Reilly home with him comes into the apartment. When he moves to the bed where she lies and starts caressing her without saying a word, she wonders about his feelings for Ivan. Her assumptions that this unknown man is desperately in love with Ivan are affirmed when he begins to kiss her and then to "lick the bud of [her] clitoris, first taking from it, too, the dried juices of [her] earlier lovemaking, and then finally paying attention to it for its own sake" (26). He goes on until they both have an ecstatic orgasm, after which Robin explains, "You are a veil through which [Ivan and I] make love to each other" (27). For her, this confession raises many questions about Robin's and Ivan's apparently unfulfilled love. Due to the fact that it is totally "uncool" to be curious – according to the Beat ethos of the 'Rule of Cool,' she tries to play the dominant role that Ivan might play if he was having sex with Robin. Finally, di Prima withdraws,

> [...] kneeling upright as I straddled him, and drinking in the desperate moans and convulsive trembling that I had set going, aware at last of the turmoil of emotions within myself: desire, aroused by the power I was wielding, and anguish and frustration that I could not complete the act I was approximating, that I was not a man – pirate or jewel thief – I had so often in the daydreams of adolescence pretended to myself to be. Suddenly I was angry at Robin for desiring Ivan, for taking no pleasure in my flesh for its own sake. *(Memoirs:* 32)

Di Prima is aware of the fact that men, especially Beat outlaws, are free to choose the life they want, which is denied to most of the women, even if they were within the same Beat circles as men. Voluntarily, she plays a stand-in for a more desired lover. Yet, she is resisting to get lost in any of these roles or to give up her female independence for the sake of male desire. Her emphasis on wanting to be worshipped for her own "female" flesh clearly shows a distinctly "unphallic" sexuality which is both assertively active and explicitly feminine (cf. Moke 1998: 153).

6.1.2 More than just Friends?

By some critics, Diane di Prima has been criticized for imitating male Beat writers by depicting explicit, often violent sex scenes. Her extensive descriptions of penises and clitorises remind the reader of the popular stereotype of Beats as sex-crazed. The lesbian scenes in *Memoirs of a Beatnik* have functions similar to male-focused pornography, as she presents females as sex objects triggering male fantasy. Salaciously, she describes having sex with her female college classmate and fellow dropout Tomi, seemingly aiming to stimulate male readers.

The narrator's joy in her own unphallic sexual agency is clearly shown in several explicit descriptions of lovemaking. In one passage, di Prima as the narrator is modeling for a portrait Tomi is drawing of her in the barn art studio of her parents' weekend cabin in Connecticut. While she poses for Tomi, she remembers afternoons they spent in their college dorm room listening to the Brahms' Requiem while making love. Di Prima remarks that it was Tomi who "galvanized the whole scene and made it come alive, by falling in love with each of us, one after the other" (46). Getting more and more excited, they enter the woods where they love each other:

> I could feel her teeth press against my pelvic bone as she strove to enter more deeply. The walls of my vagina were quivering, vibrating like an exquisitely tuned instrument to her every stroke and nuance. At last everything went totally black, a familiar fire licked from my stomach down to my groin and with long, racking shudders I came into her mouth. *(Memoirs:* 43)

Following that, the narrator falls down on the flat rock and later sees a small purple bruise beginning to show on her hip bone. In this scene, di Prima once more shows that, by making love to both men and women, she is able to take on various different sexual roles, but rejects being restricted to any of them. For the typical reader of pornography, her homosexual depictions of lesbian sex might be as erotic as the heterosexual passages with Ivan and Robin. Yet, the love scene with Tomi probably includes more intimacy and sensitivity, and she delightfully portrays her affair without shame or censorship.

Contrary to that, di Prima does find reason for censorship when depicting Tomi's upper-class family, which is so different from her own. Di Prima talks about her parents as "sensible, hard-working first-generation Italian-Americans" (Moke: 1998: 154) who, with "grim determination had put themselves through college and become 'professional people'. They were never in debt and bought nothing 'on time'. They were noisy and unpretentious". Of her large family, she writes: "I had seventeen aunts and as many uncles, and twenty-two first cousins, whom I had been taught to regard as additional brothers and sisters" (1998: 48). Even though much of *Memoirs of a Beatnik* is invented, di Prima includes concrete historical referents which represent reality and the truth. Both her family and her Beat friends justify di Prima's memoir as truthful life writing, and the reader is able to recognize the author as the historical Diane di Prima. Truthfully, the narrator depicts her own family as illiterate and loving Italians, while Tomi's Anglo-European upper-class family presents a stark contrast. Tomi's family is sexually deviant, self-destructive, and sadomasochistic. As the narrative unfolds, they draw di Prima into their perversions. Tomi's father Serge is drunk all day and complains about his wife's frigidity; Martha, his wife, knits pullovers by the fire and is completely vacant; Aunt Helen lays Tarot cards all the time; Tomi's fourteen-year-old brother William locks himself into his room and does not talk to anyone.

The scenes which follow are among the most shocking and disturbing ones in the book. In the first of these, Diane finds out about the incestuous relationship between Tomi and her fourteen-year-old brother "Sweet William" they have obviously been keeping secret for years. Observing them through a keyhole, she is appalled by the brutality of William's penetration. By watching the scene calmly, di Prima's narrator is voyeuristic, mimicking readers of pornography or erotica, as she participates in a secret taboo.

The second appalling event occurs in a later scene, when di Prima is a victim of rape during a boat excursion in which Tomi's family picnics on an island. Taking a nap in the sun, she is suddenly awakened by the weight of Serge, Tomi's father, who attempts to rape her. She finds him on top of her, sticking his tongue in her ear. At the beginning, she is disgusted by his alcohol breath and his "thick, older man's body" (67). She resists, but her fear is soon transformed into pleasure. Feeling sympathetic with "poor silly Serge, who never got to screw his wife," di Prima decides: "[…] and if he wanted to throw a fuck into me, why I might as well let him. It wasn't going to hurt me. Not a whole lot. Anyway, it didn't seem that I had much choice" (68). Faced with being raped, she rethinks her self-defense, decides to be merciful, and even enjoys her molestation, which is the most reasonable solution for her. She is astonished about the orgasm she experiences, and all other contemplations about Tomi's and William's lovemaking disappear from her mind. After the rape, Serge kisses Diane fatherly, and goes back to his family napping around the fire. By turning a rape into a pleasurable sex act, the reader gets to know another aspect of di Prima as an extremely innovative female sexual persona. Yet, this scene is also among the most shocking ones due to the fact that it is modeled on patriarchal, masculine fantasies: Rape – using the female body for sexual gratification – is accepted, and the woman gives in to the power and dominance of the male body. The rape scene also clearly shows that di Prima writes in the tradition of male-centered erotica (cf. Grace 2002: 165).

The third occasion that causes the narrator to finish the relationship with Tomi is the fact that Tomi can never be a real beatnik. When Tomi says she cannot live in a shared pad with O'Reilly and her, because her parents need her at home, di Prima points out the opportunities she might miss:

> "You know what you're giving up." I meant O'Reilley, but I meant light and freedom, air and laughter, the outside world – outside of the stuffy incestuous atmosphere of her "family life". I meant drawing tables in high white rooms, nights at the ballet or at some exotic restaurant, or simply wandering, exploring the neon streets. And mostly I meant laughter, the silliness and glee unscrutinized, one's blood running strong and red in one's own veins, not drawn to feed the ineradicable grief of the preceding generation. *(Memoirs:* 72)

Tomi does not get involved in the Beat community, in contrast to di Prima, who breaks up with her family, rents her own Greenwich Village apartment, and tries to support herself financially as good as possible.

6.1.3 City Spring and Country Summer

Living in the Village now, di Prima decides to dedicate herself to poetry only. To pay the rent, she poses for pornographic photos. For her, this job is decidedly unattractive: Due to the new Beat 'Rule of Cool', she detests devoting her time to earning money, which is clearly "uncool". Repulsed by New York's pornographic scene, she realizes that her photographer, Mr. Gay Faye, for whom she works, is nauseated by her female body. About her photos, she muses: "The productions of his camera, reproduced in full color by the tens of thousands, passed as sexy, were glued onto calendars and hung in garages and dens all over America" (78). While taking on odd jobs, she goes on writing, and, in contrast to many other still unknown female poets of the time, she becomes one of Beats' "best girl poets"[25], according to Jack Kerouac's words. Time passes quickly, and her pad becomes a favorite meeting/sleeping place for numerous Beat friends. Just around the corner, Rienzi's, a new coffee shop especially for the "young Bohemian crowd" opens up on MacDougal Street: "We all sat there in the long afternoons, reading and making each other's acquaintance, nursing twenty-five cent cups of espresso for hours, and drawing pictures on paper napkins. Intoxicated by the stories of our youth, by *Jean-Christophe* and *La Bohéme*, we thought to play a similar game," di Prima writes: "We almost carried it off" (90).

Di Prima indulges in the new subculture which emerges in the darkest and most hidden parts of the Village, letting "the blood running strong and red in one's own veins" (72), as she had foreseen it when trying to convince Tomi to move in with her. Di Prima is a typical example for the 1950s female bohemian: Dressed in black, a chain smoker and writer, sexually independent, and drinking espresso in the afternoon. In a later passage, a clichéd depiction of the Beat fifties follows, when she is invited to a party in the country, somewhere on a hill not far from the Hudson. While they all – around two hundred young bohemians – sit around the bonfire, playing bongos and guitars and making love somewhere in the Hudson River Valley, di Prima falls in love with the young guitarist, Billy. Another cliché about Beats' frequent drug use seems to be confirmed here: "There was a good, rich smell on the breeze which I recognized as pot – I'd been around it often enough, though I'd never had any. Then a fat, loosely rolled joint came into my hands and I took a drag on it" (94). When Billy asks her to stay on the farm with him and his father Big Bill, "a tall, spare, hawk-faced man in his forties, very handsome and very black-Irish" (96), she does not refuse, as di Prima had never lived in the country before[26]: "Next day I sawed the high heels off my shoes, and borrowed a pair of Billy's big, baggy jeans, which I tied with a rope around my middle to keep them on, and began to live in the country"

---

[25] In 1963, Kerouac was asked which female writers of the time he would include in a selective compilation of Beat texts. Kerouac named four females in his listing of 27 writers, among them Barbara Moraff as "best girl poet" and di Prima as "other best girl poet". He also claimed Denise Levertov and Lois Sorrells should be included (McNeil: 1996: 213).
[26] Di Prima re-enters country life in 1965 – a time not included in her *Memoirs* – by joining Timothy Leary's psychedelic community at Millbrook.

(99). Big Bill gives them a small empty house on the farm, and some time later, Little John, a Village friend, comes for a visit. Surprisingly, the narrator spends her time being a traditional 1950s girl: After the men leave for work, she cleans the shack, weeds the garden and harvests ripe vegetables, or boils potatoes for supper. Unexpectedly, she realizes that she "dug being woman to the three men, cleaning and mending and cooking for them" (100). In the evening, they often play chess or sometimes even perform staged readings of Shakespeare and Brecht. "I got used to the slow, paced rhythm of my days and for a while it seemed to me that I had never known any other place than this timeless one, days colored green by the garden, and nights colored gold by the oil lamp," di Prima depicts the time with Billy, Big Bill, and Little John: "I lost myself in my new-found woman's role, the position defined and revealed by my sex: the baking and mending, the mothering and fucking, the girls' parts in the plays – and I was content" (110).

Only for a short time, the narrator, normally subversive and non-conformist, is satisfied with the prescribed gender roles of the time. Yet, she soon starts relationships with three men at the same time, claiming that monogamy is impossible to achieve. She states that "it was good being a chick to three men, and each of them on his own trip, each wanting a different thing" (108). She goes on to say that

> I have since found that it is usually a good thing to be the woman of many men at once, or to be one of many women on one man's scene, or to be one of many women in a household with many men, and the scene between all of you shifting and ambiguous. What is not good, what is claustrophobic and deadening, is the regular one-to-one relationship. OK for a weekend, or a month in the mountains, but not OK for a long-time thing, not OK once you have both told yourselves that this is to be the form of your lives. *(Memoirs:* 108)

Refusing to be stuck in a monogamous relationship, di Prima is clearly in favor of polygamy which drives away endless, deadening discussions, boredom, and emotional pain. She does not want to live through the "horror, the nightmare in which most of us are spending our adult lives" by believing in the "one-to-one world" (109) which is the enemy of our existence. In the country, she admires the qualities of all three men: Big Bill's maturity, stability, and generosity made "me feel safe and well, as I had never felt in my life, his gallantry made me feel beautiful," she writes (109-110). She also notes that young Billy's "life force" was similar to her own, whether they were "hiking, or weeding, or fucking," while Little John, her New York City roommate, was "brother and friend" (110); Contemplating the joys of that spring from a 1969 point of view during the time she wrote *Memoirs*, di Prima seizes the opportunity to consider the claustrophobic situation one-to-one relationships can present.

In the middle of these country scenes, di Prima chooses to pick up a pedagogical theme, trying to teach the reader, and to correct. Similar to the memoirs of Joyce Johnson and Hettie Jones, she wants to set the record straight by explaining her attitudes in order to avoid misunderstandings. Like in the scene where she asks the reader to list the favorite kisses in a blank space below, di Prima's textual subversions in the following passage again have non-fictive, didactic purposes. In this part of *Memoirs of a Beatnik*, she interrupts the country idyll by including a lengthy, educational discussion of birth control, protection from disease, and the joys of pregnancy. Subtitled "Fuck the Pill: A Digression," di Prima warns her female readers who might assume that the invention of the pill is the solution for all sexual problems.

> [...] the lucky girls have the pill now, and they can do what they please, are as free as men, etc., etc. The pill, the pill, the pill! I am so tired of hearing about the pill, hearing the praises of the pill! Let me tell you about the pill. It makes you fat, the pill does. It makes you hungry. Gives you sore breasts, slight morning sickness, condemns you, who have avoided pregnancy, to live in a perpetual state of early pregnancy: woozy and nauseous, and likely to burst into tears. And – crowning irony – it makes you, who have finally achieved the full freedom to fuck, much less likely to fuck, cuts down on the sex drive. So much for the pill. *(Memoirs:* 104-105)

Depicting the disadvantages of birth control devices, she praises her personal magic ability to have sex without getting pregnant: "In fact, for the first few years of my running around town I never used anything to avoid pregnancy, and never once got pregnant" (103). Di Prima's narrator knows about the scientific advances to help liberate female sexuality, but she also wants to assert her own authority by having a different opinion. Di Prima's didactic instructions present an uncharacteristic move in *Memoirs*. Even in the revised 1988 version, di Prima sticks to her attitude that she prefers free sex. She notes, however, that she does not want to encourage young people to avoid condoms and revises her opinion on unsafe sex in times of AIDS: "Flirting with pregnancy is one thing: having a kid can be a great celebration of life; flirting with AIDS is something else: is simply courting a quick and ugly death" (103). By including depictions of birth control experiences in the 1950s, di Prima skillfully brings another aspect of historical verification into the text.

6.1.4 Luke

Di Prima's short, fiery affair with a young, heroin-addicted guitarist named Luke is a typical example for the narrator's attitude not to fulfill traditional gender roles, to love without depending on that person, and to remain true to her ethos of 'Cool'. Soon being bored about living in the country in a male household, di Prima longs for the "quick combat and hard living of the city" and for the "inexhaustible human interchange that was New York" (110). Back in New York City, she is homeless, having no pad to stay in, and therefore, she sleeps on the steps of the Washington Square Fountain: "There was a regular crew of about eight of us who slept there, four to six of the eight there on any given night, and we all got to know each other pretty well, as far as moods and habits and aura went, but we never spoke" (114). Having one's own privacy and not knowing each other by name was necessary if you wanted to keep the "code of coolness". Being anonymous is what she wants, because unfolding "our emotional lives would have destroyed the space that the indifference of the city gave each and every one as her most precious gift" (115). Di Prima would get up at ten, read for one hour, order breakfast at Rienzi's, where she would change her clothes, wash her face, and brush her teeth. She would then enjoy "drinking good, strong coffee and reading while your friends come in and out and the morning draws to a close and you write stray words in a notebook" (116). The Village was a good area for beatniks, tourists, and the Mafia, di Prima points out, but if you were an interracial or homosexual couple, things were different, as they were often threatened in the streets. When Norman Verne, the proprietor of the Quixote Bookstore asks the narrator to manage the store while they are on a canoeing trip in Canada for a month, she accepts and moves into the backroom, equipped with a stove, fridge, and an army cot. Eventually, Luke Taylor, a "very beautiful, ghost-like blonde boy" (117) who had been sleeping in the backroom, turns up, and they decide to take care of the shop together.

While some lovers disappear as soon as they have appeared, a few others are important throughout *Memoirs*. Ivan, who is di Prima's first male lover, is significant because, finally, he will be the father of her first child.[27] The sexual passages including Luke, however, are the most powerful ones, even though their affair is only short-lived. Di Prima takes this relationship seriously, yet she does not sacrifice her independence. Suddenly, however, her lover tells her he must leave the city due to some drug dealing in a Mafia-neighborhood, where he had witnessed the execution of one of his friends. Instead of lamenting her lover's misery and departure, Diane does not show her emotions. As usual, their final love making is depicted in great detail:

> [...] in the slow, hot, summer night with all the noises of August backyards and August streets exploding around us, I made love to that thick, strong, uncircumcised cock, made love indeed, called love into being, coaxed it into fullness and feeling with my mouth – I was young enough and had magic enough to do that. In love, I MADE love, and love flowered like an aureole around us both, [...] My hands were on his fine, thin waist as he came, I could feel his back arch, the electricity in his flesh, and my head between his strong, golden-haired thighs was clasped tightly, I could hear his blood – or my own – exploding in my ears, and knew this seed I swallowed for the sacrament – the holy and illimitable essence that drove the stars. *(Memoirs:* 129-130).

It is interesting how powerfully the author describes their love making. Although the narrator idealizes their affair by seeing it as "pre-matter energy," she defiantly asserts her sexual identity in ways that challenge male power (126). Di Prima's depictions of sexual affairs powerfully reflect the prevailing male Beat attitude of nonattachment. The narrator takes on the same 'Ethos of Cool' and represents a woman capable of living out female independence, free love, and freedom of spirit. Additionally, she revises the usual variations on female characterization in erotic autobiographical texts: Subtly, she represents a sexualized female who resists exploitation. She does so without even implying that her demonstration of female sexual autonomy is cast on a model of male sexuality. When Luke departs for New Orleans, two things hold the narrator back:

---

[27] Beat poet and radical activist LeRoi Jones (Amiri Baraka), husband of Hettie Jones, was the father of di Prima's second child. Di Prima and LeRoi Jones were the founders of the 'New York Poets Theater' and editors of the *Floating Bear* (1961-1963).

> One was our code, our eternal tiresome rule of Cool, that would have made it impossible for me to say those words without blowing our entire scene, retrospectively even, blowing what had gone before, so that if I had indeed gone with Luke all the magic would have gone out of our coming together – or so it seemed to us then. The other was my total, unutterable fascination with Manhattan [...].
> *(Memoirs:* 133)

The narrator is too "cool" to admit her love of Luke, and finally, her commitment to a loose Beat community makes her stay. Having gained total independence again, di Prima rents a new pad together with Susan O'Reilley: "It was a lovely pad, one of the best I ever had, and I look back on it with great fondness to this day. The life I lived in it was the simplest, kindest, and most devoted life I have ever managed to live, the friends were fine, the goals were clear and set" (136). They make a living room out of the front room, and sleep in the larger of the two middle rooms, "on a bed that was nothing but a bed frame with some wooden slats across it and an old cotton-stuffed mattress on top of that" (136-137). The smaller room is immediately dubbed "the woodshed", because it was filled with cartons and barrels of wood for the fireplace. In those days, no one had ever heard of beatniks and hipsters, and so, the construction workers who offer them wood from the construction sites are cheerful and friendly. Carrying it home with shopping carts, "[i]t took about four cartloads a day to keep us warm," the narrator tells about the harsh winter times in the cold water flat. The apartment soon develops into a party spot for various Beats in need of a place to stay. While her friends indulge in dance, acting, music, or political philosophy, di Prima dedicates her whole day to poetry. Compiling her first book of poems, *This Kind of Bird Flies Backward* (1958), her roommates discourage her by claiming that her work is not publishable due to the Beat slang in which the poems are written (cf. 173). Things, however, came differently.

6.2 Real or Made up Orgasms? Reality Versus Fiction

Chapter 13, "Organs and Orgasms: An Appreciation," and Chapter 14, "We set out," are the two last chapters of the memoir. In both chapters, di Prima depicts the ongoing changes in New York's Greenwich Village and the political situation in the middle of the Cold War: The narrator has to live through the 1956 presidential elections, "the horror of the Rosenberg executions" (174), the Hungarian Revolution, the first fallout terror, and the repressive measures against alleged communists and homosexuals. During the years of McCarthyism,

> [...] gay bars had been closed, and people cruised Central Park West more cautiously: there were many plainclothes busts. There were more and more drugs available: cocaine and opium, as well as the ubiquitous heroin, but the hallucinogens hadn't hit the scene as yet. The affluent post-Korean-war society was setting down to a grimmer, more long-term ugliness. At that moment, there really seemed to be no way out. *(Memoirs:* 174-175)

Following these reflections on society and politics, di Prima analyzes the emerging Beat subculture, the "miscellany of people" like alternative bums, jazz freaks, Beat lesbians, poets, musicians, painters, or various Poundians[28] who frequented the bookstores. Living according to the 'Rule of Cool,' they were different from the rest of the U.S. without calling themselves Beats yet. "As far as we knew," the narrator explains, "there was only a small handful of us – perhaps forty of fifty in the city – who knew what we knew: who raced about in Levis and work shirts, made art, smoked dope, dug the new jazz, and spoke a bastardization of the black argot". They knew there must be other small groups all around America, around "fifty living in San Francisco, and perhaps a hundred more scattered throughout the country: Chicago, New Orleans, etc.". Yet, their own "isolation was total and impenetrable, and we did not try to communicate with even this small handful of our confreres". More important than being connected with other subcultural groups, their main goal was "to keep our integrity (much time and energy went into defining the concept of the 'sellout') and to keep our cool: a hard, clear edge definition in the midst of the terrifying indifference and sentimentality around us – 'media mush' (175). Trying to avoid their sellout, they remained united within their groups, building small communities in anonymous pads all over New York City, closing themselves in, and non-members out.

However, could Diane di Prima really prevent the sellout she and her friends were afraid of? Even though di Prima worries about a Beat sellout, one might argue that she is not totally credible as she betrays the whole scene by writing a pornography for financial reasons only. In the author's note written in May 1969 which opens up *Memoirs*, she defends her move towards writing pornography as a way of preserving her integrity. A young, blonde college freshman who is driving her back to San Francisco after a poetry reading at Berkeley asks her, "What do you suppose happened to all those Beatniks?". The author's answer is, "Well sweetie, some of us sold out and became hippies. And some of us managed to preserve our integrity by accepting government grants, or writing pornographic novels"[29](1).

Clearly, di Prima does not see herself involved in a Beat sellout. This might be due to the fact that she gravely violates the boundaries and limits of autobiography as a literary genre. Similar to the subsection "Fuck the Pill: A Digression," the author inserts two subchapters called "A Night by the Fire: What you would like to hear" and "A Night by the Fire: What actually happened". Both insertions are part of Chapter 12 called "The Pad: Two". Di Prima's inner conflict about the limits of

---

[28] Di Prima began a correspondence with the poet Ezra Pound, visiting him daily for two weeks in 1955 at St. Elizabeth's Hospital in Washington, D.C., where he was hospitalized. In *Memoirs*, she writes that he "wanted us single-handed to change the nature of the programming on nationwide television" (1998: 173). Susan O'Reilly and di Prima continued visiting him at home after his discharge from hospital.

[29] Even though di Prima blames the hippies for a "sellout" in 1969, she played a major part in creating the bohemian literary hippie scene in San Francisco. Together with Allen Ginsberg and other major Beats like Michael McClure or Lenore Kandel, she made the step from beatnik to hippie. From the mid-sixties onwards, di Prima embraced a genuine hippie-lifestyle which was not much different from her Beat years in the 1950s. During the last years of the 1960s, di Prima was always on the move – staying at Timothy Leary's psychedelic community at Millbrook, driving through the country in a Volkswagen van, reading poetry at galleries, colleges, bars, and underground clubs (cf. Knight 2000: 126f.).

the genre becomes quite obvious here: She gives two options concerning the story line for the reader to choose, making clear that the reader cannot always trust in what he/she is reading. Here, Diane di Prima's text is subversive due to the fictive and didactic elements she includes. In the "what you would like to hear"-section, the narrator and her roommates have an orgy in a mid-November night, when "it was too cold for any of us to preserve the slightest desire for privacy or solitude" (147). Di Prima's shared pad was a Greenwich Village cold water apartment, and in the winter, it was so cold that they all slept in front of the fireplace, crawling together under a blanket in a double bed. The passage in which di Prima parodies her authorial voice as a pornographer starts as follows: "Maybe I would feel a hand in my cunt, and turn towards its owner, and in doing so I would brush against whomever was sleeping on the other side of me, and feel a hard-on against my hip in passing, and wriggle closer, opening my thighs and closing them around a prick […]" (148). The extensive orgy which follows is depicted in great detail. Leslie, Don, O'Reilley, Pete, and Diane have group sex in a double bed until just before dawn. Explicitly, di Prima points out, "Maybe we all come once and then maybe Pete sucks Leslie off, Leslie goes down on O'Reilly, while Don and I watch. I guess then Pete would build up the fire, and we would smoke some hash". Then the orgy might start all over again when "Don starts nuzzling my neck, and we fuck dog-fashion, and Leslie comes up behind Don and slips it in, and we set up some kind of crazy syncopated rhythm that gets the bed rocking again. Finally, however, "we all go to sleep, just before dawn, with one numb arm each stuck under somebody else […]" (150).

Real life, however, was quite different from this erotic passage. In "A Night by the Fire: What actually happened," di Prima tells things as they really were, teaching the reader about the reality of Beat life. She is didactic once again, explaining that usual evenings in their pad are boring and unexciting. The pad is freezing cold, and all of them want to stay warm by being as close to the fire as possible.

> Pete is poking the fire, and the cheap old phonograph is playing the same Stan Getz record over and over. Don is sitting on the edge of the bed, playing drums with the poker against the fireplace. O'Reilley is lying next to the fire reading Kropotkin's Appeal to the Young. […] Leslie is lying next to her, flat out on his back, smoking and looking at the ceiling. He has had two dance classes and is exhausted. I am on the cold side of the bed, away from the fire, but I have made up for it by going to bed in sweatpants and sweatshirt. I have a wool cap pulled down over my crew-cut and the covers up to my chin and only my nose and the lower part of my eyes are showing. *(Memoirs:* 151)

This scene, even though typical for Village Beat life in the fifties, is anything but erotic. Due to the cold, they go to bed early, turning their back to each other: "We are curled up, spoon fashion, all on our right sides, facing the fire. My nose is cold. My nose is always cold, and usually numb" (151). These two scenes clearly show di Prima's denial to bow too deeply to the standards of traditional autobiography. Her work does not stay within the boundaries of the autobiographical genre and exceeds it by merging fictional and nonfiction elements too often. In these two subchapters, didacticism is connected with textual subversion. The truthfulness of di Prima's *Memoirs* is clearly being questioned: The group orgy she depicts is fantasy; the reality for the five friends is boredom and discomfort due to the cold. By shifting the narrative view, di Prima changes the original story in order to teach a lesson.

Contrary to traditional pornographic writing, in which every passage has sexual purposes, leaving out personal details, friends, and one's life story, di Prima includes a self-reflexive element in *Memoirs*. Untypical for traditional woman's autobiography by over-embellishing scenes which were unspectacular in reality, di Prima adds various options and endings about the erotic or un-erotic night by the fire, leaving the reader unsure about the events. Following this depiction, the reader doubts di Prima's reliability. Which scenes are invented? Which passages are true? Is di Prima's *Memoirs* in general a truthful portrayal of what really happened within the Beat scene? Or does she just invent scenes in order to write a bestseller to make money? Moreover, is di Prima a trustworthy narrator? The narrator is being called "Diane di Prima" in the book, but how much does she herself as "the author writing the book" have to do with di Prima, the narrating persona?

The chapters which follow the Night-by-the-fire are among the most memoir-like and informative ones in the book. After having analyzed the two different versions about a night by the fire, readers may also question the truthfulness of the following sex orgy with Allen Ginsberg, Jack Kerouac, and Peter Orlovsky. The passages including these male Beat icons seem to be made up and contain fictional elements in order to make the story more interesting. When di Prima reads Allen Ginsberg's *Howl* (1956) for the first time, she knows that this is just the awakening of a much larger movement. Its powerful opening, "I saw the best minds of my generation destroyed by madness," indicates to her that many hipsters are hiding out, writing without getting things published, giving poetry readings in hidden basements for friends who think that their works are "unpublishable" (180). Now that *Howl* was published, however, "this Allen Ginsberg, whoever he was, had broken ground for all of us – all few hundreds of us – simply by getting this published". There were not many like her, but at least she was about to meet her "brothers and sisters" (176). In New York, the first mailing list of LeRoi Jones and di Prima's poetry magazine *The Floating Bear* included 117 artists, which means that there were very few people interested in underground poetry. In a recent interview, di Prima remembers the initially small circle of Beat bohemians:

> In the 50s there were very few of us. It took until the end of the 50s for any of us to meet each other. There were almost no poets around. There was an inspiring jazz movement. There was a beginning of a theater movement that was coming in from Europe. Then it burst into experimental theater in New York by the end of the 50s and 60s. But the writers were tucked away in little enclaves. [...] For most of the 50s, the arts were very hidden and very paranoid. The 50s were undercover time. Don't forget McCarthy, don't forget the Rosenbergs, don't forget Wilhelm Reich, who died in prison.[30]

---

[30] See Morrisey, Brian. "An Interview with Diane di Prima". *POESY – An Anthology*. April 21, 2006. http://www.poesy.org/interviews.html

After having read Ginsberg's groundbreaking work, di Prima gets into contact with him and Lawrence Ferlinghetti, who wrote the foreword to her first publication *This Kind of Bird Flies Backward*. When Ginsberg and his friends are in New York, she is eager to meet them. Kerouac, Ginsberg, and his lover Peter Orlovsky come to Leslie's apartment, where she is staying at the time, bringing with them much cheap wine and "good grass" (181). The orgy, comprised of di Prima, her friends Leslie and Benny, and Beat heroes Kerouac, Ginsberg, and Orlovsky, is probably the climax of *Memoirs*. They start getting "thoroughly stoned," and then, Ginsberg and Kerouac are reading their poetry. Due to the Beat philosophy of spontaneity, "Jack's belief, which Allen shared at the time, was that one should never change or rewrite anything. He felt that the initial flash of the turned-on mind was best, in life as well as in poetry, and I could see that he probably really lived that way". Kerouac is convinced that di Prima should follow his path, and tries to revise her poetry, rolling the "original bumpy lines off his tongue, making the stops and awkwardness beautiful," while they smoke more and more marijuana (181).

After having arranged mattresses and couches to make one big bed, things start off with hugging and kissing each other, and it is all "warm and friendly, and very unsexy – like being in a bathtub with four other people". Having her period, she plans to play "for a while with the cocks with which I found myself surrounded, planning as soon as I could to get out of the way of the action and go to sleep" (182). Being "in bed with three faggots," Kerouac "wanted some pussy and decided he was going to get it".[31] Gradually, things are getting out of hand, and "a strange, non descript kind of orgy" (181) follows. While Kerouac caresses di Prima's breasts "with his handsome head," wanting her to get rid of her tampon, Ginsberg embarked on a long speech dealing with the joys of sex while menstruating. Giving in, the narrator "pulled out the bloody talisman and flung it across the room" (182). While di Prima and Kerouac enjoy their "long, slow, easy fuck" (183) "just to prove that he didn't mind a little blood" (182), Ginsberg dedicates himself to the male bodies lying next to him.

Even though it is a fact that di Prima spent one or the other night with the male Beat icons in reality, the Kerouac-orgy seems exaggerated and unreal. After their first orgasms, Kerouac, high on more

---

[31] During the late 1940s and 1950s, Beat writers Jack Kerouac, Allen Ginsberg, Neal Cassady, and William Burroughs were exploring tangled and shifting homosocialities. Jack Kerouac was always very conflicted about his homosexual liaisons. According to biographer Gerald Nicosia, Kerouac fought against the label 'queer' all his life time: "It wasn't just a matter of defending his masculinity; for when drunk he often boasted of the men who had "blown" him, invited other men to do so, or challenged men to let him fuck them. But he believed in man's role as the head of the family, as the ruggedly honest, stoically suffering breadwinner […], the role personified by his father, as well as countless film heroes from Jean Gabin to Gary Cooper. The 'queer' stance – sniffling, sardonic, dissembling – seemed the very opposite of this" (1994: 155). Kerouac, who was probably the most traditionally minded of all Beat writers, shared this position with Ginsberg and Burroughs: For them, there were two kinds of homosexuals. Burroughs distinguishes between "strong, manly, noble homosexuals (or queers)" and the "dehumanised fags who jerk around like puppets on invisible strings, galvanized into hideous activity that is the negation of everything living and spontaneous" (Savran: 1998: 70). In Ginsberg's words there is, on the one hand, the "populist, humanist, quasi-heterosexual, Whitmanic, bohemian, free-love, homosexual" and, on the other hand, the "privileged, exaggeratedly effeminate, gossipy, moneyed, money-style-clothing-conscious, near-hysterical queen" (70).

wine and dope[32], suggests he and di Prima should try out the "Tibetan yab-yum" style, while Ginsberg "was reciting Whitman and rubbing Leslie's cock with his feet" (185). Kerouac exclaims,

> "Look, Allen"! and leaped out of bed pulling me onto him as he stood in a deep plié and we tried to do it in Tibetan yab-yum position. It felt good, was really fine and lots of fun, but Jack was drunk and high and balance not too good, and we fell over, narrowly missing a plant and went on fucking on the floor, my legs around his waist, while he protested that we should slow down and let him get into lotus position so we could try that one. *(Memoirs:* 185)

Yab-yum positions[33] or Lotus-style sex so that they could have sex and meditate at the same time – one cannot help but question the truthfulness of the account. The group sex with celebrities clearly spices the story that Olympia Press found was too dull and unamusing.

Di Prima's erotic depictions which belong to the realm of fantasy, are clearly contrasted with "historical" parts which confirm the veracity of the text. Passages like "List your favorite kisses," "Fuck the pill," "A Night by the Fire," but also depictions of people and places in the Village represent real life. In all chapters, di Prima, however, strongly relies on the illusion of memory. She sets her scenes in the past and places herself in them, using flashbacks or dreamlike techniques as a frequent pattern to introduce invented erotic scenes. This device is typical for erotic novels or pornographies: A small number of characters acts in a minimal story line which is interrupted by long sex scenes.

Yet surprisingly, blending fact and fiction is not unusual in autobiographical writing. By definition, an autobiography is a true story of a person's life written by that person. Autobiography is assumed to be non-fiction and is therefore supposed not to be filled with blatant fantasies. Often, however, they have fictional qualities which are part of people's lives, dreams, values, memories, and fears (cf. Bjorklund 1998: 30ff.). These unavoidable elements of fiction are so-called 'filters'[34]. Filters often play an important role in contributing to the message that is being conveyed and do not necessarily negate the non-fiction claim of autobiography. Even though fictional elements are included in di Prima's work,

---

[32] Even though Kerouac was a liberally minded person throughout the 1950s, he became increasingly narrow-minded when he grew older. He distanced himself from the movement he was once part of and became increasingly conservative, intolerant, and bigoted. According to di Prima, the events depicted in *Memoirs* took place in 1953-1956. As a consequence of alcoholism, Jack Kerouac died of inner haemorrhages in October 1969, the year she published the book. Before his death, he even scared off Allen Ginsberg on William Buckley's TV show *Firing Line* by being anti-semitic and anti-Beat Generation. About the flower power generation, Kerouac stated that he was in favor of their idea of spiritual enlightenment, but he opposed psychedelic drugs and leftist politics (cf. Watson 1998: 298).

[33] The women's magazine COSMOPOLITAN (May 2005) describes this position as follows: "YAB-YUM-STELLUNG: Die klassische buddhistische Götterpaar-Vereinigung. Dabei sitzt er aufrecht, die Beine gekreuzt oder lang ausgestreckt, sie sitzt auf ihm, die Beine hinter seinem Rücken gekreuzt. Nun legen beide die rechte Hand auf die Herzgegend des anderen oder legen die Stirne aneinander und sehen sich in die Augen, um die tiefe Nähe zu spüren." (2005: 66).

[34] In Maxine Hong Kingston's *The Woman Warrior*, so-called 'filters' play a crucial role. Her talk-story may be considered fiction, but it is closely connected to her true life story. The invented passages in the book are part of Kingston's life and explain both her Chinese American culture and her relationship with her mother. Mostly throughout the book, Kingston's story is considered non-fiction and verifiable. For more information, see the following web site: Huffman, Emily. "Rhetorical Analysis – Maxine Hong Kingston's The Woman Warrior". September 15, 2006. http://www.cwrl.utexas.edu/~waddington/web309/EMILY9.HTM. Also see Kingston, Maxine Hong (1989). *The Woman Warrior: Memoirs of a Girlhood among Ghosts.* New York: Vintage Books.

Memoirs generally stays within the boundaries of autobiographical writing, as the narrative contains a basic level of truth and verifiable lineage.

Even though female Beat writers generally resist being categorized and labeled, it is the literary critic's task to make sense of literary developments. The following chapter will take a closer look at feminist autobiographical writing as defined by critic Estelle Jelinek, and *Memoirs of a Beatnik* will be categorized according to various subgenres of autobiography.

6.3 Towards a Categorization of *Memoirs*

Despite its fictitious and invented passages, di Prima's *Memoirs* contains many classical characteristics of autobiography. In her revolutionary feminist compilation of autobiographical criticism, *Women's Autobiography: Essays in Criticism*, Estelle Jelinek characterizes traditional autobiographical writings. Furthermore, she analyzes how women's life writings have changed the elements normally used to define and structure the narrative of the male self[35]. Jelinek refers to the general consensus that a "good autobiography not only focuses on its author, but also reveals his connectedness to the rest of society; it is representative of his times, a mirror of his era" (1980: 7). Throughout history, males tended to focus on the progress of their professional or intellectual lives when writing an autobiography, leaving out their identity as a member of a group or society at large. Men's life stories are mostly success stories. In the book, Jelinek mentions numerous works of male life writing, like the first autobiography ever written, Augustine's *Confessions* (400), Rousseau's *Confessions* (1781), or more recent works like Malcolm X's *The Autobiography of Malcolm X* (1965). They all "stress their authors' successful professional life and concomitantly its relationship to their times" while leaving out personal details. Malcolm X, for example, tells his rise to fame, coming from a poverty-stricken and violent family. Jelinek makes clear that women's life writings – contrary to men's –"rarely mirror the establishment history of their times. They emphasize to a much lesser extent the public aspect of their lives, the affairs of the world, or even their careers, and concentrate instead on their personal lives – domestic details, family difficulties, close friends, and especially people who influenced them" (7-8). As an early example, Agrippina's *Memoirs* written in the first century focuses on her family members instead of political matters.

Personal experiences, emotionality, friends, and the bohemian scene in general play a crucial role in di Prima's *Memoirs*, whereas affairs influencing world history are mentioned only marginally. Miles Davis' moving away from Tenth Avenue into some other neighborhood seems to have a greater impact on the young bohemians than the historic events of 1956. In Chapter 14 called "We Set Out," for the first time in *Memoirs*, di Prima refers to political changes going on in the United States during the time. The Rosenberg executions and the Hungarian Revolution made them "paranoid, glued to the

---

[35] For more information about Jelinek's early publication seen in connection with *Memoirs*, see Moke 1998: 169ff.

radio, and talking endlessly of where we could possibly go into exile" (174). Wilhelm Reich was in federal prison, the first fallout terror had finally struck, and some people bought land in Montana to construct a city under a lead dome. More important for them, however, is the fact that New York's "neo-fascist city planning" ordered the area north of their pad to be destructed, making way for the Lincoln Center. "The house next door to us, which had been empty for twenty-eight years, and had functioned as our private garbage dump for as long as we lived there, was suddenly torn down, leaving a number of bums homeless and scattering thousands of rats – most of them into our walls" (174). Only at the end of the book, di Prima mentions the political changes that affected society as a whole, like the repressions under McCarthyism or the U.S. consumer society, which gradually became grimmer. These being the only historic events mentioned, di Prima goes on to talk about – Jelinek called them typical "women topics" – "domestic details" (di Prima's pads), "family difficulties" (difficulties raising money for the pad, food etc.), "close friends" (her heterosexual and homosexual liaisons with numerous fellow beatniks), and "people who influenced them" (the impact of *Howl*, Ginsberg, Kerouac, and other male Beat writers on them).

Typically for women's autobiographical writings, di Prima elides her own progress as a poet. Even if women were professional and successful writers, Jelinek points out, "we find them omitting their work life, referring obliquely to their careers, or camouflaging them behind the personal aspects of their lives" (8). Di Prima does not include her personal writing career in *Memoirs* and – in comparison to, for example, Norman Podhoretz' *Making It* (1967) – she does not describe her professional life in detail. She depicts jobs, like being a pornographic model, which are necessary in order to pay the rent, the bills, and buy food. Only in one passage, she mentions that she is a poet trying to get her first compilation of poems published. When reading *Memoirs*, the reader gets to know the 19-year-old narrator as a young, Greenwich Village bohemian only, but not as a young, aspiring poet. In comparison to many male autobiographers, she leaves out her own writing career in order to mirror New York's bohemian scene in the first place, the scene she was part of. Critic Steven Watson points out that di Prima's *Memoirs* "not only provided a vivid picture of bohemian New York life in the mid-1950s but restored to erotica real bodies, lived-in humor, and a canny comfort about sex surpassing that of the Beat males" (1995: 273).

In order to illustrate how women often underestimate their own lives, Estelle Jelinek names several early examples of women's life writings, as well as more contemporary ones, like Gertrude Stein's *Autobiography of Alice B. Toklas* and Ellen Glasgow's *The Woman Within*. She discusses several women's autobiographies to show women's autobiographical intention, namely to introspectively and intimately focus on private, personal details, while understating their professional success. Feminist critic Sidonie Smith points out the problem that females generally often sacrifice their individuality

> [...] to the constitutive definitions of her identity as member of a family, as someone's daughter, someone's wife and someone's mother. The unified self disperses, radiating outward until its fragments dissipate altogether into social and communal masks. Thus woman's destiny cannot be self-determined, and her agency cannot be recognized. (Moke. *Desires of their own:* 170)

Concerning losing one's individuality and identity, Smith's hypothesis is not true for Diane di Prima. While Smith's descriptions of women's strategies of representation seem to reiterate the descriptions of Beat women's roles presented in narratives of that era, di Prima's *Memoirs* does not. The concept of identity is crucial for di Prima: The female narrator in *Memoirs* defines herself as a member of a group rather than an individual. The narrative voice takes on the role of a communal persona, depicting Beat life as "we," yet she is not interested in depicting her own personal history. Di Prima's self is able to move in and out of various roles, offering the memoirs of a beatnik, as the title implies. She sees herself as a member of the Beat community, but she does identify herself as someone's daughter, someone's wife, or someone's mother, as women often do according to Smith. The narrative voice in the book clearly refuses traditional role models and adopts male versions of rebellion.

Many Beat women like di Prima copied a certain hipster code of 'being cool' and acting like a man. In *Burning Questions – My Life as a Rebel*, Zane, the female narrator, tells about the Beat behavior patterns that had to be followed in order not to be "uncool". After her boyfriend Marshall leaves her, she ponders over their relationship and the strict 'Rule of Cool':

> According to the strict code of Cool by which we lived, only weakness moved anyone to extend a relationship beyond the initial passion of the moment. Once a passion peaked, you were supposed to let it go like a poem that had found its form. To "work" on a relationship as people take pride in doing nowadays was considered a barbarism that would destroy not only whatever feeling might be left but whatever good had gone before. (Shulman. *Burning Questions:* 105)

Already at the beginning of their relationship, Marshall had made clear that "the trouble with women was they didn't know how to let go, they always tried to hang on after the natural end and drag everyone down to the ground. Just as they wanted to think instead of fuck and talk instead of sleep". Some of Marshall's Beat friends come for a visit to "comfort" her when he drops her, but she knows that they "had made the obligatory pass at me in the first weeks after Marshall's departure". She is well aware that "they did it more for form than desire, as I turned them down more for form than disgust, for I'd never been anything else to them but Marshall's pussy. [...] I had not come to New York to throw myself away on love" (106).

While male Beats seemed to be cool and unemotional by nature, women were often only seen as accessories for males, even though they imitated the hip, cool, hot lifestyle. The rule was clear for everyone: To act like a hipster is, for both sexes, to act like a man, to be indifferent, and to understate one's emotions. By indulging in sexual excesses in *Memoirs of a Beatnik*, di Prima refuses to be beaten down, and instead also approaches the male model for autobiography. In an interview, di Prima muses about the origins of the 'Rule of Cool':

> Why did *Cool* come about? I don't know – I guess it was the fashion. It was maybe a reaction to the oversentimentality of our parents' generation – the soap operas, Frank Sinatra ... So the jazz was cool, we were cool, everybody was cool, and if you were cool that meant that you gave everybody more space, sort of. [...] For example, LeRoi (Amiri Baraka) and I were together for three years and I think we used the word "love" only once or twice. You see there was a depth of passion to the NOT stating it that was very intense.[36]

Di Prima sees herself in the role of the strong, unemotional, "cool" character who is able to lead the lifestyle she chooses. The hipster code of their "eternal, tiresome rule of Cool" (1998: 94) is a social code that makes women collaborators with their own oppression due to the fact that the essence of cool is passivity, lack of emotion, and indifference. The 'Rule of Cool' oppressed feelings and emotions, but also prohibited the feminine in both sexes. Imitating men, di Prima acts similar to Hemingway's mannish vamp Brett Ashley in *The Sun also Rises*. Yet, this cool behavior is problematic for women: The gender binary collapses into a unitary conformity with masculine behavior. Feminist and literary critic Julia Kristeva notes that female writers often take on a "phallic position" that obtains "in a culture where the speaking subjects are conceived of as masters of their speech" (1981: 165). This position might compromise the female author by masculinizing her.

Throughout the memoir, di Prima adopts the 'Rule of Cool' attitude to present herself as a sexually active character, acting like a man. Even though di Prima first experienced eroticized sexuality with women, she depicts active female sexuality as masculine. While some female writers of the time would have had troubles to present their active, eroticized female sexuality in their works, di Prima does not: Being independent and self-confident, she enjoys her unconflicted sexual agency. For the narrator, her open sexuality is an unvexed, natural condition. It is particularly noteworthy, however, that the author has been introduced to sexual matters by females, not males. During one of the frolic Italian celebrations at home, the women in di Prima's family quite openly show their relaxed attitude concerning female sexuality: "I had had to stand for inspection while my grandmother and my mother's older sisters felt of my budding breasts, drawing them out with their fingers, or spanned my bottom with their hands, while commenting in Italian on my good and bad points as a future breeding animal. All this was done in a spirit of utter kindness and delight," di Prima writes (48). The narrator also prefers females when exploring her sexuality during her adolescent years at College. Di Prima, for example, depicts homoerotic evenings with Mara, Mathilde, Kate, Lee, Susan, Petra, and Tomi.

Decoding typically male characteristics of life writing, Estelle Jelinek points out that classical male-authored autobiography generally contains the following features: Throughout history, men's autobiographical works have mostly been coherent, unifying, linear, consistent, and progressive in

---

[36] See Di Prima, Diane (1981). "Cool". *The Shocking Tabloid Issues*. January 8, 2007. http://www.researchpubs.com/books/tab2exc1.php

terms of time and chronology. While males' present their successful careers in linear narratives filled with harmony and orderliness, "irregularity rather than orderliness informs the self-portrays by women" (1980: 17). Women's autobiographies are often disconnected, fragmentary, and organized in units, rather than chapters. At first glance, *Memoirs of a Beatnik* progresses in a certain chronological plot, starting with "February," "February continued," "February Concluded," "April," "April Continued," "April Concluded," "Country Spring," "Summer" – and finally concluding with di Prima's "We Set Out," the day she leaves New York City.

> And when the full moon shone on the fire-escape again, I didn't get my period as I should have. And as the moon waned, my breasts grew and became sore, and I knew I was pregnant. And I began to put my books in boxes, and pack up the odds and ends of my life, for a whole new adventure was starting, and I had no idea where it would land me. *(Memoirs:* 187)

In a 1980 interview done by the writer Raul Santiago Sebazco, di Prima explains that she suddenly decided to have a baby, but refused to get bored in a usual monogamous relationship. About the lover she chose as the father of her child, she says: "He was my first choice. I had 6 or 7 lovers and what happened then was I made a semi-conscious choice. The man I chose was a man I had been in love with 6 years before. He was in town only occasionally and studying at Johns Hopkins at the time. He was still an exciting person to me. I didn't intend to get pregnant that day but I did". Keeping her pregnancy secret, she did not tell him about the baby's existence until three months after the birth: "I wrote him a Christmas card that said, 'By the way, you have a daughter in New York, come see us sometime'. We were all into being very cool back then, you know"[37]. At the end of *Memoirs*, di Prima leaves for California, and eventually finishes her journey in San Francisco. Surprisingly, the book ends with a pregnant first person narrator, enriching her 'Rule of Cool' lifestyle with a typical female topic. Even though she expects a baby, she is still able to maintain her independence by setting her own rules.

Superficially, di Prima's text is clearly chronologically structured, drifting through several seasons from 1953 to 1956. Critics might argue that this chronological order in which *Memoirs* was written once again mirrors di Prima's "male-oriented" writing. However, at a closer look, the plot shows characteristics of disorder, diffusion, and diversity. Her work denies temporality, the seasonal motif being replaced by chapters like "The Pad," "Organs and Orgasms," and "We Set Out". The first person narrator cuts up scenes and time itself to present sequences of interconnected scenes. Di Prima quickly moves from one scene to the other, and memory floats in and out of time, denying any historical setting. In this respect, di Prima employs the typically female "disorder" in her memoir, which is contrasted to the "orderly" male plot and chronology, according to Jelinek.

---

[37] See di Prima, Diane (1981). "Cool". *The Shocking Tabloid Issues.* January 8, 2007. http://www.researchpubs.com/books/tab2exc1.php

Containing typical characteristics of women's autobiography – adding a cool, unemotional touch to the story, *Memoirs of a Beatnik* can be read as a chronicle of the Beat culture from a female perspective, written in memoir form. Both autobiographies and memoirs are based on a person's life experience. Generally, they differ in time and focus. Memoirs are less structured and less all-encompassing than lengthier autobiographical works. Generally, an autobiography has at its center the "life and times" of the person telling the story, while a memoir deals with more personal details, including intimate feelings and emotions. Furthermore, di Prima's *Memoirs* is shorter than a traditional autobiography, which is an extensive account of a longer period of time. Memoirs focus on a short period in a writer's life or a specific aspect of one's life, like inner thoughts, philosophies, or life-changing events. According to John A. Cuddon, the contemporary memoir often tries to focus on certain highlights or crucial events in somebody's past, often including a contemplation of the meaning of that event at the time when the memoir is written (cf. 1991: 88). This defining category is only partly true for di Prima, since she wrote her book mainly in order to make money, and because her publisher asked her to write down her adventurous Beat memories that might interest a large number of readers. After all, laying bare the intimacies and secrets surrounding the male Beat icons guaranteed public interest. By definition, memoirs are often more emotional than autobiographies and capture particular scenes or a series of events rather than document every fact of a person's life (cf. 89). Di Prima's scope of time is brief compared to other full length autobiographies which might highlight someone's whole life and all background information included. *Memoirs*, in comparison, only covers three particular years in the 1950s, which is important since this time marks the beginning of the formation of the Beat sub-culture. On the whole, *Memoirs of a Beatnik* exemplifies many of the typical characteristics of the memoir genre: The author remembers highlights of her past, and reconstructs the events and their impact in a personal way by including her extended "Beat family". Furthermore, she focuses on a brief period of time or rather a series of related events, and refuses to write down her memoirs in a lengthy, expanded autobiography capturing all of her life. The work covers some years of her life, her relationships, and jobs, but only to show how they are related to her experience in Beat New York City. It is a zooming-in of one aspect of her life, rather than an in-depth look at her entire life.

Memoirs of a Beatnik contains features of an erotic or even pornographic memoir. Due to the fact that some parts are obviously made up to spice up the story, the term 'semi-autobiographical' might be considered appropriate. As one would expect from erotic autobiography, di Prima makes the private public – even more significantly than in other narratives of the self. She enriches the story of her subcultural bohemian environment with her intimate sexual depictions. Moreover, she sees herself taking part in a larger cultural setting. At the same time, while being the strong, unemotional main protagonist of the narrative, di Prima also adopts the role of communal persona, telling the story of the awakening of the Beat Generation and so chronicling a specific historical moment. The young narrator sees herself as determined, sexual woman, but some readers might also consider her "cliterocentric," seeing her as *the* sexual subject in the book. Due to the many unexamined assumptions about women's intellectual, creative, or even sexual inferiority, di Prima is particularly outstanding, as she is a sexually liberated female and a clear forerunner of the feminist revolution which would occur a decade later.

One could also go further and argue that *Memoirs* is clearly a pornographic memoir. As a literary genre, pornography is writing that has sexual arousal as its primary aim. Erotica or erotic writing, in comparison, are works with artistic pretensions. Therefore, the descriptive term *pornography* also contains "a statement about intentionality and instrumentality without reference to merit, whereas the term *erotica* is evaluative and laudatory"[38]. In *Flesh and the Word*, John Preston more baldly says, "The only difference is that erotica is the stuff bought by rich people"[39]. Other sources do not distinguish erotic writing and pornography. For some critics, erotica is fiction dealing mainly with the sex lives of its characters and featuring graphic descriptions of sex acts, while pornography is only a subculture product. Due to the fact that the distinction between the two genres blurs, *Memoirs of a Beatnik* can be assigned to both. Erotic writing has become a mainstream genre since the 1990s, when many bookstores began stocking erotic works on their shelves. During the prim 1960s, when *Memoirs* was written, the effects on the reader must have been even more shocking than nowadays.

Pornographic works are not always easy to determine. Robin West states that even if we cannot clearly define pornography, we can say that something is pornographic. She points out that pornography can be defined by three distinguishing attributes: Primarily, pornography is an aid to sexual pleasure and satisfies a sexual interest. Furthermore, pornography has a commercial nature, as it is a commercial product which is produced, bought, and sold on the market. Third, pornography is offensive, it is "an assault on a relatively widely accepted conception of sexual virtue" (West: 1987: 682); Thus, it is shocking and of low value. All three points can be applied to di Prima's narrative: *Memoirs* might be written for those readers who are interested in finding sexual arousal when reading erotic narratives. Di Prima clearly places the female as the sex object in male fantasy. The text's lesbian sex scenes, for example, have similar functions as in male-focused pornography: They salaciously trigger male sexuality. Due the title of the book, it is also likely, however, that readers rather try to get background information about the famous, rebellious Beat Generation through reading the book. Kerouac, Ginsberg, and Burroughs became heroes after years of rejection, and therefore, the lurid title should tempt the reader to buy the book. West's second argument, money matters, also plays a crucial role for di Prima. Being short of money, she commercializes the Beat Generation looking backwards from 1969 to 1953. At the end of the 1960s, the Beats, or what was left of them, were either "domesticated" or had turned into hippies. Di Prima had financial problems at the time and was urged to sell her Beat life as a commercial product, writing a "spicy" memoir that promises to reveal new details about a

---

[38] See "Erotica and Pornography". *An Encyclopaedia of Gay, Lesbian, Bisexual, Transgender & Queer Culture*. September 7, 2006. http://www.glbtq.com/literature/erotica_pornography.html
[39] See "Erotica and Pornography". *An Encyclopaedia of Gay, Lesbian, Bisexual, Transgender & Queer Culture*. September 7, 2006. http://www.glbtq.com/literature/erotica_pornography.html

whole literary movement. Asked in an interview about why *Memoirs* was written, she claims that "it deliberately made money for Olympia Press," but it also got herself out of financial distress. She goes on to say that the book "was the only thing I ever wrote for money and it's earning money to this day"[40]. West's third defining category is also true for *Memoirs:* Even for the contemporary reader, the book might be shocking, offensive, and scandalous, as it defies traditional concepts about sexuality, monogamy, and partnership.

Di Prima's pornographic memoir is clearly male-centered, which is proved in two particular scenes: First, when Tomi is more or less voluntarily raped by her brother while Diane watches voyeuristically through the keyhole, and second, when di Prima is raped by Tomi's father Serge during a boat trip. These rapes can be read as cultural devices to depict sexual pleasures, on the one hand, but, on the other hand, they legitimize rape. *Memoirs of a Beatnik* shows connections to pornographic literature as her characters act within a minimal story line which is often interrupted by long scenes depicting various kinds of sex. In many chapters, a certain pattern takes shape: Creating the illusion of remembering passages exactly, she sets certain scenes in the past and places herself in them. In dreamlike flashbacks, she introduces certain sex scenes. Di Prima seems to have copied this device from pornographic fiction. She distorts reality and repeatedly slips from fiction to history, from novel to memoir. In effect, di Prima rather shows how to be a Beat than reporting about what it was like to be part of the Beat Generation, in contrast to Joyce Johnson's and Hettie Jones' memoirs.

Di Prima, however, is also skillfully reinventing the masculine genre of pornography to present a woman's coming-of-age from a very personal point of view. She embraces heterosexual intercourse and homoerotic affairs, rejects patriarchy and sexism, and tells square U.S. society that women are free to choose their own sexual identity. She is confessional and among the first women memoirists who openly talk about taboos like lesbian sex, pornographic jobs, or abortion. By doing so, she scoffs at male Beats' constructions of sexuality.

Beside being an erotic or pornographic autobiography, *Memoirs of a Beatnik* can also be called a quest narrative. In Kerouac's scandalous autobiographical novel *On the Road*, the two main protagonists Sal and Dean are breaking down barriers all across the United States and Mexico in order to experience more and more kicks. Similarly, di Prima is breaking down barriers of sexual confinement, shocking America's rigid and paranoid postwar culture. Her strength is to stay independent, authentic, and true to herself. Same as Dean Moriarty, di Prima is autonomous and on a spiritual trip. Their quest leads them to similar experiences, yearning for more and more kicks like drugs, sexual excesses, and a "cool," independent lifestyle. For di Prima, the non-conformist 'Rule of Cool' is a revolt for personal freedom, finally leading to her participation in second wave feminism. Her quest is crucial also in the sense of being part of the intimate Beat circle which offers her a site of authority from which to write her *Memoirs*.

---

[40] See Morrisey, Brian. "An Interview with Diane di Prima". *POESY – An Anthology*. April 21, 2006. http://www.poesy.org/interviews.html

6.4 Diane di Prima – A Female Neal Cassady?

When taking a closer look, certain similarities can be recognized between the lives of Diane di Prima and Neal Cassady, Beat hero and icon of several Beat narratives. In their intensity, Neal Cassady's road adventures could be taken from di Prima's *Memoirs of a Beatnik*. Both di Prima and Cassady embraced the so-called 'Rule of Cool': The lives of both authors were full of sexual excesses, they were "cool," did not show any emotions, and devoted their lives to the Beat "carpe-diem"-attitude only.

Already in his lifetime, Neal Cassady (1926-1968) achieved the status of a modern folk hero, a contemporary legend. Both during his life and after his death, that legend has found expression in a number of written works, on film, and in popular song. Walt Whitman wrote that before he produced *Leaves of Grass* (1855) he had been "simmering, simmering" until the influence of Ralph Waldo Emerson brought him to boil. Cassady, too, had the same effect on Jack Kerouac and Allen Ginsberg. Poet Gary Snyder describes the impressions Neal Cassady left behind:

> My vision of Cassady is of the 1890s cowboys, the type of person who works the high plains of the 1880s and 1890s. [...] He is the Denver grandchild of the 1880s cowboys with no range left to work on. Cassady's type is that frontier type, reduced to pool halls and driving back and forth across the country. Cassady was the energy of the archetypical west, the energy of the frontier, still coming down. Cassady is the cowboy crashing. (Charters. *Kerouac*: 286)

Similar to Diane di Prima's experiences in *Memoirs*, Jack Kerouac would later observe that for Cassady, "sex was the one and only holy and important thing in his life" (1991: 28). In his autobiography, Neal Cassady writes that he was sexually initiated at the age of nine. Accompanying his father to the home of an alcoholic friend, Neal and his brothers were encouraged to have sexual intercourse with as many sisters as they would please. During that night, all sexual limits evaporated, as Neal shared women with his father and brothers (cf. Wilson 1998: 79f.).

Sex, cars, and theft were the main influences in Neal Cassady's adolescence, all connected in what he called "Adventures in Auto-Eroticism". Between fourteen and twenty-one, Cassady had stolen over 500 cars in the state of Colorado. Arrested ten times and convicted six, he spent fifteen months in reform schools. Unrepentant, he would be released, see a car, and once again indulge in his "soul-thrilling pleasures" of driving all through the desert (Cassady: 1981: 170). Similarly, di Prima also experiences her personal "Adventures in Auto-Eroticism". She is a female Beat writer who dares to write about herself in the first place. She herself as the narrating persona is the main protagonist of many poems and narratives, but she is also the main focus of her two autobiographical works, *Memoirs of a Beatnik* (1969) and *Recollections of my Life as a Woman: The New York Years* (2001). Like di Prima, Cassady started to write an autobiography called *The First Third* while imprisoned in

San Quentin in 1958/1959[41]. In *Memoirs*, di Prima talks about herself as the center of a chosen bohemian family, about her body, bodily pleasures, and her "sexual power" (43).

Like di Prima, Cassady also boasted about his sexual activity throughout his lifetime. Being a handsome sportsman, he attracted both men and women. Kerouac compared Neal's face to the U.S. entertainer Gene Autry, also called "The Singing Cowboy," but Cassady could not afford good clothes. Kerouac recalled, "his dirty workclothes clung to him so gracefully, as though you couldn't buy a better fit from a custom tailor but only earn it from the Natural Tailor of Natural Joy" (1991: 10). Cassady's seductions were directed at both men and women. Falling in love with innumerous girls even though he was married to Carolyn Cassady, he would always find someone to adore, if only for a moment. Beat friends like Allen Ginsberg were also sexually attracted to him. Even though Diane di Prima cannot be called a "womanizer" or "manizer," she attracted both men and women. Before experiencing her first heterosexual intercourse, she had several affairs with female college friends.

The greatest mystification of Cassady was, of course, by Jack Kerouac. In *On the Road*, Cassady's sexual drives and frantic womanizing play an important role and are depicted in detail. Gerald Nicosia explains that "Jack promoted Neal as a myth figure, just as Allen had done for Jack; in effect, Jack and Neal's relationship became a mirror image of the intense, almost priestly bond between Jack and Allen" (1994: 250). In *On the Road*, Neal Cassady, Dean Moriarty in the novel, has a very ambivalent role. Representing social and individual energy in destructive form, he is living out the ecstasy of jazz, articulating the holiness of sexual intercourse, and the eternal hope of renewal after a divorce. Cassady is a devil and an angel at the same time: eternally loved by women and men, but hated if he abandons them.

In *On the Road*, Dean Moriarty can keep three women satisfied simultaneously, and he can make love any time and anywhere. For Sal, Dean represents "the holy GOOF" (194), a prophet and saint who totally rejects responsibility. When a girl complains about his lack of "any sense of responsibility for years" (182), Dean just giggles and starts dancing. Moriarty's hyper-masculine behavior can be seen as both the cause and result of his manic lifestyle. He frantically loves – preferably – teenage girls, because his personality will not allow him to settle down in one monogamous relationship. Similar to Moriarty, di Prima's narrator in *Memoirs* also refuses tiring one-to-one relationships, and has affairs with several lovers at the same time. Although Dean is married three times in *On the Road*, he is adulterous all the time, and always looks for new "chicks" for Sal and himself:

---

[41] Neal Cassady's autobiography, however, remained unfinished. It was first published by the small San Francisco Beat publishing house City Lights in 1981 after Cassady's wife Carolyn Cassady had released the manuscript. See Cassady, Neal (1981). *The First Third and Other Writings*. San Francisco: City Lights.

> He darted the car and looked in every direction for girls. "Look at her!" The air was so sweet in New Orleans it seemed to come in soft bandannas; and you could smell the river and really smell the people, and mud, and molasses, and every kind of tropical exhalation with your nose suddenly removed from the dry ices of a Northern winter. We bounced in our seats. "And dig her!" yelled Dean, pointing at another woman. "Oh, I love, love women! I think women are wonderful! I love women!" He spat out the window; he groaned; he clutched his head. Great beads of sweat fell from his forehead from pure excitement and exhaustion. *(On the Road:* 140)

Dean's pursuit of Beat "chicks" is part of the role he has among his East Coast friends, as Sal Paradise sees him as "a new kind of American saint" (39). Sal and Dean can clearly be seen as two hyper-masculine travelers. Both are selfish, irresponsible, and abusive towards women who sometimes accompany them on their road trips, but who are excluded from their male kicks. Moriarty is constantly juggling his time between multiple lovers, as he can never stay too long with one partner. As depicted in *On the Road*, Dean's frantic love making requires a detailed schedule. Carlo Marx (Allen Ginsberg in real life), who himself had an affair with Dean, explains that while he comes off work,

> [...] Dean is balling Marylou at the hotel and gives me time to change and dress. At one sharp he rushes from Marylou to Camille – of course neither of them knows what's going on – and bangs her once, giving me time to arrive at one-thirty. Then he comes out with me – first he has to beg with Camille, who's really started hating me – [...]. Then at six he goes back to Marylou –and he's going to spend all day tomorrow running around to get the necessary papers for their divorce. Marylou's all for it, but she insists on banging in the interim. She says she loves him - so does Camille. *(On the Road:* 42-43)

Throughout *On the Road*, Dean has three wives (Marylou, Camille, and Inez) and several other girlfriends and affairs. His attraction towards women is unbroken, even if he leaves his wives, only to come back half a year later to apologize. Here, a connection to Diane di Prima can be spun. Throughout *Memoirs of a Beatnik*, Diane di Prima has numerous female and male lovers. There is Ivan, a West Village man who was "quiet, rather thin, dressed in clean dungarees and blue work shirt, his wet hair neatly combed" (1998: 10), and who would be the future father of her first child. There is Robin, Ivan's friend, who suddenly appears in the apartment and seduces her. Furthermore, there are Tomi and several other female college friends who have homoerotic liaisons with each other. In another episode of the book, Diane does not say "no" when Tomi's father rapes her. Then there are Billy, the country guitarist, and his father Big Bill: They start a triangle relationship on their farm in the Hudson River Valley. Back in New York, she falls in love with "a very beautiful, ghost-like blonde boy named Luke Taylor, who played a very heavy shade blues guitar and shot a lot of heroin – 'horse' as we called it then" (117-118). Chapter 13 of *Memoirs of a Beatnik* is called "Organs and Orgasms – An Appreciation": At the time, di Prima has six or seven lovers at the same time, but unlike Neal Cassady, she does not have a fixed schedule that arranges when to meet each of them:

> In the Spring for a while I found myself the sole occupant of Number Six, Amsterdam Avenue, and it was then and there that I instituted the custom of giving keys to all my lovers; there were at that time six or seven of them. At this time I got a real double-bed mattress and box spring, and I put them under the window in the front room, and we would watch the moonlight fall on the fire-escape [...]. Everyone came in differently, everyone took me on a different trip; it was like six mythologies, six different worlds. *(Memoirs:* 159)

There was Georgie Dunningham, whom she had met at a jam session. Georgie brought along Antoine. Furthermore, there were Don, Pete, Ivan, and Dirty John, all of them "would come, each of them the same, but all of them different" (170). Even though parts of the memoir are made up, di Prima had numerous relationships at that time in real life. Apart from the sexual scenes in the book that are exaggerated, the included people and the affairs she had are true accounts. In comparison to Moriarty, di Prima does not have a fixed daily schedule. Dean's long time schedule is frequently a result of his decision to travel hundreds of miles to see a distant lover or friend. One afternoon, for example, after having spent a frantic night out, Dean presents his new schedule for the near future: "I'm going to divorce Marylou and marry Camille and go live with her in San Francisco. But this is only after you and I, dear Carlo, go to Texas, dig Old Bull Lee [William Burroughs], that gone cat I've never met and both of you've told me so much about, and then I'll go to San Fran" (48).

Similar to the narrator in *Memoirs* who also seems unattached and reckless, Dean is only interested in sexual kicks. "You have absolutely no regard for anybody but yourself and your damned kicks. All you think about is what's hanging between your legs and how much money or fun you can get out of people and then you just throw them aside" (193-194), Sal's girlfriend Galatea attacks Dean, but this only confirms Sal's own opinion that "sex was the one and only important thing in his life" (4). As Galatea points out, he is sexist, but she finally also leaves Sal in Mexico because of his misogynous behavior. Dean himself states that he does not care about anything "so long's I can get that lil ole gal with that lil sumpin down there between her legs" (10). The accusations that he cares for nothing but his "damned kicks" (194) is easy to see right from the start, but this is the basis of his sex appeal. The women accusing Dean of just caring for himself, appear "sullen" and "mean" to Sal, who devalues them as "nothing but a sewing circle" (193). Women in *On the Road* are often left in the position of paying for male irresponsibility, especially Dean's wife Camille, who is left alone in San Francisco raising their two children and paying the bills. Sal, too, does not take his road affairs too seriously and continuously defends Moriarty's irresponsible behavior. But even if Sal is dropped by a girl, he can always call some "rich girl [he] knew" who pulls "a hundred-dollar bill out of her silk stocking" and says, "'You've been talking of a trip to Frisco; that being the case, take this and go and have your fun'" (181). Obviously, Dean's and Sal's charms could not be rejected by any woman. After having married Inez in Newark towards the end of the book, Dean, immediately after the marriage, "jumped on a bus and roared off again across the awful continent to San Francisco to rejoin Camille and the two baby girls. So now he was three times married, twice divorced, and living with his second wife"

(305). Actually, "there are as many marriages and divorces in *On the Road* as in the Hollywood movie colony (must be that California climate)" (Theado: 2001: 78).

Di Prima's *Memoirs* is similarly in favor of this certain 'Ethos of Cool'. She creates a self-portrait of a new kind of woman: She is independent, brave, and uses her lovers as she pleases – same as Cassady. She is a woman who longs for the same adventures shown in *On the Road*, but she also experiences them herself. Unlike many other women among the Beats, di Prima did not drown, but remained an accepted and equal member of the predominantly male "boy gang". Considering all that, di Prima can definitely be called a "female Cassady".

The preceding chapter, including its subchapters, analyzed and categorized Diane di Prima's bold work *Memoirs of a Beatnik*, a text which was clearly shocking and confrontational for the "chaste" postwar audience. Di Prima's first person narrator represents a new type of woman, namely that of the uncommitted, careless hipster obliged to the 'Rule of Cool'.

The two women being in the spotlight in the next chapters also belong to that new group of self-confident Beat women whose major aim is to speak for a whole generation of silenced women. Joyce Johnson published her Beat memoir *Minor Characters* in 1983, Hettie Jones followed with *How I Became Hettie Jones* in 1990. Their life writings were released rather late in life, offering the two authors the possibility to reflect on their young age from a distance. Beside their long running personal friendship, both women share having been the girlfriend/wife of two outstanding Beat icons – Jack Kerouac and LeRoi Jones.

7 Joyce Johnson and Hettie Jones: Confide in me!

Sharing a number of similarities, *Minor Characters* and *How I Became Hettie Jones* are probably the most famous and well-known memoirs by female Beats. Both authors ponder over the question whether there was anything "to become" for a 1950s female teenager – and how: "What should I do now," Jones wants to know, "What should I do now to make myself happen? What's next?" (1997: 27). Successfully, both Johnson and Jones were determined to escape the fifties plot scripted for talented girls. Both Joyce Johnson's *Minor Characters* and Hettie Jones' *How I Became Hettie Jones* directly refer to the historic period generally known as the Beat era, which can be roughly dated from 1944 to 1964; each was written several decades after its historic focus, which is typical of life writing; and each work is aware of its responsibility to tell the truth about their life stories as nonfictional reliable accounts. In contrast to Diane di Prima, who often floats out of time and into imagination, their narrators speak as verifiable historical referents set in the middle of Beat times, presenting themselves as trustworthy and believable memoirists.

Paradoxically, *Minor Characters* and *How I Became Hettie Jones* contradict this claim by showing that the autobiographical act is an interpretation of past experience, as their stories also creatively manipulate facets of remembered experience. Sometimes – similarly to *Memoirs of a Beatnik* – the borders between fiction and nonfiction blur in Johnson's and Jones' life writings. Both works clearly conform to Patricia Hampl's definition of memoir as "the intersection of narration and reflection, of storytelling and essay-writing". In her essay "Memory and Imagination" (1996), Hampl refers to the memoir genre as one of the most open forms in literature, "inviting broken and incomplete images, half recollected fragments" to present life experiences, reflect on them, and consider their meaning in retrospect. The masses of details which create initial bafflement shape this confusion, and so, powerful works of art are created. In Hampl's two memoirs, *A Romantic Education* and *Virgin Time*, she moves back and forth in time and chronology, inserting flashbacks and fragmented bits of memories, complying with general assumptions in feminist autobiographical criticism that women's life writing is unorderly, confused, and elliptical. Seemingly agreeing with Hampl's definition of memoir, both Joyce Johnson and Hettie Jones are unsuccessful in presenting the truth, the whole truth, and nothing but the truth about their life in their memoirs. Hampl goes on to say that "we all sense that we can't grasp the whole truth and nothing but the truth of our experience". When we go back to write about our memories, the whole truth can never be remembered, as personal history is like a projector "flashing images on the wall of the mind," and these images are very selective. "What can be achieved, however, is a version of its swirling, changing wholeness," Hampl continues (209). Due to the fact that memory and personal history are full of confusion and subjective flashes of remembrance, a memoir can never be an accurate truthful account of what happened in the past. The piece of work that is being put together is "not necessarily the truth, not even *a* truth sometimes, but the first attempt to create a shape". Hampl complains about "the appalling inaccuracy" of her own autobiographical texts, however, she states that she is not ashamed of creating an inaccurate account of memory (210). Usually, as she begins to revise her first autobiographical draft, she remembers new, formerly hidden details. Gradually, she then begins to develop a relationship between her former self and the present self. Both Johnson and Jones see themselves as historians reporting on the events happening during the Beat era, adding a dimension to Beat literature men could not offer – a woman's perspective. They continuously revise and reinvent their writing selves, trying to correct general assumptions about the Beat Generation and give lessons about the male Beats, Beat bohemianism, and female creativity. Yearning to be intimately connected with the female reader, Johnson and Jones try to satisfy reader expectations circling around identification and sympathy.

Through their life writing, Johnson and Jones present important social and historical documents about New York's subcultural scene of the time, but their writing process also fulfills another purpose: Both authors depict their personal and intimate coming-of-age as writers until both manage to be totally visible as recognized artists at the end of their works. Joyce Johnson so turns from a "minor character" into a "principal performer," and Hettie Jones' "poetics of lack" eventually gives way to literary recognition. By writing their memoirs, they finally and successfully assess their presence in the Beat historical moment. During the time of conservative ideals, women had few opportunities to make use of their artistic talents: Johnson and Jones were outstanding, as they both speak as female rebels of the time, breaking rules women had to obey if they wanted to receive respect and approval. Due to the ostracism and rejection many Beat women had to encounter, their memoirs succeed in correcting general assumptions about the Beat Generation.

7.1 Joyce Johnson's *Minor Characters*

> Most of [the Beat women] never got the chance literally to go on the road. Our road instead became the strange lives we were leading. We had actually *chosen* those lives. *(Minor Characters:* xiii)

"This is the muse's side of the story. It turns out the muse could write as well as anybody," Angela Carter remarks in the blurb of the 1999 edition of *Minor Characters*, which describes Johnson's coming-of-age from 1945-1959. Troubled by her own and her female friends' silence, Joyce Johnson decided to write *Minor Characters* (1983) to speak for all women of the Beat Generation, helping other female Beats to make their hidden lives visible, and serving as a catharsis for nearly all of them, plagued by omission and disregard. In the foreword of Brenda Knight's *Women of the Beat Generation*, Beat poet Ann Waldman refers to the memoir as the most dominant literary genre of female Beats: The "quintessential 'rasa' or taste of the historical period is often captured by the diaristic accounts" (1996: xi), which provide historical viability by depicting the crucial moments of a whole literary movement from a completely new perspective.

Johnson's claim is not only to tell her own story, but also to immortalize talented women of the time, who were suffering as a result of the 'feminine mystique': Joan Burroughs and Elise Cowen did not survive, in part because they internalized their male Beat models too intimately; Hettie Jones postponed her own public career as a poet and writer to encourage that of LeRoi Jones, then her husband. Despite the repressions of the time, Johnson explains the importance of the lives and deaths of these women, which are vital to understand the processes within the Beat Generation more fully. *Minor Characters* tells the reader how a number of Beat women found themselves in each other, discovering the cultural ground their male peers had cleared for their own self-expression.

In 1951, after graduation from Hunter College High School, a competitive school for girls, Joyce Johnson, then Glassman, set out for her freshman year at Barnard College. At that time, not yet sixteen, she already intended to start a writing career. In 1953, while a junior at Barnard, Johnson was told by her male creative writing professor that she and other girls in the class should collect experiences before starting to write. As she describes him, he is a "middle-aged man, who no doubt wishes he were standing before a class at Harvard". "How many of you girls want to be writers," he asks in a "tone as dry as the crackers in the American cultural barrel". All the hands go up, including some flashy engagement rings. It is 1953. "The air is thick with the uneasiness of the girl students," Johnson writes (80). Realizing the girls' anxiety and ambition, he makes clear: "first of all, if you were going to be writers, you wouldn't be enrolled in this class. You couldn't even be enrolled in school. You'd be hopping freight trains, riding through America". The hands go down. The message seems to be that only experience, exploration, and adventure could provide the background information to become a successful author. Disencouraged by her professor's words, Johnson goes on, "the young would-be writers in this room have understood instantly that of course there is no hope" (81). Johnson did not fully grasp the meaning of that statement at the time. Her parents lived around the corner from the Barnard Campus on 116th street and so – being an only child – she lived at home, not in a dorm. Restless in school and avid for experience, Johnson scandalously escaped from parental control by moving out to live on her own without finishing her senior year. Wanting to be the heroine of her life, and not just another Barnard girl suffering from what Betty Friedan calls the "housewife syndrome," she moved into a room of her own. For Johnson, real life was not to be found in her all girls' school: "Real life," Johnson writes, "was not to be found in the streets around my house, or anywhere on the Upper West Side, [...] or in my school of girls grubbing joylessly for marks, hysterical about geometry exams and Latin homework, flirting ridiculously with the seventy-year-old elevator operator, the only male visible on the premises" (30). In 1957, Johnson for the first time realized the significance of her professor's words: Allen Ginsberg, a former Columbia student, helped to arrange a blind date between Johnson and Jack Kerouac at a restaurant in Greenwich Village, shortly before she published her first novel at Random House – now aged 22. 1957 was also the breakthrough year for Kerouac, when Gilbert Millstein talked about the publishing of *On the Road* as a "historic occasion" in the New York Times (Kerouac: 1991: viii). Johnson was with Kerouac when *On the Road* was released, walking to the newsstand to read the review with him. Over night, his autobiographical novel brought him fame and suddenly put the word Beat into media currency. Now, it seems, Johnson realizes the meaning of 'real life' she had wanted for so long:

> Real life was sexual. Or rather, it often seemed to take the forms of sex. This was the area of ultimate adventure, where you would dare or not dare. It was much less a question of desire. Sex was like a forbidden castle whose name could not even be spoken around the house, so feared was its power. Only with the utmost vigilance could you avoid being sucked into its magnetic field. The alternative was to break into the castle and take its power for yourself. *(Minor Characters:* 30)

This 'Real Life' was the opposite of what her parents called the 'Real World', by way of discouraging any fantasies of sexual experience. This 'Real Life' which her parents had never known themselves, sent Johnson from upper Manhattan to the Village in order to explore life. "As a writer, I would live life to the hilt as my unacceptable self, just as Jack and Allen had done," she writes. In this passage, trying to find the meaning of life, it becomes quite obvious that Johnson tries to write an initiation narrative rather than a traditional memoir. Johnson's "initiation," meaning her search for individuality and identity, is a major theme in the book. Johnson goes through a growing-up process from a young, timid teenage girl to a self-confident, bohemian young woman. In 1983, the year *Minor Characters* was first published, Johnson's memoir was being advertised as "A Young Woman's Coming-of-Age in the Beat Orbit of Jack Kerouac," but she herself intended her book to do more than just document her love affair with Kerouac. By writing *Minor Characters*, Johnson celebrates the lives of several little-known women friends who were aspiring authors and artists in the 1950s, but who – instead – became the 'minor characters' in the background of more famous male beatniks. Beat poet Elise Cowen is one of the tragic examples for the omission of female Beats, as U.S. literature characterizes her only as Ginsberg's mad girlfriend and typist of "Kaddish". In *Minor Characters*, Cowen is able to speak for herself, first to Johnson in a letter dated 1959 from Berkeley, and then to the reader through her inserted poems.

7.1.1 A Side Glance: Elise Cowen (1933–1962)

> [A] woman from the audience asks: "Why are there so few women on this panel? Why are there so few women in this whole week's program? Why were there so few women among the Beat writers?" and [Gregory] Corso, suddenly utterly serious, leans forward and says: "There were women, they were there, I knew them, their families put them in institutions, they were given electric shock. In the '50s if you were male you could be a rebel, but if you were female your families had you locked up. There were cases, I knew them, someday someone will write about them. (Stephen Scobie quoted in Knight. *Women of the Beat Generation:* 141)

Elise Cowen, even though dead for 45 years now, has become alive through numerous Beat texts which include her as a main protagonist by providing insight into her life. Being Johnson's classmate at Barnard College in 1950/1951, she was born in Long Island into a wealthy Jewish family. In accordance with her family's plans, Cowen attended college, but did not succeed in the ways her parents had hoped. When Johnson first met Cowen, her first impression warned her to avoid her. Cowen's "bad," rebellious period started soon after her thirteenth birthday, ending her "good" period abruptly: She was a "silent, obstinate girl who holed up in her room and read poetry," and who "smoked and took no trouble with her appearance," wearing black-rimmed glasses and being totally uncommunicative (Johnson: 1999: 55). At the age of sixteen, Cowen lost her virginity, she "had actually gone all the way to that mysterious stage," Johnson writes (56).

Becoming increasingly involved with the Beat circle, she immediately recognized a "twin soul" with Allen Ginsberg after their first meeting. Even looking alike during that time, they started a passionate affair in the spring and summer of 1953, when Ginsberg followed a doctor's advice to indulge in heterosexuality in order to be cured from homosexuality (cf. Trigilio 2004: 119). After they split up right before the composition of "Howl" due to Ginsberg's first homosexual encounters, Cowen was never able to let go. As Johnson explains the situation, "Elise was a moment in Allen's life. In Elise's life, Allen was an eternity" (1999: 78). Cowen appears in some of Ginsberg's texts, but her role is mainly restricted to being among the few heterosexual try-outs for him. When Ginsberg and Peter Orlovsky became a couple, Cowen's mental state worsened. She wrote hundreds of poems herself, but did not publish any during her short life. After college, she worked as a typist in New York City, then quit, and moved to San Francisco. According to her friend Leo Skir, she lived with a drunken Irish artist and spent most of her time at a bar called "The Place". She got pregnant, had a hysterectomy, returned to New York, and eventually moved back into her parents' home in Washington Heights. In and out of mental institutions, Cowen was suffering from auditory hallucinations and paranoia.

On February 16, 1962, Cowen, aged 28, jumped through a closed window from her parents' living room in Washington Heights and died immediately. She had just been released from Hillside Mental Hospital. Subsequent to her death, eighty-three poems were found in a box in Leo Skir's apartment in Minneapolis and have been published; the rest of her poems and her journals, however, were destroyed by her parents soon after her death, as they were angered by the lesbian and bisexual subject matter in their daughter's work. Cowen's literary relationship with Allen Ginsberg suggests that her legacy is complex, despite the fact that a huge number of poems are irretrievable. Since her suicide, Beat critics have tried to approach her literary legacy for contradictory reasons: On the one hand, her literary work is preserved through posthumous publishing, but on the other hand, her poetry is generally included in larger narratives of Ginsberg's life and work. Among her last poems is the following: "Alone/ Weeping/ I woke weeping/ Alone/ In black park of bed" (257). The dark misery of the lines shows her frustration and madness about not knowing what to do with her ambition and anger. As a last massage to Johnson and other Beat friends, Cowen composed the tragic lines, which read like a suicide note:

No love
No compassion
No intelligence
No beauty
No humility
Twenty-seven years is enough

Mother – too late – years of meanness – I'm sorry
Daddy – what happened?
Allen – I'm sorry
Peter – Holy Rose Youth
Betty – such womanly bravery
Keith – Thank you
Joyce – So girl beautiful
Howard – Baby take care
Leo – Open the windows and Shalom
Carol – Let it happen

Let me out now please -
- Please let me in

(Knight. *Women of the Beat Generation:* 165)

When Cowen died, Ginsberg was in Bombay, searching for religious insight. Leo Skir wrote him the same night and got the following reply about a week later:

Dear Leo,
Thanks for your letter, I received it and Irving's the same day, & was a little emptied for a few days to hear about Elise [...] I hope everybody is not scared or plunged further into painful dreams by Elise's hints. None of the dream system is real, not even death's. The Self that sees all the plots is worth attention, not the plots. That's as far as I know. Good luck, Allen (Knight. *Women of the Beat Generation:* 144)

Cowen ends up a character in Joyce Johnson's memoir, in several of Leo Skir's works, and in Ginsberg's journal, where she gets added to his list of the dead. He writes,

Bounced out of Mboyas Wedding feast for not wearing ties
    & Jackets
in the marvelous Nairobi heat – cool nights near the movies
    turning a corner from the Indian restaurant –
a big square we walked, saw doctor for germs –
or the study of logistics, or Cosmic Paranoia
the inhumans talking over Microphone Consciousness –
They got Elise? – She's where the dead are that went to the
    burning ghats
or suffered "Chinese brutality" in the Himalayas

(Minor Characters: 258)

Beat criticism, in general, overemphasizes Elise Cowen's biographical role within the Beat Generation, while neglecting the discussion of her poetry, their textuality, and historicity. Through including her in *Minor Characters*, Johnson completes her woman's story with the help of Cowen, as her life as Kerouac's girlfriend has gradually lost its potency towards the end of the memoir. Finally, it is female friendship which represents continuity.

7.1.2 Distorted Memory and Fluid Time

By including snapshots from her past, capturing particular moments in time, Joyce Johnson creates a text which is only superficially unlinear, fragmented, and incoherent. At a closer look, however, Johnson's present and past tense zoomed pictures represent a complete narrative whole, in which photography as a central aspect concerning cultural and personal history and memory plays a crucial role. At the beginning of *Minor Characters*, the narrator is looking at a book showing a snapshot of four young men posing on the Columbia University campus in 1945, showing Jack Kerouac, Allen Ginsberg, William Burroughs, and Hal Chase. The speaker is a forty-seven-year-old Joyce Johnson, contemplating the image of the men who seem to have grown younger, while the author herself has grown older. "The snapshot is in a book now," Johnson is well aware of the importance of the photo: "Four young men on the Columbia campus on a day in 1945. Early spring, maybe, because the coats of three of them are open at the collar and the tree in the background is bare. They're boys, really". She describes Burroughs, who is wearing a black bowler, Hal Chase, whom she never met, and Ginsberg, who is "all adolescent gawkiness and misery". Jack Kerouac is in the middle, wearing no overcoat, just a cheap "baggy suit," stretching his arms over Chase and Ginsberg, a cigarette dangling from his mouth. For Johnson, Kerouac is "the only one of them totally connected to the moment" on the photo (1).

This passage and the next fifteen pages introduce the basic structure of Johnson's text: She continuously slides back and forth from past to present tense constructions of memory, which finally combine two narrative strings. On the one hand, the story focuses on her two-year love affair with Kerouac, but on the other hand, her coming-of-age as a young 1950s woman and writer is being zoomed in. Alternately, Johnson describes what is going on in her life, and, for example, what Joan Vollmer and Edie Parker living around the corner might be doing. "Simultaneities. Take the West End, for instance […]," she writes (8). In 1944, Edie Parker likes to go to the cafeteria on Broadway and 113th, while "Jack, who's been shipping out in the merchant marine, is often away at sea for months" (9). Contrary to that, Johnson, merely ten years old at the time, is roller-skating, reading, or weeping over *Black Beauty*. Through connecting various life stories, the author skillfully presents imaginative constructions of real people from her Beat past.

In Johnson's memoir, present and past tense images are closely connected to each other. Instead of standing in opposition with each other, they rather complete the remembered picture, creating harmony and unification. Both tenses focus on the recreated image. More than a dead artifact, the past therefore becomes alive, as the major request is to contemplate on the temporality of human existence. Joyce Johnson is well aware of the fact that her Beat past is a fragmented story. She knows that the disappeared components or "memory lapses" can only be filled with reconstructed, yet made-up conversations, scenes, and pictures.

Johnson, for example, imagines a scene where Elise Cowen is waiting for her beloved in his living room. Before Cowen got to know Allen Ginsberg, she started an affair with her philosophy professor, Alex Greer, who had a child, but no apparent wife. He introduced her to his many friends going in and out of his messy apartment, while Elise cleaned up and baby-sat for his two-year-old son. Greer had called her to come over and stay with his son, while he had to get out of the house. Johnson reconstructs the scene, making it alive by using the present tense:

> There is a winter night that from this distance looks inevitable. Lying under an old army blanket in her sweater and half-slip, Elise is stretched out on the couch in Alex's living room. The skirt she'll wear to classes tomorrow is folded over a chair; her glasses are on the coffee table. [...] Too late even now for her to go home on the subway. She'd told her parents she's babysitting for the Greers again [...] She's scared a little – only because she can't measure her own hunger. Sometimes just talking to him, she feels faint with it; her body opens to him secretly. She's only slept with one person so far, and that was two years ago, and this will be different – very. *(Minor Characters:* 60-61)

In her memory, Johnson imagines unmovable picture-like scenes. The reader can easily visualize Elise lying under the blanket, waiting wishfully for her lover to arrive. In this passage, Johnson's writing technique directly and openly problematizes memory and time, illustrating the extent to which what is known as past remains a vivid present picture through what she herself calls "the strangeness" of memory (77). Johnson recalls the scene she has not personally experienced as if she is part of it, and as if things are happening now, in the present time. She vividly imagines a scene from the past, probably wishing to bring the picture of her dead best friend back to life. Similar to the photograph of Kerouac and his friends, which is described at the beginning of the memoir, this particular scene in which Elise is lying on the sofa creates the impression of a historical moment. The passage can be compared to a photograph stuck into an album. On the photograph, however, it is not Kerouac and his friends who are being zoomed in this time, but it is Cowen. Like the work of a photographer or a painter, Johnson captures "the look of things, the look that conveys their meaning, to catch the color, the relief, the expression, the surface, the substance of the human spectacle" (12).

Minor Characters rests upon this certain "strangeness of memory" and the power of imagination in order to reconstruct past events, but also to develop Johnson's autobiographical self. Johnson's textual self in *Minor Characters* relies upon fixed images which float in and out of time. Similar to, for example, Jack Kerouac, Johnson focuses on the visualization of particular places, describing them in the present tense to make them alive. She depicts, for example, the famous Waldorf Café, where she spends numerous weekday and Sunday afternoons. It "was a dreary-looking place," "being a uniform grey-brown," having "none of the chrome-and-brass art-deco fittings of the Automat, or the bountifulness of Jewish cafeterias like Hektor's near Times Square [...]" (38). Another image Johnson creates to point out the depressiveness of being under parental control is a philistine room in her parents' apartment on 116th Street. The room she is painfully thinking of is dominated by a huge piano. The colors red, green, and gold are forever etched in her memory; the red couch wears a green slipcover, the Oriental rug – bought just before the Depression – is vacuumed daily, the table is in the style known as French provincial, and the Chinese lamp on it is covered with cellophane. Above the piano hangs the portrait of the eight-year-old Joyce Glassman:

> There's the terrible poignancy in this room of gratifications deferred, the tensions of gentility. It's as if all these objects – the piano, the rug, the portrait – are held in uneasy captivity, hostages to aspirations. If the slipcovers ever come off, if the heavy drapes are drawn aside letting in the daylight, everything that has been so carefully preserved will be seen to have become frayed and faded anyway. *(Minor Characters:* 14)

This passage is a typical example to show the different selves Johnson represents: First, there is the self that she was as a child, second, the critical self she has become, and third, the self she could have been if she had not moved out of her parents' apartment. All three selves are equally part of Johnson's life writing (cf. Grace 2002: 147).

While the Glassman living room is a museum of inanimate, dead relics of the past, other memories are full of life. Even though Johnson did not graduate from Barnard, because she was tired of all the boredom and stiffness, she agrees to come to a class reunion. In her present tense narration of this experience, she meets classmates whose lives have passed quite differently from hers. Johnson meets the class of 1955, whom she last saw capped and gowned the day of her non-graduation. When asked what they do, a middle-aged woman answers, "I live in Scarsdale". "Well, that's an occupation, I suppose," Johnson imaginatively comments (98). Her former classmates report news of marriages, births, deaths, divorces, and promotions. "Barnard was evidently their great time," she continues (99). Although sarcastically depicting white-haired, chubby women sipping wine and pretending interest in each other, Johnson's description fulfills another purpose: Meeting her former classmates reanimates her Beat friend Elise. Even at the time Johnson wrote *Minor Characters,* she says "it's sometimes a shock to remember Elise is dead and I can't pick up a phone and talk to her" (53). Through the literary act of merging language and memory, Johnson linguistically transcends death and brings Elise back to life. Similarly to other dead Beats like Joan Vollmer, Cowen is presented vividly, as if still alive, and their conversations give the impression as if they are taking place at that very moment. Johnson perceives her friend as if she had lived into her thirties: "Any time now Elise will appear, swinging her black handbag, her hair streaked with gray, cut shorter than ever, as she used to threaten she'd wear it after she'd passed her thirtieth birthday – but maybe she changed her mind and let it grow long after all, twisted into a knot," Johnson is pondering. Imagining Cowen to be at the Barnard reunion, Johnson visualizes that they would "laugh at the folly of finding each other here, the insanity of meeting, all grown up" (100).

Johnson is aware of the fact that these visions are only illusionary. No matter if internal recollections like memories or external ones such as photos, they deviate depending on who positions them and how they are positioned. Several times throughout the memoir, she juxtaposes her own memory with someone else's record of memory. In the night Johnson first meets Kerouac, she describes herself as a "very young woman in a red coat, round-faced and blonde". Nevertheless, she is not sure what Kerouac really saw when looking at her while having their first date.[42] Johnson's recollection aligns with Kerouac's memory of her: In *Desolation Angels*, she is being described as an "interesting young person," "a Jewess, elegant middleclass sad and looking for something – she looked Polish as hell" (Grace: 2002: 148). Johnson is puzzled and asks herself: "Where am I in all those funny categories?" (1999: 128). The two images make self-awareness even more difficult. They both alter reality and thus the historical construction of the Beat Generation.

Although male Beats offered women refuge from the stifling silent generation, Joyce Johnson criticizes that Kerouac, Ginsberg, and Burroughs often crossed out the female when gender was an issue. She asks herself what is missing from New York's Beat scene, and comes to the conclusion that women are being excluded. Johnson is particularly interested in reconstructing the Beat years of Kerouac's wife Edie Parker[43] and Burroughs' wife Joan Vollmer Adams, and so she constructs her own pictures based on the stories she has read or heard about them. Even though Johnson does not know either of them, she imagines Edie Parker to be full of enthusiasm and good humor, even though already fearing that Kerouac would always prefer his male friends to her. Vollmer and Parker were best friends, roommates, and the connective links for Kerouac, Burroughs, Ginsberg, and Carr. Kerouac and Parker had been living together on and off since 1941. "It was all over between them, though, by January of 1945, and then Edie vanishes – at least from the literary histories," Johnson writes. She imagines Edie Parker as follows:

> [...] I've always had an image of Edie as one of those girls who tries almost fatally hard to be a good sport. You can't help liking her, though. She's even cute in the way girls aren't cute anymore, a sweater girl in saddle shoes, her light brown hair in a pompadour. There's been something determinedly spunky in the way she confronts bizarre circumstances, trying on a life that doesn't fit her. What became of Edie? Eventually she recovered, I hope, in her next three and a half decades. *(Minor Characters:* 3)

Even though she does not know what became of Parker, she is well aware of the tragic fate of Joan Vollmer Adams. She definitely would have loved her if she had known her, Johnson says. "She's as

---

[42] During their first date, Kerouac – quite unromantically – was eating frankfurters, home fries, and baked beans with Heinz ketchup on them. Johnson writes, "I keep stealing looks at him because he's beautiful. You're not supposed to say a man is beautiful, but he is" (128). Johnson paid the bill: "I've never bought a man dinner before," she goes on: "It makes me feel very competent and womanly" (127).

[43] Edie Parker was Jack Kerouac's first wife. They married in 1944. Their marriage, however, only lasted for two months. As Johnson notes, Edie Parker Kerouac was no fifties' housewife. Indeed, along with Joan Vollmer, Edie was the center of the intellectual and creative movement that produced the new consciousness of the early Beats. "And this is something Edie knows, most likely – an unarticulated sadness," Johnson writes in *Minor Characters*, even though she has never met her personally. "That Jack, despite her dreams of marriage and 'Oh, we'll have our Bohemian period and then we'll settle down and he'll write books and we'll love each other forever', is unpossessable. Edie's got her resourceful spirit, though. She's even had her own adventures, working as a longshoreman while Jack's at sea, and as a cigarette girl on Forty-second Street," Johnson remarks (1999: 10). Parker's autobiography *You'll be Okay* remains unpublished until today. She was extremely disappointed that no publisher wanted to hear about her marriage with Kerouac. At Kerouac's funeral in 1969, she announced: "I am Mrs. Jack Kerouac!" (Knight: 2000: 79). Before her death in 1992, she was married four times.

familiar to me as another woman very like her whom I once knew and loved, and as alien as the person who still lives on in the most dangerous depths of myself," she writes (5-6). Comparing Joan Vollmer Adams' wit to the intellectual capacities of Elise Cowen, Vollmer was "a great reader of Korzybski, Spengler, Kafka, etc., startling the men by holding her own in their discussions," Johnson points out (3-4). Married to William Burroughs, both got deeper and deeper into legal troubles due to their drug addiction: "She matched him as well in her growing interest in drugs, staying high all day on Benzedrine-soaked cotton from nasal inhalers". Johnson goes on speculating, "Perhaps Bill first showed her how you could crack open the inhaler case like a nut and get out the little pad that could be swallowed down whole with your morning coffee, quite transforming the wintery grey courtyard light and the littered kitchen […]" (4). Her intelligence and interest in philosophy and literature matched Burroughs' point by point. On September 6, 1951, both were at a party in Mexico. Everyone had been drinking for hours when Burroughs announced that it was time for their William Tell act. Joan Vollmer put a water glass on her head. Burroughs, however, missed the glass. Vollmer died instantly, not yet thirty years old (cf. Knight 2000: 52f.). Was her death "a knowing, prescient act of suicide on Joan's part, the ultimate play-out of total despair?," or her final act a "demonstration of her faith and trust" and a "final gift to Bill," Johnson wonders (5).

Creating and reconstructing her life story through those of other women of the time is central to Johnson's discourse. By including the stories of other women, she manifests her own coming-of-age. Sharing this strategy with Beat friend Hettie Jones, Johnson connects various narrative strings. Hettie Jones' *How I Became Hettie Jones* similarly circles around some of her best friends, like Joyce Johnson or Helene Dorn, to name just two. By speaking for a whole generation of silenced women, Johnson creates a kind of solidarity through both lived and imagined experiences. By doing so, she suggests that the self can only be invented by creating others. The interwoven stories about Elise Cowen, Joan Vollmer, Edie Parker, and Hettie Cohen (later Jones), who defied racism by marrying a black poet, complete and connect Johnson's memoir. The stories of these women represent the red thread which winds through Johnson's narrative.

One of the major writing techniques that Johnson uses to construct her memoir is an ironic point/counterpoint strategy that brings events which have originally been unconnected into significant relationship with each other (cf. Grace 2002: 149f.). This particular technique is used to emphasize the restraints and drawbacks women in the 1950s had to face. Several times throughout the book, Johnson compares her own or a female friend's situation at a particular point in time with the experiences of male Beats like Kerouac or Ginsberg during the same days or months.

Two examples for Johnson's point/counterpoint strategy illustrate my point. In Johnson's creative writing class at Barnard college in 1953, she learns from her professor that female students should not be sitting in his classroom, but instead they should experience real life, like hopping freight trains. While Johnson is getting bored with the daily schedule at college, yearning for a life she is not allowed to have, Allen Ginsberg takes to the road. As a man, he can travel wherever he pleases. "By January of

1954, Allen Ginsberg is on the move in the Yucatán," Johnson compares his thrilling life with the dreariness of her own. He is obviously living the professor's instructions many female students could not follow, experiencing poetic visions of his mother and his tragic Beat friends. Lying in a hammock high on paracodeine, he stares into the Mayan night and sees his mother's face, "young and darkhaired, at a piano at a party, close up, facing me, svelte and in rapport with life" (81). In June, Ginsberg crosses the Mexican border, making the notes "Enter U.S. alone naked with knapsack, watch, camera, poem, beard". He resembles exactly that "archetypal male vagabond/writer of Professor X's imaginings," Johnson writes regretfully, as she herself does not have the chance to be on the road (82).

The second example of juxtaposing male and females versions of Beat experiences is even more troublesome: Johnson links her own abortion experience[44] with Kerouac's adventurous journey to Desolation Peak in Washington State, where he would spend the summer as a fire guardian for the United States Fire Service in isolation, alone with God and nature. Kerouac portrays the solitude of this summer in *The Dharma Bums*. By contrasting these two events from two different lives that took place at the same time, Johnson stresses the injustice Beat women of the time had to face. Kerouac is bored because of the solitude and lack of entertainment, suffering the horrors of a classically male natural solitude; Johnson, in contrast, is confronted with different kinds of dismay, namely the horrors of an illegal abortion. In her down-to-earth world, there are no beautiful butterflies, comic chipmunks, and there are no singing birds which are a reality in Kerouac's gorgeous mountain landscape. At the time Johnson has her abortion, Kerouac is "thirty-four years old – a Zen pilgrim in Salvation Army clothes and new hiking boots with soles that would be worn to nothing by the end of his sixty-three days of solitude. There were envelopes of Lipton's dried pea soup in his rucksack, and a copy of *The God That Failed*[45]" (112). Being alone in the mountains, Kerouac tries to regain his inner solitude and dispose of his constant paranoid sense of mortality. Instead of enjoying nature's beauties, Johnson has

---

[44] In memoirs by female Beats, motherhood and abortion are prominent themes. Like Joyce Johnson, Hettie Jones cannot carry out her first baby: "There was no way in the world I could have this baby," she confesses when she realizes she is pregnant (1997: 52). She underwent an abortion, because she was afraid to be the white mother of interracial children. Years later, however, she gave birth to two colored girls. Diane di Prima had similar experiences. In the poem "Brass Furnace Going Out: Song, After an Abortion," she tries to cope with her abortion, regretfully proclaiming: "will/you/come here/again/my breasts prepare/to feed you: they do what they can" (see http://www.angelfire.com/mn2/anarchistpoetry/Diprimadir/Diprima3.html; January 19, 2007). Leo Skir's depiction of Elise Cowen's abortion is shocking and horrifying: The fetus had grown too big while all doctors were on Christmas vacation, and so she had to have a hysterectomy (cf. Peabody 1997: 40). In his poem "Fragment: The Names II," Allen Ginsberg refers to Cowen's "poor unmarried body broken on that ground Manhattan Heights" when she finally commits suicide (1984: 261). Brenda Frazer is another tragic example: She aborted two children while being a prostitute in Mexico. In many cases, children were the price Beat women had to pay if they wanted to lead lives that were as exciting as those of Beat men.

[45] *The God That Failed*, edited by Richard Crossman, is a classic work and crucial document of the Cold War that brings together essays by six of the most important writers of the twentieth century on their conversion to and subsequent disillusionment with communism. In describing their own experiences, the authors illustrate the fate of leftism around the world. André Gide (France), Richard Wright (the United States), Ignazio Silone (Italy), Stephen Spender (England), Arthur Koestler (Germany), and Louis Fischer, an American foreign correspondent, all tell how their search for the betterment of humanity led them to communism, and the personal agony and revulsion which then caused them to reject it. See Crossman, Richard, ed. (2001). *The God that Failed*. New York: Columbia University Press.

her first abortion in an illegal clinic. Lying helplessly on her back, she is despising America's social system that denies women legal abortions. The painful abortion is performed in secret by a doctor whose professional self-esteem clearly depends on his open contempt for her predicament. "But don't ever let me catch you back here again, young lady!," the doctor from Canarsie calls after her, while she staggers down the cement steps of the abortionist's house (110). She writes, "It was noon in Canarsie, an ordinary day in July" (111). Her abortion is carried out while Jack Kerouac spends another ordinary day on beautiful Desolation Peak. Later on in life, she is horrified about Kerouac's repudiation of his own daughter Jan[46]. He could not face his daughter and pretended that she was not his child, to relieve him from obligations until a blood test proved the opposite. He strongly suspected that every woman's primary aim was to bring new life into the world, "a child who was only going to suffer and die" in the end (Johnson: 2000: 25). Johnson thinks of her unwanted child "scraped out of me," and asks, "Could I blame Jack more than I blamed myself? […] For me, too, freedom and life seemed equivalent" (109). In both examples, the frustrating classroom episode and Johnson's abortion, the image of Johnson in a dismissive, restricted surrounding is contrasted to the images of Kerouac and Ginsberg free to explore the world.

Throughout the memoir, Johnson's experiments with reality and fiction are hazardous. Her memoir is full of scenes that render imagined accounts. However, Johnson is a memoirist who does not fool her readers by claiming that every word she tells purports to be true. According to Henry James' *The Art of Fiction and other Essays*, life writing always bears the burden of truth telling (cf. Johnson 2002: 150). By including the stories of other Beat women, Joyce Johnson is concerned with creating a different kind of truth. As she is clearly aware that it is impossible to completely retell the past, she aims at telling what she and female Beat friends of hers felt in the first place. By depicting the male and female life stories of others, Johnson reveals much of herself as the supposed main protagonist of the story. But is Johnson really the main character of the memoir? Similar to di Prima's *Memoirs of a Beatnik*, Johnson takes a back seat in *Minor Characters,* as the memoir mainly centers around her female Beat friends and her connection with Jack Kerouac. Johnson as a character is in the spotlight only if her personal story crosses Kerouac's life or the lives of Elise Cowen and Hettie Cohen. In *Minor Characters,* the truth of her historical discourse merges with powerful feelings for her beloved friends. Thus, the reader can judge the work's validity through its claim for historical truth, as Johnson includes historical sources such as letters, journal entries, or poems. Additionally, her claim toward an emotional representation of the time can be verified by the felt response of author and reader.

---

[46] Jan was born in 1952, shortly after Kerouac's relationship with Joan Haverty, his second wife, had broken up. Kerouac had hastily married Haverty to realize his ideals of a perfect family, but after 7 months, the marriage ended in divorce. Jan Kerouac was Kerouac's only child. She also became a writer herself. Two of her autobiographical novels, *Baby Driver* and *Trainsong*, are similar to the narrative style her father employed; however, she writes in a less confessional style. Aged 15, Jan left her family to be on the road. "She was […] traveling everywhere, lecturing and reading her work, going through men, drink, drugs, and every sort of experience at a frighteningly fast pace" (Knight: 2000: 313). In 1996, Jan Kerouac died of kidney failure after continuing health problems.

Probably the most important imaginative reconstruction Johnson creates is that of the life of Jack Kerouac's mother, Gabrielle Kerouac. In Kerouac biographies and other critical works on the Beat Generation, only little information is available about Gabrielle Kerouac, also called "Mèmére"[47] by her son. While being sexist towards many women in his life, Kerouac's most constant lifelong relationship with a woman was with his mother. He was dependent on her throughout his life. Working hard in a shoe factory to support the family which grew poorer and poorer from year to year, she financed her son's idle beatnik lifestyle until *On the Road* – he was 35 by then – gave him a modest financial success. Even after the publication of *On the Road,* Kerouac let his mother control his finances, mainly out of guilt over her having to support him for so long. When he began to receive enough income, he perpetually moved her from house to house, from East Coast to West Coast, from North to South and back again – even if this was rather his interpretation of "taking care" of her than her own. About Kerouac's Oedipus complex, Johnson writes: "Interestingly enough, the only woman Jack Kerouac ever actually took with him on the road wasn't me or Edie Parker or Carolyn Cassady or any of the dark *fellaheen* beauties of his longings, but Gabrielle L'Evesque Kerouac, age sixty-two [...]" (1999: 155). Gabrielle Kerouac was probably the only person in his life with whom he could be completely himself, able to do and say anything that came into his mind uncensored by how it would affect the audience or his readership.

Gabrielle Lévesque was born into a French-Canadian family. A devoted Catholic, she attended church regularly. Even though many French-Canadian workers in Lowell were unsatisfied with the Catholic Church, his mother immersed Kerouac in strict Catholicism. What is found in biographies about Kerouac presents his mother as a tyrannical woman trapped in working-class domesticity who cannot let go of her grown-up son. Gabrielle Kerouac believed her son to be drawn into the Beat scene by having the wrong friends. She therefore tried to destroy Kerouac's Beat-connections throughout his lifetime. In 1959, Kerouac's mother wrote a vitriolic letter to Allen Ginsberg and Bill Burroughs, worsening their relationships for years. Warning them not to mention her son's name in their future "dirty" books, she threatens: "You miserable bums, all you have in your filthy minds is dirt, sex and dope. [...] I'll sue you and have you in jail. I raised Jack to be decent and I aim to keep him that way. [...] We don't want sex fiens or dope fiens around us" (Sandison: 1999: 130). In Kerouac biographies, she is depicted as exaggeratedly motherly and feels threatened by her son's girlfriends and wives[48]. One Saturday morning in late May 1958, Johnson sets out for Northport, where Kerouac lives with his mother at the time, to have lunch there. Johnson's first and last encounter with Mèmére is unpleasant:

---

[47] A French Canadian slang term for grandmother, this is what Kerouac usually called his mother.
[48] For the first forty years of his life, Kerouac had failed to sustain a longer relationship with a woman, although he was well-known for having affairs with many women. He was married three times, to Edie Parker, Joan Haverty, and Stella Sampas. The first two marriages ended within months. In the mid-1960s, he was married again, but this time to a motherly older childhood friend from Lowell, Stella Sampas, who he wished would help around the house as his mother was growing older.

> Memere greeted me at the door with a blunt, inhospitable question: "What train are you going back on?" She was a grandmotherly figure in her housedress and apron – short and squat, with thick round glasses and iron-gray hair pulled into a bun. She told me she had been cooking since early that morning. As I entered the house, I could smell meat roasting in the kitchen. A heavy meal was being prepared even though it was a hot summer day. (Johnson. *Door Wide Open:* 141)

To her disappointment, Kerouac is depressed and drunk. Being dissatisfied with Johnson's "profligate New York way of washing dishes," Mèmére finally "shooed [her] out of the kitchen," and so Johnson goes back to the dining room, "where Jack was still passed out with his head on the table" (144). Too drunk to accompany her to the station, Johnson leaves to catch the bus by herself.

Even though Kerouac's mother ignores her when they meet, Johnson's narrator in *Minor Characters* presents Mèmére more positively than expected. Johnson feels sorry for Kerouac's mother and shows her sympathy by entering Mèmére's body and mind. Skillfully, she visualizes the broken heart of a mother who has lost her oldest son Gerard, who had died in 1926 when Jack was 5 years old. After Gerard's death, "I can see how she must have clung to the younger boy, taking him to bed night after night for comfort – breaking all the Freudian rules. But what did Gabrielle Kerouac know of such sophistications? There was her own need, the warmth of her own need, the warmth of her small son's light body curled into her own, the dreamy fragrance of his hair," Johnson imagines the desperation (1999: 17). Johnson's narrator ponders over the excitement of driving from east coast to west coast: "Memere's thrilled by the small adventure of an overnight stop in a run-down hotel that humiliates Jack by its cheapness. It's all luxury and gaiety, not hardship. With her boy Jackie beside her, she's seeing the world at last. What had she known but work and poverty and Sunday masses?" (155-156). Having moved her to San Francisco's bay area, Gabrielle Kerouac was not satisfied with the place her son had chosen for her. Johnson imagines the situation: "Memere hated Berkeley, hated the hills and the morning fog that kept the clothes from drying on the line, hated the crazy strangers that kept dropping in to lure Jack away from her, hated the sound of the typewriter behind his shut door" (156). Finally, Johnson confronts the inevitable moment when Kerouac dies of internal bleedings. She imagines Mèmére being there for him during his last hours:

> In the room where another child has died, a small boy, Jean Louis Kerouac, lies waiting for his Memere. She will kiss him and turn out the light, abandoning him to the dark that has taken his brother. One day he will go to sleep and never wake up, for all the prayers of the nuns at the school and the priests in their black suits and his mother's weeping. […] She's thinking, I'll never let this one go. I'll protect him from everything bad.
> The stone comes down upon him, turns into flesh.
> There is no one to blame here. *(Minor Characters:* 227-228)

The depicted experiences, whether real or imagined, show the growing understanding Johnson has for Kerouac's development. Yet, they also reveal her own desire to explore the United States, move across the country, and the sorrow about their break-up and his early death aged 47. The filters or invented parts also indirectly tell another part of Johnson's own life-story. By including others, she gives meaning to her own recollections. Thus, the image the reader has of the author's coming-of-age is not like a mosaic any more, but gradually turns into a narrative whole.

Towards the end of the memoir, Johnson's life as Kerouac's girlfriend has lost its importance: It is female friendship which is decisive for her development from a young teenage girl to a reflective, middle-aged writer; it is Elise Cowen who turns up again at the end of the book to help Johnson to complete her Beat woman's story. Farewell is the major theme of the last pages, as the narrator re-experiences her best friend's suicide by quoting from letters, poems, newspaper clippings, parts of remembered conversations, and images of their last meeting. Elise Cowen, even though dead now, is able to speak for herself: First, she speaks to Johnson in a letter dated 1959 from Berkeley where she was living at the time. Second, she speaks directly to the readers through her poetry. The texts Johnson inserts create a whole picture of Cowen's death. The way her friends tried to cope with her suicide is to emphasize the traces upon which knowledge of one's own past is based. Johnson's own words are powerless, she knows, and so she lets others speak out the truth.

The ending of *Minor Characters* is not unhappy, even though the male hero of the book, Jack Kerouac, and the female heroine, Elise Cowen, die tragically. This is because Johnson lets us know that her spirits did not decrease after her affair with Kerouac ended. Johnson and Kerouac had split up on a street corner in the fall of 1958. "There had been too many separations, too many drunken, chaotic nights, and always that confusing distance in him that was both paternal and rejecting – 'You do what you wanna do'," Johnson explains their split-up (253). In the 1960s, Johnson married James Johnson, who died in a motorcycle accident soon after their marriage. The original ideas of the Beat Generation suffered a temporary eclipse in the 1960s. Johnson laments that the 1960s were not her time: "I saw hippies replace beatniks, sociologists replace poets, the empty canvas replace the Kline". Furthermore, "Ecstasy had become chemical, forgetfulness could be had by prescription. Revolution was in the wind, but it never came […]" (261). The counterculture had its own ethos of conformity and was hostile towards the "camaraderie of loneliness" (xxviii). Psychedelic drugs and a kind of "Do your own thing"-attitude had little to do with her experience of taking innumerable risks and nonmarketable rewards. On the last two pages of the memoir, Johnson – once again – looks at a snapshot, showing a young girl in black stockings, black skirt, and black sweater. The picture shows Joyce Glassman, twenty-two, "with her hair hanging down below her shoulders, all in black like Masha in *The Seagull*," but unlike Masha, "she's not in mourning for her life": "How could she have been, with her seat at the table in the exact center of the universe," Johnson reflects on herself as a young woman (261). She is a young Beat woman full of expectancy, happy to sit with a group of men whose voices rise and fall. Johnson looks at her picture and is optimistic:

> As a female, she's not quite part of this convergence. A fact she ignores, sitting by in her excitement as the voices of the men, always the men, passionately rise and fall and their beer glasses collect and the smoke of their cigarettes rises toward the ceiling and the dead culture is surely being wakened.
> Merely being here, she tells herself, is enough. *(Minor Characters:* 262)

Joyce Johnson, now forty-seven years old, wishes to abandon her female silence. Even though she is non-conformist, she is left alone knowing that the past can never be told as the memoirist would like, as indicated in the last sentence of the memoir: "If time were like a passage of music, you could keep going back to it till you got it right" (262).

7.1.3 The Kerouac – Johnson Connection

Johnson's ironically titled *Minor Characters* (1983), which received a National Book Critics Circle award in 1983, was one of the first books to focus upon the lives of Beat women. Johnson was Kerouac's lover during 1957 and 1958. While her epistolary novel *Door Wide Open* (2000) focuses almost completely on the love affair with Kerouac, he is only one protagonist among others in *Minor Characters* – a fact which might be disappointing for those readers who primarily aim at peeping behind every single intimacy between Kerouac and Johnson. In fact, Kerouac's first encounter with Johnson is being depicted late in the book on page 126, even though Kerouac's road trips are juxtaposed to Johnson's own life story from the beginning onwards. Johnson does not tell her story from the perspective of a despised lover, having been abandoned by *the* icon of a whole generation. She is also not in favor of trying to arouse pity. Her standpoint is that of a woman having experienced many enjoyable, but also many dispiriting moments together with her friends Jack Kerouac, Elise Cowen, Allen Ginsberg, Herbert Huncke, Gregory Corso, or LeRoi and Hettie Jones. They are merely her friends and not depicted as celebrities, as the reader might find out disappointedly. The people who later became icons of a whole generation are described from an insider's perspective. Due to the fact that the perspective is female, it is particularly valuable, as it represents one of the few women's documents about the Beats.

Having started her writing career at the age of twenty, Johnson – not having met Kerouac yet – later found out that her own agent had rejected three manuscripts of Kerouac, including *On the Road*. Considering this, it is important to remember that several other women Beat writers, most notably Johnson and di Prima, were working in "Beat" directions before any of the major Beat works were published. When di Prima read Ginsberg's *Howl* in 1956, the work served less as an artistic inspiration than as a reassurance that she was not alone, that a movement was beginning. She realized that "[a]ll the people who, like me, had hidden and skulked, writing down what they knew for a small handful of friends […] would now step forward and say their piece" (1998: 176). A year before she met Kerouac, Johnson had already begun her first novel, *Come and Join the Dance* (1962). Its heroine, Susan Levitt, whose story parallels Johnson's own experience, turns her back on her family and her college career to find the liberating experience she craves amid a group of male and female dropouts: 'Outlaws,' she calls them, a mysterious underground brotherhood. At the end of the novel, she departs for Paris on her own.

Johnson found her way to the core of the Beat Generation through her Barnard classmate Elise Cowen, who had started dating Allen Ginsberg in 1952, two years before Ginsberg had fallen in love with Peter Orlovsky, who became his longtime companion.[49] In January 1957, Ginsberg arranged a blind date for Kerouac and Johnson; the 21-year-old Johnson and the 32-year-old, road-weary Kerouac met at Howard Johnson's in the village.

> I push open the heavy glass door, and there is, sure enough, a black-haired man at the counter in a flannel lumberjack shirt slightly the worse for wear. He looks up and stares at me hard with blue eyes, amazingly blue. And the skin of his face is so brown. He's the only person in Howard Johnson's in color. I feel a little scared as I walk up to him. "Jack?" I say. *(Minor Characters:* 127)

That very same night, right after their first encounter, Kerouac moved into Johnson's apartment. "When we got to the door, he didn't ask to see my manuscript. He pulled me against him and kissed me before I even turned on the light," Johnson confesses intimately. "I kissed him back, and he acted surprised. [...] 'The trouble is,' Jack said with his voice against my ear, 'I don't … like … blondes'" . Johnson laughs and replies, "'Well, in that case I'll just dye my hair' – wondering all the same if it was true" (130-131). Kerouac did not have many belongings, owning only a sleeping bag, a knapsack in which there were some jeans, a few old T-Shirts, and some notebooks he had bought in Mexico City. He did not even have a typewriter and therefore was borrowing other people's typewriters. Wishing to be dark-haired and dark-skinned, Johnson envied Kerouac's dark fellaheen women he had written about. About her time with him, she writes that she was "everydayness, bacon and eggs in the morning or the middle of the nights, which I learned to cook just the way he liked – sunny side up in the black iron frying pan," and she would buy slab bacon in the grocery store like the one he always had in Lowell: "He took extraordinary pleasure in small things like that" (131-132).

For nearly two years, she and Kerouac lived together intermittently between his trips to Tangiers, Paris, San Francisco, Mexico City, and Orlando/Florida. More than anything, she wanted to go on the road with him; but, disappointedly, Johnson realizes: "Could he ever include a woman in his journeys? I didn't altogether see why not. Whenever I tried to raise the question, he'd stop me by saying that what I really wanted were babies. That was what all women wanted and what I wanted too [...]" (136). He would depart enthusiastically for each destination, write her a letter or two trying to convince her to join him, but then he would suddenly find the "vibrations" too sinister, and therefore move on. Due to his frantic traveling, Johnson never had the chance to follow, as he moved too quickly from A to B. Wanting to be with his male friends only, he was clearly fooling Johnson by telling her to follow, but then leaving before she could arrive. These scenes are typical for Kerouac's

---

[49] In 1954, San Francisco painter Robert LaVigne introduced his model and companion, Peter Orlovsky, to Ginsberg. Soon after this first meeting, Orlovsky and Ginsberg became lovers and moved in together, defining their relationship as a marriage. Despite periods of separation, this arrangement remained intact until Ginsberg's death in April 1997. Orlovsky has written poetry on his own, though he never fully established a literary identity for himself that transcended his status as Ginsberg's lover.

sexist attitudes towards women. Kerouac had become famous over night when *On the Road* was published on September 5, 1957. After having mailed Kerouac thirty dollars for the bus ticket from Mexico City to New York, Johnson is the one who is with him at the newsstand, reading the book's review in *The New York Times*.

> *On the Road* is the second novel by Jack Kerouac, and its publication is a historic occasion insofar as the exposure of an authentic work of art is of any great moment in an age in which the attention is fragmented and the sensibilities are blunted by the superlatives of fashion (multiplied a millionfold by the spirit and power of communication). (Gilbert Millstein quoted in *Minor Characters:* 184)

Kerouac himself had mixed feelings about the publication, as the book had been written six years ago, the work of a young man, depicting his road kicks with Neal Cassady. Sending Cassady one of the first copies into prison, his old friend was disappointed about the work due to the fact that the Viking editors had violated much of the book's initial spontaneity. Kerouac's reaction at the newsstand was not all too euphoric: "He didn't look happy, exactly, but strangely puzzled, as if he couldn't figure out why he wasn't happier than I was. We returned to the apartment to go back to sleep. Jack lay down obscure for the last time of his life. The ringing phone woke him the next morning and he was famous" (185).

Unsuccessfully, Johnson tried to take care of Kerouac by fending off the world: Answering the ever-ringing phone for him; opening the piles of letters outpouring hatred, love, or yearnings, like "I am dying in this little hick town. If I could only meet you, touch you […]" (Charters: 1983: 624); going to parties where men wanted to fight him and girls wanted to go to bed with him. About their relationship, Johnson writes, "I loved him – and knew, with some strange twenty-one-year-old wisdom, that it would not be permanent, even the few times we talked of marriage. We were better at being friends than anything else, not that I realized it then […]" (624). To read about their two-year love affair is to hope against hope that somehow Johnson will be able to save Kerouac from unwanted bad reputation, from his paralyzing emotional dependence upon his mother, and from alcohol. It was not meant to be. In the end, she lost him to his mother, who represented home and safety to him. Johnson last spoke to Kerouac on the phone in 1964, five years before his death. He was drunk and "lonely wherever he was, and what he said didn't even make much sense. Something about how I'd never wanted anything from him – which wasn't really true, of course – 'You never wanted furs or anything, just a little ol' pea soup'," Johnson remembers: "Still I could feel the sweetness there, and I cried after he hung up" (623).

Retrospectively, Johnson discovered that she was sometimes freed from the small, continuous acts of female subordination in the 1950s since Kerouac fulfilled few, if any, of the conventional demands of his masculine role. In the mid-1950s, he could not support himself, much less a girlfriend, and Johnson notes the perverse, but real pleasures of buying him dinner or lending him money. Though Kerouac was not faithful, neither was she. Most important for her was to be there at the moment of a cultural revolution, in the "exact center of the universe" (1999: 261). While Johnson laments the silence imposed on Beat women, never does she suggest that any other cultural site could have offered her as much stimulation.

7.1.4 The Process of Writing a Memoir

> What's my process of writing? Just do it!
> (Joyce Johnson quoted in Grace. *Breaking the Rule of Cool:* 194)

In a 1999 interview, Johnson admits that if she had written *Minor Characters* in her late twenties or early thirties, she probably would have written a novel about a sad love affair. In the 1960s and 1970s, Johnson was not thinking about writing a memoir at all. Johnson takes Virginia Woolf as an example: In *Moments of Being*, she writes about the same events at 25 and again at the age of 50. At 50, Woolf is "remembering so much more, it seems," and she is able to "see around the events, the things that happened to her" (Grace: 2004: 185). Asked about the meaning of fabrications in memoir writing, Johnson is aware of their troubling effects. For her, there are things you do for the sake of form. She could have put in everything that happened to her during the years she was writing about, but she rather wanted to have a focus. "As much as I could," she affirms, "I tried really hard to remember what happened as close as I could get, apart from one's lapses in memory. I didn't consciously invent in *Minor Characters*. I sort of re-created, which is different" (185). In comparison to Kerouac, who had an excellent gift for memorizing, Johnson is a very selective rememberer. There are some things that are stamped on her mind, but there are also many scenes which are simply lost. However, as she states, she remembers places very easily. For example, she can close her eyes and see her parents' living room, "the red couch with a green slipcover, the baby grand piano and needlepoint piano bench" (186). Due to the fact that some people she knew rather well slipped from her memory, she had to read her diaries of the time in order to facilitate remembering. Kerouac was different in that respect, as he had a gift for re-visualizing places, people, and experiences. His memory was always available to him, a reason why he could write down things that happened years before accurately and without hesitation. The publication and selling of *Minor Characters* clearly profited from the memoir boom which started in the 1980s and still has not reached its climax. The 1990s and post-millennium years have brought a new age of confession, and confession seems to have become the norm. Johnson and her fellow Beat memoirist di Prima were among the first ones to publish autobiographical Beat writings – *Memoirs of a Beatnik* appeared in 1969, *Minor Characters* in 1983. Brenda Frazer's *Troia – Mexican Memoirs*, which was published in 1969, is also an early document of a Beat woman struggling to survive in a male-dominated Beat world. The memoir stands apart as a work that in form and content may be the most troubling and provocative of female Beat life stories.

For Johnson, memoir writing is only possible if the writer distances herself from the events she writes about, and this can only be done decades later. Nowadays, confessional writing has become accepted by a broad readership, and so effects of shock and surprise are clearly diminished. When Kerouac and Ginsberg were first writing their confessional works, the audience was mostly appalled. During the end of the 20th and beginning of the 21st century, the reader has become accustomed to intimacies being revealed in public. According to Johnson, the current interest in memoir writing rests upon the fact that memoirs "are often more surprising and more interesting than a lot of fiction that's around". Authors of fiction are getting more and more unimaginative, as they seem to have a content problem: "If you read a lot of contemporary fiction you seem to feel after a while that the same kinds of things are being endlessly written about. Where real life is full of quirky surprises, messier". Today, writers are "especially casting about for content right now" (187), but once the author clearly knows what the content of the work will be, the form can easily be determined. For Johnson, one problem of writing *Minor Characters* was how to include Jack Kerouac in the story without interrupting it. Finding a solution to the problem, she points out: "Then I hit upon the device of following myself and following him as two separate streams, then converge. Then, we diverge at the end. That was the form" (188). Inspired by second wave feminism, Johnson suddenly recognized that her female friends' stories and her own coming of age were important for the whole women's movement. However, women writers' networking obviously did not work as well as that of Beat men. Writing more or less privately, she admits: "I don't know that I talked to Hettie about my writing. She knew that I wrote, of course. She didn't talk with me about hers. I didn't talk with Diane di Prima about my writing. I knew Diane. I had known Diane in high school" (198-199).

In the preceding chapters, Joyce Johnson's *Minor Characters* was presented as a forerunner of feminist autobiographical Beat writing. Concentrating on the textual analysis of her work, it is quite evident that her Beat friends and particularly Jack Kerouac have been of major importance for her development as a writer. In the following chapters, another woman representing the 'epitome of cool' is being zoomed in – Hettie Jones: Black-stockinged, intellectual, and essentially Beat. Being a feminist before the term was even coined, her pads and parties provided a safe refuge for many Beat writers and artists.

7.2 Hettie Jones' *How I Became Hettie Jones*

7.2.1 The Joneses' Search for Identity

> The idea […] is to change first of our own volition and according to our own inner promptings before they impose completely arbitrary changes on us. (Jane Bowles. *Two Serious Ladies*, quoted in *How I Became Hettie Jones:* 3)

In Hettie Jones' memoir *How I Became Hettie Jones*, roughly seven years (1957 – 1964) of a life in and around poetry are recorded. For Jones, the work is a testament to an experience of passing through poetry while remaining "in it," but at the same time writing little of it. On the one hand, the memoir details the life and times of Jones and the literary scene in New York as the bohemian 1950s evolved into the countercultural 1960s. On the other hand, the dividing line between private and public experience is central. Both Jones' marriage with the African-American poet LeRoi Jones (now Amiri Baraka) as well as the book's overarching question, "Who is Hettie Jones?," point to the significant problematic of identity. The problem of searching for one's identity seems to be evident for both authors: In Jones' memoir, the emergence of "the poet" LeRoi Jones is depicted in its precise cultural context, as he moves from what he called the "aesthetic" period of his avant-garde work to the Black Arts movement and a new identity as Amiri Baraka. Similar to LeRoi, Hettie Jones also undergoes a transformation. Not only through marriage, Hettie Cohen transforms into Hettie Jones, but also because of her Beat companions and her personal coming-of-age as a writer. For her, this shift of identity in racial and cultural terms is completed by writing *How I Became Hettie Jones* in 1990.

Not only concerning their friendship, but also when writing their life stories, Hettie Jones and Joyce Johnson share several similarities. Jones' memoir rests upon some of the same writing techniques, including a similar scene setting, an intense contemplating on how tricky memory is, or the emergence of various textual selves located in the middle of a floating time concept. Jones' work, however, does not include snapshot-like images, but instead uses textual fragments to construct a self. The precisely ordered textual pieces of her life story have therapeutic effects: By including them, she can so cope with society's racism, her parents' rejection of her interracial family, and Roi's abandoning of her because of her whiteness. The tormented self which turns up through the painful story-telling process is transparent, vanishing and reentering the stage every time the reader closes and opens the memoir. The reader soon realizes that the self telling the fragmented story intends to reveal everything about the past, no matter how painful the experiences might have been.

In order to point out that the present and past are totally clinging to each other, Jones – similar to Johnson – arranges alternating scenes using both tenses. At the beginning of her life writing, Jones presents a short present tense image of herself as a young woman on the day she first meets Roi. She interconnects the "small, dark, twenty-two-year-old Jew" Cohen, who has just left her family in Laurelton, New York, to find liberation in the Village, and the fifty-five-year-old Jones, who is still musing about her past days and who refuses to distance herself from her younger self (2). This narrative device to open the book by going back to her job as a Subscription Manager at the *Record Changer* – naming the date March 1957 – is powerful for the reader, as she immediately sets the scene and time. During the next chapter, Jones re-lives her childhood when remembering weaving a basket with clouds in the sky when she was six years old, ironing pillowcases and handkerchiefs with her mother, being a Jewish outsider among Laurelton's Irish, and experiencing racism for the first time at Mary Washington College in Virginia. All experiences are relics of her past, which is a fragmented record of events. Yet, despite her depriving suburban environment, she knows that at least she "was going to *become* – something, anything, whatever that meant":

> By 1951, the year we labeled the Silent Generation, I'd been recommended to silence often. Men had little use for an outspoken woman, I'd been warned. What I wanted, I was told, was security and upward mobility, which might be mine if I learned to shut my mouth. Myself I simply expected, by force of will, to assume a new shape in the future. Unlike any woman in my family or anyone I'd ever actually known, I was going to become – something, anything, whatever that meant. *(How I Became Hettie Jones:* 10)

Appearing like mosaics, Jones' chapters consist of subchapters of varied lengths, some being very short. Jones' time jumps convey the impression of constant motion, turbulence, restlessness, and disharmony – aspects Estelle Jelinek refers to as typical features of women's life writings. The reader soon realizes that Jones' Beat life seems to be exciting, diversified, and full of ups and downs. Concerning temporal and corporal text manipulations, Nancy M. Grace refers to the so-called "chronological code" of French literary critic Roland Barthes (cf. 2002: 153f.). Similar to Barthes, Jones' textual self lives in three realities at the same time: First, there is her past self which re-experiences past events, second, the self which emerges as a poet and writer, and third, the middle-aged self still living in an apartment in Greenwich Village, writing the memoir. Jones perfectly manipulates Barthes' code, which is clearly shown in the way her marriage with LeRoi Jones brings along many transformations for her.

When Jones first met Cohen, he was happily surprised to find his interviewer reading Kafka's *Amerika,* and she was pleased to encounter someone so smart and direct, "his movements were easy, those of a man at home not only in skin but in muscle and bone," Jones writes. "And he led with his head. What had started with Kafka just went on going" (1997: 2). Jones had been raised in a middle-class Newark family, attended Rutgers and Howard University, and served as a gunner in the U.S. Air Force. Profoundly alienated, his mood began to improve when he read "Howl," calling the poem the most important poetic influence of the period (cf. Watson 1998: 267).

When Hettie Jones marries LeRoi, she, on the one hand, reflects on her name that will be changed from Cohen into Jones, but on the other hand, she is also aware of the fact that other transformations will occur. "One night, introducing me to someone, Frank O'Hara called me Hettie Cohen," Jones writes. "Her name is Jones now," Roi interrupted.

> Despite the shared name, there were different transformations awaiting us. He would remain, like any man of any race, exactly as he was, augmented. Whereas I, like few other women at the time, would first lose my past to share his, and then, with that eventuality lost too, would become the person who speaks to you now. *(How I Became Hettie Jones:* 65)

When moving into Fourteenth Street, she finally leaves behind her old name Cohen. As she owes a sizable sum of money to the telephone company and as the phone was listed under her old name, she simply says she does not know Hettie Cohen when the bill collector calls her office. Rejecting her past, she declares: "Yes, she did work here, but I don't know where she is now". At first, she is shocked about her words and "felt a terrible loss, as if I'd dismissed an old friend. But it was done;

that was it for Hettie Cohen". After hanging up, she calls her husband, who "made a big, comforting joke about her departure" (115).

Change of name is a central concern for both Hettie and LeRoi Jones. However, different cultural logics are inscribed in changing their first names and surnames. Hettie Cohen is only fully Hettie Jones after writing her autobiography, shown by the title *How I Became Hettie Jones*. This does not happen by simply marrying LeRoi, but it is rather a question of resolving authorship and marriage: Toward the end of their literary/marital partnership, as their marriage got into deep troubles due to Roi's extramarital affairs and increasing radicalism, Roi introduced Hettie as H. Cohen-Jones in the last *Yugen* issue of the year 1962: "He gave me a new name that year – H. Cohen-Jones – and surprised me with it on the last *Yugen* masthead. I liked it – it was funny to have the least aristocratic hyphenated name in America, although the up-front initial H, somehow left out the woman whose mouth I was trying to open [...]" (168). LeRoi Jones obviously wanted to give his wife back at least some of the identity she lost by accepting her new name when marrying. On the other hand, LeRoi Jones also changed his name from Everett Leroy to LeRoi Jones at the beginning of his literary career, calling it his "transitional" period. He later on changed his name into Imamu Amiri Baraka in his Black Nationalist phase (1965-1974). From 1974 onwards, he dropped "Imamu" while in the Third World Marxist phase. However, he kept "LeRoi Jones" as authorial in both editions of his autobiography and in his selected writings[50]. The names "LeRoi Jones" and "Amiri Baraka" are results of cultural politics. Hettie Cohen did not become Hettie Jones in the same way that LeRoi Jones became Amiri Baraka, even though the two transformations are connected with each other. Her act of self-naming does not take place in an act of authorial framing outside the text, but within her narration (cf. Watten 2002: 100f.). Cohen transforms into Jones due to the numerous Beat artists, writers, musicians who are her friends, due to the Greenwich Village Beat scene she is part of, and due to the interracial family that strengthens her self.

Jones' narrative self is writing consciously from the present, but then moves into the past. In comparison to the agile narrator, LeRoi is envisioned as an immobile masculine character being stuck in the past. Jones sees herself as a flexible character which has to get rid of her past so that she can continue living. However, she does not want to lose that individual past completely. In several paragraphs, the present collapses into the past: In one scene, Jones as the memoirist in her 50s is looking down from her window at the image of herself as a young person, walking along the sidewalk toward her favorite Beat café, the Five Spot (cf. 1997: 65). In these few lines, Jones once more captures time and space. Continuously throughout the book, her past and present are brought together, creating a coherent whole.

Jones is fierce about the necessity to reconstruct her past. Memory, however, fails her several times. Remembering is a must, but she cannot always exactly retell her own life or the stories of her female

---

[50] This periodization is continually referred to by Baraka himself, and is also schematized in the table of contents of his selected writings, *The LeRoi Jones/Amiri Baraka Reader*, edited by William J. Harris.

Beat friends. In life writing, the author always comes across blank spots in memory. Both Joyce Johnson and Hettie Jones are very skillful in trying to elude these moments by turning to private documents like diaries, photographs, or letters written at the time. These texts are tools that facilitate reconstructing scenes that could have taken place, but did not. The reader has to take for granted what might have been, but is left unsure about reality. When writing about the day Roi told her he was leaving her because she was white, Jones admits that all that is left in her memory is the "open door behind his back". "Memory's so tricky," she confesses (218). Against this image of just seeing an open door behind Roi's back, she places remembered parts of their conversations and excerpts from Jones' *The Autobiography of LeRoi Jones/Amiri Baraka* which was first published in 1984. The fragmented scene she constructs is a credible depiction of what might have happened that day. She creates this rearranged scene in order to powerfully express her emotional sorrow, but also her desire to cope with that depressing part of her life.

> "I can't take you," he said. "I don't want to."
> I could feel it coming, like an awful tide. I said "Why?" and then there it was:
> "Because you're white."
> "As if the tragic world around our 'free zone' had finally swept in and frozen us to the spot," was the way he told it later. My eyes, he said, showed such pain he almost covered his face.
> And he should have, I guess, since he'd shattered my life.
> *(How I Became Hettie Jones*: 218)

The Joneses' interracial relationship had been put to the test for years. When Hettie Cohen had married LeRoi Jones on October 13, 1958, her family was appalled. She describes the decision to marry Jones as inevitable and simple, because she loved him. It was, nevertheless, a daring decision, for even in the Village's accepting milieu, there were only some interracial couples living there in the 1950s. So offended was the Italian community just south of Washington Square that gangs of male rowdies sometimes threatened them. The difference between this and other Beat liaisons was that, as Hettie Jones observed, they "made acquaintance *through work* rather than simply *as wife*" (129). The Joneses' separated in the early 1960s, and when LeRoi asked for a divorce in 1965, many regarded the break-up as a symbol of the crumbling civil rights coalition of blacks and whites. After the murder of Malcolm X in February of that year, LeRoi became increasingly involved in the politics of black separatism and soon changed his name to Amiri Baraka.

The Joneses split up at a crucial historical moment. In 1965, the Civil Rights Movement was at its climax, as black leaders were not only known regionally any more. LeRoi Jones' play *Dutchman* was first performed at Howard University, and his first full-length play *The Slave* was awaited impatiently. In every interview about his work, he was asked about his relation to his white woman Hettie. She writes, "Sometimes I got a dependent clause: 'Jones, who is married to a white woman.' Or my name: 'his white wife, the former Hettie Cohen.' Used against him I blurred his indictments: why in 'all you white folks' was I the exception?" (217). During the seven years Hettie Jones had known LeRoi, she could not have imagined that the so-called "black rage" could turn on her and her black children Kelly and Lisa. More and more, LeRoi Jones was put under pressure by the public: "Now some people were beginning to say that hypocritical Roi talked black but married white. Others, more directly, said he was laying with the Devil" (218). Seen from this perspective, the end of their relationship seemed to be an inescapable consequence.

7.2.2 Setting up Scenes

Jones' scenes which defy temporality in all respects are set up very skillfully. She masterfully visualizes particular places and persons: As an autobiographer, her narrative is like scanning a photo album; she zooms in past moments. This special writing technique of alternating past and present tenses, of creating powerful images, of reanimating her internal recordings and photograph-like recollections is surprisingly similar to Johnson's way of writing. Very often, her paragraphs open with setting up a present tense scene. Remembering the Laurelton Jewish Center where her family regularly attended mass, she creates a present tense scene: "It's warm for late September, I don't mind my bare arms, or the thin crepe of my chemise, already the only dress that still fits. Beside me my father's hands, dark and thick-nailed, rest on the open *machzor*, the liturgy. My mother's at his right, with rough cheeks and powdered nose. As usual I feel older than both of them" (61). Another example for presenting past scenes vividly in present tense is, "Tense, low-voiced, frowning, facing each other a foot apart, up to our ears in mutual, prideful life, we're standing, Roi and I, with the threshold of the kitchen doorway between us" (122). Another scene starts with "Now he's on the couch in the living room, his face with its bones and planes all contorted, his arm around me like an awkward boyfriend. 'I want to come home,' he whispers, 'but Diane [di Prima] told me you went to bed with A. B. and I couldn't stand that.' *Me*? [...] This man is crazy! Are all men *crazy*?" (140). After having given birth to her second child, Jones sets the scene as follows: "At the curb on a corner of Fourteenth and First, late one fall afternoon. It's beginning to rain. Hurrying people eddy around me, I'm a convoy in a traffic dilemma: I've got a baby carriage on the sidewalk, a shopping cart piled with clean laundry in the street, and a fallen sheet getting mucky in the gutter" (145). Being a working mother in the 1960s was rather unusual. Jones has a job interview at *Time* magazine and opens the paragraph with "It's a bright fall noon but not where I am, nineteen floors above Sixth Avenue at Fifty-first Street, in a corridor that makes me think of death row. Suddenly I feel something wrong: it's my chewing gum. I reach for something to stick it to" (204). Jones' opening scenes aim at getting the reader directly into the narrative. By depicting certain houses, people, streets, and by stimulating all five senses, the reader feels included into the story:

> Apartment 20 gets morning sun and I'm soaking it up in the window, on the window sill, eating the first peach of the season. I've got a snatch view of the corner market on Bleecker, where the peach comes from and where an old Italian lady who likes me is setting out more of them. When I buy things from her she pats me and adds

> extra to the bag, and when I protest she says, "You too little already." *(How I Became Hettie Jones:* 29)

Within one scene, Jones speaks to all five senses: She includes gustatory senses, like eating the first peach of the season, visual senses, like "I've got a snatch view of the corner market," olfactory senses, as she is soaking up the sun and smelling May air, senses of touch, when the old Italian lady is patting her, and auditory senses while listening to the turmoil on the street below her window.

Jones is continually making efforts to pull herself and the reader back into the present. The act of writing the story is an experience of the present: She shows this by asking the reader to actively take part in her narrative. The first sentence of the book is already calling on the reader's attention: "Meet Hettie Cohen" (1). Rather than speaking to herself of herself, which would be typical of life writing, she opens up her narrative with what might be perceived as a request, an order, or even an invitation. From the opening sentence onwards until the end of the book, the reader is on one level with the narrator, creating a we-feeling between herself and the audience. "Meet Hettie Cohen" serves as the basis for the intimate author-reader-relationship which is supposed to develop. Together with the fifty-five-year-old Hettie Jones, the reader is being invited to get to know Hettie Cohen, "a small, dark, twenty-two-year-old Jew from Laurelton, Queens, with a paperback book in [her] hand. Kafka's *Amerika*" (2). Her narrative depends upon the reader's presence and cannot exist for its own sake. To achieve this, Jones creates a confidential tone of openness and trust. Without the collaboration between author and reader, *How I Became Hettie Jones* cannot speak for Jones and the culture of her time. The introducing line is both friendly, loyal, and open, but also directive. For Jones, the present becomes a perfect place for living out her talents as a teacher and educator, being an expert on 1950s cultural history: The race relations of the time, the bohemian Beat scene, but also the beginning of second wave feminism play a crucial role, even though Jones is not yet aware of the radical changes for women's emancipation. She is also an excellent preacher who tells the reader that nothing is wrong about having a biracial family, that giving birth to black children even though she is white is nothing to worry about. Speaking to the reader using the second-person "you," she declares, "For those who still don't believe it, race disappears in the house – in the bathroom, under the covers, in the bedbugs in your common mattress, in the morning sleep in your eyes" (36). Even though thirty states still had miscegenation laws in the 1950s, Hettie and LeRoi were not afraid to be seen together in public, even though, "there weren't a half-dozen steady interracial couples in the Village" at the time (36). By using the second-person "you," the reader is directly addressed to join Jones' life story: "Look at us there, if you will, in that chilly spring dawn. Two twenty-five-year-old kids with a kid, in the middle of a lot of commotion. Do you see race in this? Have you forgotten? It would get worse" (104). Sometimes, it seems, Jones is desperate to communicate with the reader:

> Why am I so glad to see him, even after these five years? After lies and infidelities, and other large and small betrayals, hardly discussed, little understood, on both our parts. How do you feel about this, really? It can't be self-hate that's causing my heart to leap at each bound of his legs. It can't be that I've paid – what can it be? Why am I happy? Do you call it love as he gathers me up and we push through the door and crash to the bed in a quick, shivery, clothes-on connection? Can you lust for the one you love so domestically? *(How I Became Hettie Jones:* 166)

Jones asks the reader for help. Why does she still love Roi, even though Diane di Prima has already given birth to their child in the meantime? Why is she still happy, consciously knowing he cannot be faithful? Jones writes that she was not surprised to hear that her husband and Diane di Prima had been lovers for quite some time, but "the first affair cuts the cake, nothing else is ever as sharp" (98). They split, but after some time, LeRoi decides to move in with Hettie and the children again. Jones was jealous of di Prima, whom she knew well, as di Prima was everything that she was not:

> To begin she was single, and single women know, as the blues say, when to raise their window high. I liked her because she was smart and quick to laugh, and enjoyed her bisexual life (although she tended to wear lovers like chevrons). Unmarried, she was raising a daughter. Unusual, her family hadn't turned on her; she took me to Brooklyn once to meet her grandmother. I never knew how she lived, working only occasional odd jobs. But Diane's life was her lit.
> At first I thought it had to be all my fault. Because the two of them loved Ezra Pound and as a Jew I just couldn't. *(How I Became Hettie Jones:* 98)

Jones does not demand that he ends the affair, knowing that he makes his own decisions. "Among my friends I counted as many affairs as marriages, everyone was hot and mixed up," she describes the Beat scene, and thus tries to forgive her husband's infidelity (99). For Jones, there is clarity in separation, too, as "you begin to see what you miss" (166). Through directly conversing with the reader, the connection gets intimately close. The "you" incorporates the reader into the story, so that an escape is not possible any more, as she/he is being asked for advice. Another exemplary scene for the close You-I relationship takes place in a late September morning: "We're hanging around, reading the paper. Roi's in a chair, one of the two the landlord said I might keep, and which, were we your typical fifties couple, we would now think of as 'our furniture'" (41). There are no answers to the questions she asks the reader, but the presence of the reader is of utmost importance.

Similar to Joyce Johnson, Jones is also a skillful player with language and inserts various types of texts into her memoir. Several times throughout the book, Jones gives up her own voice to let others speak, which is often more effective. Personal correspondence, her journal entries of the time, poems of various Black Mountain poets, or her own and Roi's poems are connected with the narrative, sharing Johnson's affinity for the contemporary skeleton-trend of life-writing. However, Jones uses the additional material more generously and frequently than Johnson, and so, the impact on the reader is different. Many inserted parts of *How I Became Hettie Jones* are written by different artists of the 1960s, including Charles Olson or Robert Creeley, Michael McClure, Billie Holiday, Ron Loewinsohn, or her husband LeRoi Jones, who are representatives of the literary and political culture of the Beat Generation. For her, other authors' texts can effectively speak for the Beat era, as the power of these artists' words seems to her greater than her own. Same as in her book, Beat history has always been intersected with other artistic movements like the Black Mountain School, the San Francisco School, or the New York School of Poetry. Jones' self is relational and seeks herself in others. At a Dexedrine-soaked party in Twentieth Street, Jones takes out the last issue of *Yugen* and quotes Michael McClure:

> Matchflame of violet and flesh …
> … clear bright light.
> … stars outside.
> … long sounds of cars.
> … the huge reality of touch and love.
> … real as you are real whom I speak to.
> *(How I Became Hettie Jones:* 77)

In times of crises, she also finds comfort in Charles Olson's powerful words "What does not change/ is the will to change" (116). Through her husband's poetry, she becomes aware about the way he thinks about their relationship when they grow more and more apart. He writes, "To say/ I love you & cannot even recognize/ you" (86), which reflects his own inner conflicts. In harmonious times, he writes a poem about Hettie giving birth to their first child:

> My wife is left-handed.
> Which implies a fierce de-
> termination. A complete other
> worldliness. IT'S WEIRD BABY ….
>
> & now her belly droops over the seat.
> They say it's a child. But
> I ain't quite so sure.
> *(How I Became Hettie Jones:* 89)

About Hettie's love of singing to the baby, Roi writes, "… your voice/ down the hall, through the window, above/ all those trees a light/ it seems/ & you are singing. What song/ is that The words/ are beautiful" (93). The intersected works written by LeRoi Jones have the effect to reveal intimate details about their often problematic relationship. By showing both perspectives, she therefore gives her husband the chance to defend himself against unjustified charges.

A poet herself, Jones admired Denise Levertov or Barbara Guest, but she knew she could never approach the sophisticated metaphoric poetry they wrote. Moreover, she also felt a close affinity towards William Carlos Williams or Robert Creeley, whose words "Let me be my own fool/ of my own making, the sun of it/ is equivocal," are also included in her memoir (148). Being inspired by the "language equivalent to Miles's pretty, ambivalent notes," she also finds wisdom in Kay Boyle's belief that – when writing down memory's "dreamy, evasive eyes" – "there's no way even the honest among us can be trusted" (185). Memory is dishonest and may deceive you, but by intersecting various artistic voices of the time and personal documents, her story becomes credible.

The result of her collaged writing is that another persona different from her self emerges out of her initial self: The communal Beat persona, already well known from other Beat memoirs, arises out of the dialogic blending of voices. Her unified persona is like Whitman's all-encompassing "I" or Ginsberg's "I" in "Howl". Similar to her best friend Joyce Johnson and her rival Diane di Prima, Jones speaks for a whole generation of women like herself: Beat, underdog, female, underestimated. The memoir catalogues women who were part of the male-dominated Beat culture, but got lost in history, even though many of them were poets or writers themselves. The sheer mass of this group of women and their relative anonymity suggest the distortions of official Beat history. In Jones' history, she includes, among others, her friend Helene Dorn (pages 128 to 131). Married to Ed Dorn, a former Black Mountain student from Santa Fe, she joined her husband who had come to read at the 92nd Street Y, which was having an avant-garde poetry series. "She'd wanted to paint, but in the forties lucky girls married early. So the War Bond Queen moved up in the world, to the bigger house on the hill, had a son the first year, then a daughter, then left her wealthy husband to paint again, and almost too soon, it seemed, took up with Ed" (129). They had a son and went back to Black Mountain, where she painted, typed, and edited. Further on, Jones writes about her encounters with Sara Blackburn, wife of poet Paul Blackburn (pages 99-100 and 201) and playwright Aishah Rahman, who was the Joneses' neighbor at 27 Cooper Square. Beat author Bonnie Bremser, later Brenda Frazer, who wrote *Troia: Mexican Memoirs* (1969), turns up on page 110. Her husband Ray Bremser had learned to write in jail, and was paroled when LeRoi Jones hired him to write for their magazine *Yugen*. Frazer was a "pretty, snub-nosed, brunette chick," who was "so in love that sometimes passion overwhelmed her; she'd close her eyes to contain it, press her head against his sleeve" (110). Even in bohemia, Frazer yearned for everything a woman could do: She bore a baby, but they soon had to flee across the border to Mexico due to a false rumor concerning Ray's parole. Jones writes that she never met Bonnie again, the "bleached, broke, skin-and-bones Bonnie about whom she wrote in her memoir, *Troia*"[51] (111). There is no romance in her road life as she finally escapes to the U.S. again, putting up their daughter for abortion. Jones also includes her poet friend Rochelle Owens (page 111), whose work would be soon included in Totem's *Four Young Lady Poets*, and Rena Oppenheimer Rosequist (pages 81-83, 110), then Joel Oppenheimer's wife. Rena was like a big sister to Jones. "One day in her eighteenth year she hitched to Black Mountain, with a friend who'd heard of the place," Jones remarks (82). In the early fifties, Black Mountain was the spot for avant-garde art, an experimental community which was home to many writers, composers, choreographers, painters, and sculptors. Rena eventually fell in love with Joel, but her Catholic family disapproved: "The morning Rena left home to be married, her mother stood in the doorway threatening suicide. The priest had been sent for. But Rena – amazingly nicknamed Sissy – slipped away before God's hand could stay her" (82). Rena was an extremely important influence for Hettie Jones, because she was self-confident, and becoming an artist's wife had not stopped her own career. Moreover, like Hettie, she combined working, being married, taking

---

[51] Mexican slang for adventuress or whore

care of her children, and being an artist. In a 1999 interview, Jones notes that she had just had lunch with Oppenheimer, who is now called Rena Rosequist, some days before, and they are close friends until today. Recalling the past, they remembered their parents' repelling attitude towards young female Beats. Jones does not remember one single female friend, who, if she was still in touch with her parents, was on good terms with them. The majority had left home and disappeared (cf. Grace 2004: 159f.). Diane di Prima (pages 98 and 190-191) also plays a crucial role, because she was Roi's lover; they had a child – di Prima's second one – and founded a mimeographed subscription newsletter called *The Floating Bear*. Here, they published the works of many Beat writers, both those who became famous and those who have slipped into obscurity. However, it seems that Jones refuses to put too much weight on the affair; therefore, di Prima is only mentioned twice in *How I Became Hettie Jones*. She recollects a situation when she first meets di Prima and LeRoi's baby: "I then came face to face, buggy to buggy, with Diane di Prima, who had her new baby out, which didn't look like *her*, either". Jones is often approached by passers-by who say her two African American babies look cute, but "sure don't look like *you*" (190). Similarly, di Prima's baby named Dominique is also black, but LeRoi Jones does not accept fatherhood and denies the existence of his child. Yet, Hettie Jones still envies di Prima's independent spirit, even though she is also the mother of two toddlers now.

> I admired Diane – why not? She wrote. Her self-directed life included a lot of good work. But her plans for Roi were far from his own. He'd written – in the story "Going down slow" – that when he was with her he always knew where his pants were. Which hardly mattered now, since by the time he put them on he'd risked his history. I looked at the dark brow, the familiar features of Diane's baby. It was hard – *hard* – for me to admit she existed. *(How I Became Hettie Jones:* 190)

Probably one of the most important characters in the memoir, but also in Jones' life, is Joyce Johnson (pages 79-81, 154-156). Jones and Johnson had met on a snowy, cold winter day in 1957 when Jones was putting up fliers for a reading her husband was giving. Jones had recognized Johnson as the woman who had been with Jack Kerouac when she had met him at Jazz on the Wagon. That affair was over now, and Johnson lived alone on First Avenue and was writing a novel which was already under contract at the time. Jones immediately liked Johnson, because like her, "she took her independence for granted". Moreover, "Both of us were paying the rent. Neither of us had ever considered wanting a man to support us. And having sex hadn't made us *bad*". They shared what was most important to them as young independent women: Common assumptions about their uncommon lives. "We lived outside, as if. As if we were men? As if we were newer, freer versions of ourselves? There have always been women like us. Poverty, and self-support, is enough dominion," Jones is convinced (81). Even though Johnson was among her best friends, they did not talk about each other's writing process. The two authors are still as close as ever today, whereas "a lot of other people have moved away or remained married or something like that," Jones points out (Grace: 2004: 172). Jones also enumerates other interracial couples such as, for example, Ia and Marzette Watts (pages 169-172). Marzette Watts and his red-haired Swedish wife, Ia, had moved in on the first-floor of 27 Cooper Square and were the

Joneses' neighbors. Marzette, who became a well-known jazz musician later on in life, "was a sight in those days, as he had stopped combing his hair". His style, "though not uncommon now, hadn't been seen here since slavery, and in 1962 seemed improbable on this tall, dark, affable guy from Alabama" (169). Other interracial unions were Garth and Archie Shepp (pages 170-171), who was an African American jazz musician and professor in the African-American Studies department at the University of Massachusetts, Amherst, where he taught both music and music history from the 1970s to the early 2000s. Diana Powell and actor/director Douglas Turner Ward (page 202) also had two black children. For Powell, having an interracial family is like being "disguised in your own skin" (202). African American painter Bob Thomson and his wife Carol Plenda (pages 135-136), a clothing designer, or Vertamae Smart-Grosvenor and painter Bob Grosvenor (pages 155, 193), who also had two black daughters, were also among the Joneses' friends. With these names, Jones makes the presence of women visible. In more common Beat accounts, these names remain unrecognized.

7.2.3 Jones' Coming-of-Age

In *How I Became Hettie Jones*, Jones' coming of age as a writer plays a crucial role. As one of the "minor characters" Johnson describes in her memoir, Jones soon turns from an independent full-time subscription manager for the *Partisan Review* to a part-time working mother. Her own poetical aspirations are soon sacrificed to Roi's career and the well-being of their two daughters. Serving her husband's career for so long and neglecting her own aspirations, Jones gets more and more frustrated with her role as a mere housewife, or as she put it, "I was an energetic young person of twenty-seven, serving others" (1997: 148). After her job, she comes home to help her husband run *Yugen*, the experimental magazine they published together, and Totem Press, which fostered the "new consciousness in arts and letters" (Charters: 1992: 482).

"To one of us a job is a slave," Jones writes in her memoir, "to the other it's a guarantee of freedom" (1997: 123).[52] This attitude was common in the Beat scene, because often, Beat men viewed having a steady job as a social constraint, or simply another way they were tied to a society they deemed repressive. Therefore, many hipster men would take jobs only when absolutely necessary, if at all. To many women, maintaining full-time work was a liberating opportunity for freedom from mainstream views that a woman should stay at home. For many women of male Beat writers, however, being responsible for bringing in money was a pessimistic prospect for the future. Even though Jones expresses the financial frustrations of being the sole wage earner for her family, she never blatantly expresses being upset that she had to work outside the home (cf. 114; 204-205). The types of jobs

---

[52] Occasionally, LeRoi Jones supported his family financially; he wrote for journals, published his works, and made money himself. However, his income was only sporadic, and to him, the luxury of not holding a full-time job was possible since his wife had a full-time job. Thus, he was able to take time to focus on his writing. In "Hymn for Lanie Poo," a poem to his sister, he writes "It's impos-/ sible to be an artist and a bread/ winner at the same time" (Baraka: 1991: 7).

Jones, Johnson, Cowen and others held were often those considered typically feminine, such as secretaries, assistants, typists, and dressmakers.[53] What emerged in the avant-garde scenes, then, was an interesting role reversal. Women became the active wage earners, often assisting men with financial support, as many male hipsters viewed the notion of holding a job as a distraction.

When LeRoi Jones wrote in *The New American Poetry*, "MY POETRY is whatever I think I am […] I CAN BE ANYTHING I CAN" (1960: 424), that was simply not the case for Hettie. In her memoir, she describes this quite modestly as a matter of writer's block. While one can argue that Hettie Jones' problem was not lack at all, but instead the various conditions that constrained her poetic production, it is clear that the memoir explores the following: she discusses her "lack" of her own writing as a problem experienced in real time and space where she has to overcome her non-writing-self first. Being a recognized poet often came with the privilege of being male, as recognition, in terms of race and gender, was male.

Hettie Jones tried to write poetry herself, and so the formula "his wife is a poet too" would not work for her. Coming from a household that regarded her interest in books with a certain suspicion, she started reading seriously late in her life. "But then, ah! Gluttonous, directionless, I read anything and everything I could get my hands on," she says. At the age of 25, her love for poetry was sparked by the publishing of Donald Allen's anthology *The New American Poetry 1945 – 1960,* and she was convinced that "here was a process I could, and would, join as a writer. I would write poems, I vowed, and eventually I did. And prose as well, in books with spines, and it all still feels like a miracle".[54]

Even though she often willingly plays the role of a helpmate to foster her husband's career, she struggles to start a writing career of her own. One of the virtues of her narrative is the exactness with which she describes the frustrations of not being able to find a voice as a poet. Her husband reads this as a claim to martyrdom and later on states: "She said, as well, that she was a writer, but she had sacrificed her writing, even hidden it from me, because of the crushing weight of my male chauvinism and her selfless desire to forward my career" (Baraka: 1984: 59). First, she sees her problem as a lack of self-confidence; second, as a lack of means; and last, in terms of a specific lack of sympathy or encouragement (cf. Watten 2002: 101).

In interviews and several of his autobiographical works, LeRoi Jones makes his wife a figure of non-identity and lack. For Hettie Cohen, this lack is, to begin with, her non-literariness: She is not positioned as a poet, and she cannot come to terms with writing poetry. Furthermore, LeRoi Jones describes her lack of identity in terms of decisive social factors, referring to her Jewish middle-class background. For him, all Jews are yearning for a certain Americanness. As they historically do not belong anywhere, they try to be assimilated. Moreover, LeRoi Jones depicts his wife as a figure of

---

[53] Both Jones and Johnson worked as editorial assistants. Joan Haverty Kerouac supported herself and Jack Kerouac, her husband for a time, as a dressmaker and department store salesgirl.
[54] Jones, Hettie. "The Book that Changed my Life". *National Book Foundation. Presenter of the National Book Awards.* March 22, 2006. See http://www.nationalbook.org/bookchanged_hjones_nbm.html

lack when he equates "White Supremacy" and "anti-Semitism" (Baraka: 1984: 213). Both factors create the internalized self-hatred that – visible everywhere in his work – is identified with the American middle-class. Hettie Jones' lack of identity and lack of poetry end up in rejection by her husband. Over the course of their marriage, which creates the time line of her memoir, LeRoi Jones – from his point of view – undergoes an enormous transformation. While Hettie Jones portrays her husband as static and unmovable while she is the one who takes on various identities throughout the book, he sees things differently. His rejection of Hettie can be seen in the withdrawal of the poet in purely personal terms. For example, "Whenever Roi came to take the children he would speak to me from across the room, as if he didn't want to get a good look" (1997: 228). But soon, this rejection will be shown more publicly.

> As if to refute the fact that he'd ever settled elsewhere, his new book, a collection of essays, was titled *Home*. He would neither speak to me nor send money, and wrote instructing me to reach him only through his parents. He did not call the children; they were driven to see him by emissaries. Eventually he changed his name to Imamu Amiri Baraka, and someone told me, though I never saw it, of a newspaper interview in which he denied my existence. *(How I Became Hettie Jones:* 231)

At the beginning of his autobiography, LeRoi Jones[55] describes his rejection of his family as a slow process. Gradually, their relationship deteriorates: "It was the feeling that Nelly[56] [Hettie] was outside my concerns, that we did not connect up [...] I had begun to see her as white! Before, even when I thought she was white, I had never felt anything negative" (1984: 287). His transformation was inevitably reinforced by the world at large: "According to many biographies and accounts of my life, it ended, both the living of it and the writing in reflection of it, when I left the 'white world'. They would not honor my life or work" (425). Recognition is a major motivation for both Hettie and LeRoi Jones. In her portrayal of her husband, she is extremely reserved, seemingly not wanting to hurt him in retrospect. In her account, LeRoi is presented as an extremely successful poet: He arrived on the scene with the appearance of *The New American Poetry* (1960) and his first book, *Preface to a Twenty-Volume Suicide Note* (1961). His success was also clearly prefigured by the literary networks constructed by both himself and Hettie through the editing and publishing of *Yugen* and Totem Press (cf. Watten 2002: 103).[57] Yet, the Joneses' cultural collaboration was dangerous during times of open racial injustice: "I realized we might get hurt or killed – and him more likely," Jones feared (1997: 37).

---

[55] In this work, I will use Baraka's original name LeRoi Jones in accordance with *How I Became Hettie Jones*. In general literary criticism, the name LeRoi Jones is used when talking about the 1950s up to his change of name in the spring of 1968, and Amiri Baraka from then up to today.
[56] In his *Autobiography*, Amiri Baraka calls his wife Hettie Jones "Nellie Kohn," as if completely denying her identity.
[57] In his 1984 autobiography, Baraka dismisses the two periodicals *Yugen* and *The Floating Bear* – which he co-edited with Diane di Prima – by giving them the pseudonyms *Zazen* and *The Fleeting Bear*. Positively, he remarks, "The magazine and Nellie and I were at the vortex of this swirling explosion of new poetry" (1984: 234).

Nevertheless, their relationship was always open and progressive, and most readers of *How I Became Hettie Jones* will probably understand LeRoi's identical crisis in terms of cross-racial identification.

After the success of his radical plays, LeRoi Jones' transformation gained momentum. His theatrical career started with the March 1964 production of *Dutchman*. His play *The Slave* was also immensely popular. Changing from poet to playwright meant a conscious shift to more agency and protest. From the mid-60s onwards, LeRoi Jones wanted to go beyond poetry, as poetry is an "impossibility" for him: "I can see now that the dramatic form began to interest me because I wanted to go 'beyond' poetry. I wanted some form of action literature" (1984: 275). As action theater, his drama results in a direct response, which was so important for him, because "the inner-circle hauteur that only the cognoscenti who read *Zazen* […] could appreciate had now been replaced by a wider circle of public talk" (280). Jones' fame brought a change from literature to politics, particularly after the death of Malcolm X: His move uptown to Harlem and the founding of the Black Arts Repertory Theater/School in March 1965 followed (cf. Watten 2002: 103f.). His "horizon shift" to Harlem becomes the blind spot in *How I Became Hettie Jones*, as he openly rejects her now that he is a real celebrity. He simply disappears from her memoir. Together with the rejection of poetry, LeRoi Jones rejects his family. In LeRoi Jones' *Autobiography*, he claims that poetry in its "impossibility" becomes the negative of action. An example for his views are given in *The Slave:*

> EASLEY: You're just filth, boy. Just filth. Can you understand that anything and everything you do is stupid, filthy, or meaningless! Your inept formless poetry. Hah. Poetry? A flashy doggerel for inducing all those unfortunate troops of yours to spill their blood on your behalf. But I guess that's something! Ritual drama, we used to call it at the university. The poetry of ritual drama. (Watten. "What I See": 104)

While poetry fails for LeRoi Jones, as its influence on the politics of the time is only minor, Hettie Jones struggles hard to become a poet and to get recognition for her poetic attempts.

Jones' personal coming-of-age is a long and painful process. In an important moment at the beginning of her memoir, Jones is lying on her back in the grass. Retrospectively, she realizes that this is the moment she "started leaving home," even though she is only six years old and weighs only thirty-eight pounds (1997: 5). She is startled when her parents come to visit her unexpectedly in the grass, and from this particular moment, a huge gap between herself and her parents emerges, as she now fully grasps how different she is from them. Leaving home at very young age, she rejects the fifties ideal for good girls: First, she attends a women's college in Virginia where she studies drama, then she moves into the Village, working at the *Record Changer*, a jazz magazine, and the *Partisan Review*.

For Jones, the process of life writing provides the opportunity for self-knowledge. Her own emergence as a poet is a crucial element of this process. In contrast to Joyce Johnson, whose authorial voice knows that her memoir does not have to call attention to the author's success as a writer, Jones uses her memoir to discuss the question of whether she is a writer or not. Additionally, she tries to find out whether she is a novelist or a poet, or nothing at all. Regretfully, she claims to have failed to participate in the bohemian Beat call to dedicate life to art only. In contrast to other female writers of the time, she considers herself ungifted, and even in the enriching environment of the *Partisan Review*, her own poetry does not prosper. She transfers her enthusiasm – and distribution contacts – to the publication of *Yugen*, begun in 1958: "Few magazines out of New York, to that date, had promised the new consciousness that everyone downtown agreed was just what the world needed. I know mine was raised by the very act of press-typing each quarter-inch character of *the new consciousness in arts and letters*" (53-54). Press types, T-squares, "a rickety IBM with erratic adjustable spacing," and cash accounts become symbols of the "new consciousness," "put together [...] on my old kitchen table". While her literary labor was displaced from expression, it indeed led to a new knowledge of the world: "If I hadn't yet managed to speak for myself, here at least were these others". Her hard work of editing and publishing resulted in the long yearned "*recognition*, to which [her] whole being responded" (55). Jones' writing career started relatively late. She had never liked keeping a journal and therefore gave it up, because she thought she could never write prose. However, writing letters was different. Similar to Neal Cassady and Jack Kerouac, Jones wrote piles of letters to her friend Helene Dorn, narrating long, detailed, and continuous accounts to her. This is how she gradually realized that – beside poetry – she was also able to write good prose texts:

> Long past midnight, having been absorbed for hours with trying to *tell*, I'd been conscious suddenly, and almost surprised to see the dark shapes of the poverty trees at the windows. Something in language went, now, where nothing else could go. So I owe it to Dear Helene, my fellow tailor (and eventual sculptor), that I ever left Singer and took up the pen. *(How I Became Hettie Jones:* 130-131)

How I Became Hettie Jones clearly proves that Jones is both a gifted novelist and poet, being in favor of Charles Olson's "Projective Verse". It seems that her own career could only be started after her divorce from LeRoi. The three early poems she includes into her memoir imply an unassertive self-reflexivity in connection with the creation of her literary text. The reason why she fits in the poems is her claim to be a poet. At the time she was writing the memoir, she had only published one small book of poems. Following that, she was not very ambitious about sending out her poems to publishers, as she rejected the existing poetry scene in the U.S.:

> For one thing, I wasn't a Language poet. I was much too logical and much too old-fashioned and much too linear – What are my other faults? But the poems expressed my state of mind, and then I thought the poems that I included by other people expressed the state of mind that was current in the culture at that time, or the culture I was trying to show. So I put them in at some risk, but it worked. (Grace. *Breaking the Rule of Cool:* 162)

Jones' intersected poems are powerful reminders for both herself and critics that she was already spending much time in the late 1950s and 1960s trying to be a writer, even though she found herself untalented. Her first work embedded in her memoir is a short, imagistic poem from the late 1950s composed after she had met Roi.

```
       night            sky
             sleep            lover
                      one,   two,    three
             lights-
    in the city
```
(How I Became Hettie Jones: 50)

The poem might remind the reader of William Carlos Williams' poetry, whom Jones admires a lot. Both this poem and the fairy tale prose text, in which she links herself as a writer to Charles Olson, mirror her continuous attraction towards male canonized literary figures. Instead of being inspired by women poets of the time, she turns to men during her period of artistic validation, which was full of self-doubt. In an interview decades later, Jones explains why she was not interested in women's poetry in the 1950s and early 1960s. At the time, she mainly read the Black Mountain poets Olson and Creeley or the male Beat authors who were published in *Yugen*, but she only seldom read Adrienne Rich or Sylvia Plath. She found H.D., for example, as too focused on the classics and too formal. She sometimes read Amy Lowell, but the poetic influence came from men only. She writes, "I read her [Lowell] in college, but the models for the form of the poems I eventually wrote were the guys all around me – LeRoi Jones in particular. But what to say? That was the big question. You know, writing a woman's life, you know" (Grace: 2004: 163). Jones' untitled "night sky" poem is quite different from the two remaining poems which follow. Through the façade of life writing, Jones displays the development of her own poetics. One poem, written while she lived at Cooper Square, captures life as a 1950s housewife:

My dearest darling
will you take out
the garbage, the fish heads
the cats
wouldn't eat

the children are sleeping
I cannot hear them breathing

Will you be my friend
and protector from all evil

the dead fish
take them away

please

(How I Became Hettie Jones: 209)

In this poem, it becomes obvious that the lyrical I needs a husband who takes care of her, who is like a fairy tale prince who comes to save her from all distress. The poem's narrator uses every day life as a major theme: Like many surrealists and dadaists, she elevates the mundane of the domestic, mostly female sphere into art. The act of taking out the dustbins, together with the yearning for a fairy tale prince to protect her, are central. Calling on somebody to assist her so becomes a plea for a tranquil and harmonious life. Due to the fact that she finds herself untalented, she never showed this poem or any others to her husband, as "most weren't good enough" (209). Of the poem, Jones says the following in retrospect: "The poem that's in my book that I wrote a thousand years ago – 'my dearest darling will you take out the garbage?' – when I wrote that, I never dreamed of publishing it. I just thought no one would want to publish this. I just assumed no one would want to. That didn't keep me from writing" (Grace: 2004: 163). In the style of Charles Olson, the lyrical I in "my dearest darling" follows the natural breath of the poet. It is Olson's idea of projective verse that can be found in each of her poems. There does not necessarily have to be something she fits the poem into, "everything must be made to fit into the poem; that is, the poem itself" (163). In "How you Sound," an article published in Donald Allen's *The New American Poetry*, LeRoi Jones had written down the original words: "I must be completely free to do just what I want, in the poem. 'All is permitted.' [...] There cannot be anything I must fit the poem into. Everything must be made to fit the poem" (1960: 425).

A year before, Jones had had enough of domestic constraints and the self-neglect of her own professional career. A poem written earlier during the Fourteenth Street years with Roi is critical of the myth of domestic bliss:

> I've been alive since thirty-four
> and I've sung every song
> since before the War
>
> Will the press of this music
> warp my soul
> till I'm wrinkled and gnarled
> and old and small-
>
> A crone in the marshes
> singing and singing
>
> A crone in the marshes singing
> and singing
>
> and singing
> and singing
> and singing
> and singing
> and singing

(How I Became Hettie Jones: 150)

The poem written in iambic meter shows Jones' coming-of-age as a feminist, but her feminist stance is unfulfilled at the time. A young woman, born in 1934, who has gone through many ups and downs in her life, will finally turn into an old shrunken and wrinkled lady – a "crone". Her transformation, represented as music, is connected to the World War II image of perfect motherhood: While the sons and fathers are out on the battlefields, the mother bravely takes over male responsibilities. When the men come back, however, the mother/wife devotedly returns to the domestic sphere, and is gradually pushed outside of society (cf. Grace 2002: 159). Through Jones' connection with Beat outlaws, she similarly exiled herself from her middle-class Jewish family. Yet, Jones does not give up: She predicts that her singing does not stop, meaning that her writing is eternal. She clearly envisions her older and much wiser self who lives independently and embraces the new identity as a poet.

The unpublished poems she wrote in the 1960s and 1970s incorporate themes of racism, identity, motherhood, and love. In *Women of the Beat Generation*, Brenda Knight published several others of Jones' early poems. The brief, but impressive poem "Words," for example, speaks of love and loss:

> Words
>   Are keys
> or stanchions
>   or stones
>
> I give you my word
> You pocket it
> and keep the change
>
> Here is a word on
> the tip of my tongue: love
>
> I hold it close
> though it dreams of leaving
>
>   (Knight. *Women of the Beat Generation:* 195)

The poem explores the power of words as "keys/ or stanchions/ or stones," and the thought of speaking of love reveals her vulnerability. In "Sonnet," her view of love is in part disillusionment, commenting on the power of emotion, rather than the over-romanticized beauty. "Love never held my hand/ like those summertime couples/ palm to palm, the perfectly/ interlaced fingers/ the pressures," she writes in the first stanza. "Love was a grandmaster though,/ and he laughed when he came on/ like gangbusters, who/ could refuse him, ah," she goes on in stanza three. "I knuckled under, no regrets/ but I've always wondered" (193): There is no anger in the poem, as might be assumed after her divorce in the spring of 1968, but rather confusion and contemplation, reflecting the imbalance of the relationships so characteristic of the movement. Jones further explores the power and beauty of women in "Untitled (Teddy Bears on the Highway)," in which she presents the dilemma, "itself the solution," to young women: "I have always been at the same time/ woman enough to be moved to tears/ and man enough/ to drive my car in any direction" (192). Same as in the previous poems, these lines reveal a common theme in women's writing of the 1960s, that of the young woman breaking away from her role and taking her own path. Although the presence of a man as a love object is constant throughout many of her poems, Jones' writing also reflects the forced independence of many Beat women.

Eventually, at the end of her memoir, Jones' is able to make conclusions about her self-identity as a woman/writer and her place in the Beat movement. This is because she carefully places the pieces of the memoir in a structure bringing new alternatives to her life. For this process, two aspects are of major importance: First, the fragments of memory, and second, the power of naming things. Is she LeRoi Jones' white wife, the former Hettie Cohen, as she is described in literary histories? Is she H.

Cohen-Jones, the professional name Roi gave her for the *Yugen* masthead? Is she Mrs. Hettie Jones, the name given to her by *The Chicago Manual of Style*? Is she E. L. Jones, the name given her by the telephone company after her divorce? Eventually, she realizes that only one word stands for continuity: Hettie, the only signifier that is elegantly centering all other names. In this respect, Jones' creation through that of others serves as both a confession and praise. She traces her past, fills in gaps that open up, gives form to blank spots, dares to ask why she did not write more when she was young, and why she – and so many other female Beat writers – remained silent for so long. Finding answers to her questions is a complex process. The woman who has now "come-of-age" has always been 'Hettie,' who stands as a symbol for the great process of becoming.

Finally, decades after her first poetic attempts, Jones becomes what she always wanted to be: An approved writer who publishes prose texts, children's books, literary criticism – and poetry. In the late 1970s, Jones began to share her work with other writers for the first time. Aged 44, she gave her first public reading in 1978 at New York City's PS 122. Another dimension of becoming Hettie Jones was the publication of *Drive* (1998), a collection including her earlier chapbooks and more recent texts. Her second collection of poems, *All Told*, followed in 2003, and received the Norma Farber First Book Award from the Poetry Society of America.

In *Drive*, her poetics of transformation is clearly visible. Beside her personal transformation, social matters are another major theme, as she pinpoints social injustice to a broader audience. Everyday details – cars, lovers, relatives, kids, the materiality of things – but also the juxtaposition of similarity and difference play a crucial role. In all poems compiled in the book, her identification and solidarity with women in other patriarchal contexts is made clear. She distances herself from the overarching "importance" of poetry, which makes her writing provoking. Having arrived on the poetry scene relatively late, her poetry complements absence and loss. Due to gaps and interruptions over four decades, the amount of her poetic output is relatively small. Discontinuity, however, is an acknowledged aspect of Jones' work. Yet, she is not simply a tragic witness to the position of women in history. Her poems are examples of retrospective clarity, even as reconsidering her twenties might be agonizing:

> Over and over the mind returns
> to the bent shoulders of the young woman
> who types, over and over, the poem
>
> until it is perfectly placed
> on the page, the name
>
> of her husband, the name
> of her lover
> the guilty thrill
> of juxtaposition.
> *(Drive:* 73)

In this poem, Jones returns to the subordinate role she played in the male-dominated culture of poetry. She is typesetting Frank O'Hara's "Personal Poem" for *Yugen*, which names both "LeRoi" and "Mike Kanemitsu," with whom she was sexually involved. The poem might be a revenge for all the infidelities of her husband, but content is not the formal interest of the poem. The poem rather aims at showing the transformation that has happened in herself as a wife and lover. This transformation is visible throughout the poems collected in *Drive*. By creating a longitudinal section through her own life, she continuously compares the young Hettie with the older one. Jones' transformation is, for example, also shown in the various cars she has owned over the years, which she describes in "The Woman in the Green Car" (1998: 12).

Finally, Hettie Jones gets the literary acknowledgement she has always been yearning for. In contrast to LeRoi Jones, who has always been a renowned dramatist, poet, and prose writer, she was struggling hard to step out of his shadow. In his rejection of interracial bohemia and in his representation of real time black politics from Harlem to Newark, LeRoi Jones has achieved historical agency by being a secured author in the literary canon. Similarly, recognition has also arrived for Hettie Jones, but in other terms. First, there is the recognition she confers on herself in *How I Became Hettie Jones*. Yet, the reception of the work leaves questions about how her memoir can be categorized: is it an exemplary autobiography, or, as quoted in a *New York Times* review on the back of the paperback edition, "a valuable social document"? Does this imply that the book is rather a document than a literary work in its own right? As a social document of the 1950s up to the mid-sixties, the memoir has taken its place to contribute to women's writing, as well as to make visible the women on the Beat scene.

In the chapters before, Jones' artistic development as a poet and prose writer has been depicted in detail. Even though women writers are often completely excluded from the general canon of American literature, Jones' memoir claims her place in literary history and the New American canon. What has so far been left out of this analysis, however, is the meaning of 'home' for female Beats, which presents a central theme in much of their life writing. Paradoxically, domesticity – often rejected and despised – also became an economic reality for Hettie Jones. In order to understand the meaning of 'home' in bohemianism in general and specifically for female Beat writers, the following chapter exemplarily analyzes the importance of Beat meeting places for the development of the literary Beat scene.

7.2.4 Past Places in *How I Became Hettie Jones*

Not only for Hettie Jones, but also for many other female writers of the time, the concept of 'home' has always played a crucial role. Particular places, night spots, artists' cafés, galleries, 'pads,' and Beat communes are often depicted in great detail. One of Jones' central parts of her story is the focus on places which exist as temporal realities. Jones writes, for example, about 402 West Twentieth Street:

"Twentieth Street was a young time, a wild, wide open, hot time, full of love and rage and heart and soul and jism" (71). After poetry readings, they often bring home artists and writers like Kerouac and Ginsberg to their once elegant six-room parlor facing the Episcopal Seminary.[58] The marking off of spaces – in this case of certain streets, apartments, and bars – triggers memory and facilitates the creation of the self. Places play such a crucial role that they are even name-giving for the titles of the various chapters in *How I Became Hettie Jones:* Morton Street, Twentieth Street, Fourteenth Street, and Cooper Square – the place where she is still living today.

Seven Morton Street, #20, was Jones' first "room of her own". On New Year's Eve 1957, she moved in with a mattress, a gooseneck lamp, a phonograph, and pots she never used. Some days later, her parents gave her the kitchen table they were throwing away. Most often when she was at home, she sat in front of the fireplace, burning vegetable crates from the Bleecker Street markets, eating Wheat Chex, and worrying about her future. What was to become of her?

> I had just read William Carlos Williams, concluding that my own poems were not only bad but worthless. I missed the small, easy challenge of CMC's "promotional literature". Because what – or who – was the subject of Morton Street? My single-minded coming of age lacked conflict, I thought. If, as Aristotle claimed, the plot was the soul of the action, what was mine? What could be said of me? That I'd managed to get where I was? And where was that? Dick suggested I keep a journal. I wrote small impressions, likes and dislikes, about wanting to live unencumbered by things. I made a list of the men I'd slept with, to see if I could shock myself (I couldn't). *(How I Became Hettie Jones:* 24-25)

Her next pad was just off Ninth Avenue, where a lot of New York's art scene was taking place, and they had "nothing but party space to offer" (70). In Twentieth Street, Cohen – then pregnant – moved in together with LeRoi for the first time. Over the sink in their kitchen was an oversize window of sooty smoked glass, so that "the brightest day came through dulled" (72). Onto the window frame, LeRoi tacked a poem by Ron Loewinsohn their publishing company Totem Press had first released. It begins,

> The thing made real by
> a sudden twist of mind:
> [...]
> thunders into
> the consciousness

---

[58] Recounting the episode she first met Jack Kerouac, she writes about a party in their apartment after Kerouac's reading in the newly opened Seven Arts Coffee Gallery, "a second-floor storefront on Ninth Avenue in the forties, the transient neighborhood near the bus terminal" (69-70). Only about thirty people, mostly friends, were attendant. Unexpectedly, Kerouac was sober at first, and Jones decided for herself that she "liked this good-looking, friendly man whom everyone loved and admired". Not knowing to whom this pregnant woman was attached to at the party, Kerouac asked Ginsberg and got an answer: "The music was on and a few people were already dancing. Suddenly he [Kerouac] ducked and wove his way through them – fast, as if in a scrimmage – to Roi, who was at the other end of the two adjoining front rooms. Then dragging bewildered Roi by the hand he maneuvered back to me and grabbed me too, and then, with amazing strength, he picked us both up at once – all 235 pounds of us, one in each arm like two embarrassed children – and held us there with an iron grip and wouldn't let go!" (70-71).

> in all its pure & beautiful
> absurdity,
> like a White Rhinoceros.
>
> *(How I Became Hettie Jones:* 72)

"The poems *were* our lives," Jones makes clear. In October 1960, the Joneses moved into Fourteenth Street: "Manhattan has many real and imagined boundaries, but Fourteenth Street in 1960 seemed one of the clearest: a straight road the width of the island, east to west between uptown and down" (119). Many twentieth century artists had lived in the street. Hettie, LeRoi, and their child Kellie rented a parlor floor above a vacant store with dusty, discarded shoeboxes in the windows. Jones writes, "I called Fourteenth Street the Court: hard to live in but great for games". Life was not easy for them, because the pad was mostly unheated and ice cold. Leading a life in poverty, it was hard to manage the fifty dollars for the rent. For some time, until they got a water heater, Hettie sat in the deep side of the double kitchen sink to bathe, with her feet in the shallow side and water poured from pails on the stove.

27 Cooper Square is the last 'home' being described. According to Jones, Cooper Square is not a square, but a long triangle with its base the old brown Cooper Union building. When she first entered number 27, it had been vacant for years. Steep narrow stairs led up to the next two floors. In some of the rooms there were sections of the narrow pipe once used for gaslight, but none for cooking and heat. "In fact," Jones says about the dreary place, "it felt colder inside than out" (164). Nevertheless, Jones was immediately enthusiastic about living in a skylighted garret.

> From Fourteenth Street we'd have to salvage gas heaters, toilet, stove – even the kitchen sink.
> Which like me remains on Cooper Square but linked to an earlier time and place. So that tonight, at the dishes, though twice her age I can also see that person I was at twenty-seven, bathing in her kitchen sink, with all of downtown at her back, and the morning sun ablaze in the poverty trees. *(How I Became Hettie Jones:* 164)

Community gathering spots, including famous Beat bars like the Cedar and the Five Spot, which was also only a stone's throw away from Cooper Square, receive almost equal attention. All those places stick to her memory as reminders of happy days in the past. They play the role as symbols of memory: Places where famous and infamous beatniks gathered; where the literary and visual art scenes had their parties; where she and Roi lived happily together, raising their children; where she spent endless days typing their literary magazine *Yugen* that promoted many young Beat authors.

Before writing her memoir, Jones was hesitant to use home as the structural focus of her memoir: "I thought, oh god, people are going to think this is corny! You know, women always talk about their homes". However, she finally decided to use the 'home'-concept for several reasons: "I wanted this to be a woman's book. I thought men would not focus on their homes. But here I mean 'home' not just in terms of where we lived, but 'home' as the art scene. So it seemed like the likely place to locate not only my life but the literary life. And also because of the business of race, where things come together in terms of race. So it seemed very logical" (Grace: 1999: 124).

Throughout the memoir, Jones depicts the places she calls home in vivid detail. She describes floor plans, the shape of rooms, furniture, the color of walls, or the nearness of her "own" space in connection to that of others. She carefully links one space that opens into another by the presence of her husband and children. Kitchen, sink, toilets, heaters, mattresses, desks, or chairs are carried from one place to the other when the family moved. Having no money, Jones is even happy about an old pair of sneakers she finds abandoned by the previous tenants of 27 Cooper Square. They fit perfectly and assume new life. Being well aware that domesticity is often a cliché in women's autobiographies, she, nevertheless, found it a useful tool to depict the Village's 1960s art scene that represented 'home' to her. Jones sees the domestic sphere in ironic terms and inverts the Beat belief in home as something from which to escape. 'Home' stands for the powerful rebuilding of her Beat past. By remembering past places, her memories are being nurtured.

Similar to the Joneses' inviting apartments, many Beat women's pads also functioned like communes, as many muses, wives, and lovers of male Beat writers tried to provide a "perfect home" for their men. The meeting/sleeping places of Kerouac, Ginsberg, Burroughs, or Cassady were therefore often located in women's apartments.

Throughout history, women's salons in which intellectual discussion takes place have played a crucial role in literary bohemia. Historic examples of salon women in Paris were Madame de Rambouillet (1599-1665), Madame Geoffrin (1699-1777), or Madame de Staël (1766-1817). Together with Alice B. Toklas, Gertrude Stein[59] hosted avant-garde artists and writers from all over Europe and the U.S. Another important salon woman was Natalie Clifford Barney[60] (1876-1972), an American expatriate who is best known as the hostess of a weekly literary salon in Paris with famous guests like Ezra Pound, T.S. Eliot, William Carlos Williams, Rainer Maria Rilke, Djuna Barnes, F. Scott Fitzgerald, or James Joyce. For the Beat Generation, salons were replaced by "pads" located in the center of Manhattan. They often served as "communes"[61] or bohemian meeting places. Particularly noteworthy are the spacious pads of Joan Vollmer, Hettie and LeRoi Jones, and Diane di Prima. These places were immensely important for the flourishing of Beat literature, as literary critics were always around. Poems and prose were read out aloud to the others, writers and new publications were being discussed in great detail, and the wittiest reviewers were always directly and personally available. Within an instant, serious feedback on your writings could be received.

---

[59] In the 1920s, Stein's salon at 27 Rue de Fleurus in Paris, with walls covered by avant-garde paintings of contemporary artists, attracted many of the great artists and writers, including Ernest Hemingway, Thornton Wilder, Sherwood Anderson, Pablo Picasso, Henri Matisse, or Georges Braque. Her salon was a favourite meeting place for expatriate U.S. writers.

[60] For more information on Barney's salon at 20 Rue Jacob in Paris' Latin Quarter, which was held from 1909 until her death, see Orenstein, Gloria Feman (1979). "The Salon of Natalie Clifford Barney: An Interview with Berthe Cleyrergue". *SIGNS* 4.3: 484-496.

[61] According to *Meyers Grosses Taschenlexikon*, a commune is a "Lebens- und Wohngemeinschaft, die bürgerliche Eigentums-, Leistungs- und Moralvorstellungen ablehnt" (1999: 178).

One early beatnik commune was Joan Vollmer and Edie Parker's apartment half-block away from the Columbia campus. This apartment was the first in a series of pads that would provide an open forum for the exchange of new ideas and attitudes.

> In 1944 and '45, her [Vollmer's] apartment on 115th Street was an early prototype of what a later generation called pad – a psychic way station between the Village and Times Square, or between Morningside Heights and Lower Depths, in the mental geography of those who came together there, lived there sporadically, made love, wrote, suffered, experimented with drugs, in those six big rooms where Joan had lived alone with a newborn baby until Edie introduced her to Jack. *(Minor Characters:* 3)

From 1945 to 1948, the apartment soon became an uptown outpost for an elite group of Beat writers, prostitutes, drug addicts, and petty criminals. Most of them had grown up in upper-middle to upper-class environments, with parents being wealthy bankers, judges, or entrepreneurs. Vollmer herself had revolted against the boredom of her upper-class bourgeois upbringing, escaping into marriage to a law student who was drafted when the Second World War broke out. In the meantime, she got pregnant by a Columbia student, but decided to carry the baby to term. Although predominately homosexual, Burroughs was fascinated with Vollmer's intellect and wit. Burroughs' brilliant mind, his proclamations about literature and society, and his sinister air attracted Vollmer, and he soon moved into her rambling apartment. With him, he brought a group of hustlers and drug dealers who introduced the group to various kinds of drugs, and it was then that Burroughs started his lifelong addiction to heroin. Kerouac and Ginsberg had already lived in the apartment at the time and found the open exchange of ideas inspiring. Burroughs regarded Vollmer as the smartest member of the group and the only one capable of inspiring him to take up new pursuits. As Ginsberg recalled: "It was warm, very friendly, very family" (Schumacher: 1992: 52). The roommates shared their money for home-cooked communal meals; they slept together, both chastely and having sex; they conducted "Dostoyevskian confrontations" and engaged in psychoanalysis. The old-fashioned, rambling, high-ceilinged, five-bedroom apartment that Vollmer had rented for $115 a month became the center and unofficial hangout for the Beat writers. For a short time, Kerouac was married to Edie Parker, who also lived in the apartment. Parker supported the beatniks who lived in their commune by working as a cigarette girl in nightclubs, but soon escaped to a more stable life with her grandmother. Kerouac, however, remained a fixture in Vollmer's apartment. The beatniks living in Vollmer's apartment became increasingly involved with benzedrine, being introduced by Vicki Russell, a Times Square prostitute coming from a rich Detroit family: The cheapest way to get high was to "buy over-the-counter Smith, Kline, and French inhalers, meant to last six months, crack the inhaler, remove the three-quarter-inch Benzedrine-soaked accordion strip of paper, and drop it in a cup of coffee or simply swallow it whole" (Watson: 1998: 61-62). Vollmer herself, however, took more benzedrine than any of her roommates, developing sores all over her body, and having grave mental problems. With a whisk broom, she compulsively swept the apartment for hours and hours, while she heard strange voices. Even though all the others had moved out or were in jail, Vollmer stayed in the apartment. Kerouac visited her one day and found her "out of her fuckin' mind on Benzedrine[62]." She stripped and asked, "Who are you, strange man?" (Morgan: 1988: 132). Nevertheless, Burroughs and Vollmer married a year after that episode and moved to New Waverly, Texas, where they lived on a marijuana farm in order to escape legal problems in New York City. Their future plans to make money by growing marijuana was not successful, as they mostly entertained guests, including their old friend Herbert Huncke, "who came to 'sharecrop', do drugs, and play with guns" (Knight: 2000: 51).

Actually not a commune, but another important meeting place for bohemian artists and writers was Hettie and LeRoi Jones' apartment at 402 West Twentieth Street. Both their founding of the magazine *Yugen* and the establishment of an informal salon in their large apartment were crucial factors to build up a homogeneous Beat identity. In 1958, LeRoi Jones initiated the idea to found a magazine which would publish the work of young writers. Inspired by "Howl," he wrote a letter to Allen Ginsberg on toilet paper, asking him if he would contribute some of his works for the new magazine. Ginsberg enriched the magazine by drawing from his broad network of friends: Soon, the Joneses' close circle of friends included Frank O'Hara, Jack Kerouac, Diane di Prima, Gregory Corso, Gary Snider, Philip Whalen, or Joel Oppenheimer. In March 1958, the first issue appeared. Both the magazine and the Joneses' apartment gradually became a meeting point for the Beats' New York group. In eight issues, which appeared irregularly until December 1962, *Yugen* published not only Beats, but the San Francisco poets, the New York poets, and the Black Mountain poets. The Joneses' party guests included the regulars of the Cedar Bar, painters, jazz musicians, and writers. Ginsberg described the atmosphere as "an acme of good feeling. A lot of mixing, black white hip classic" (Miles: 1989: 252).

The apartments of Diane di Prima were also important Beat meeting places. Di Prima's New York City pads were frequented by a large number of Beat artists, including painters, writers, or photographers. She remembers the first pad of her own:

> My pad gradually filled up, as pads generally do. A collection of oddments – souls with no home and no particular merits – about whom the most I could say was that they were not boring, slept on the floor, or in the big double bed with me. The bed would hold up to four of us comfortably, and out of this fact grew nuances of relationship most delicate in their shading. *(Memoirs:* 87)

---

[62] Benzedrine became Kerouac's drug of choice. He was frantically searching for a new "method" of writing, and benzedrine helped him to write continuously, day and night. *On the Road* was initially typed on one single roll of paper in one 250-foot single paragraph as to be composed in an unavoidably linear fashion. There is no argument about the fact that Kerouac wanted his prose to sound like jazz. Composing without editing, replacing standard punctuation with dashes, and frantic speed typing are features of Kerouac's "Essential Spontaneous Prose". Not paying attention to spelling, punctuation, or syntax, Kerouac mainly concentrated on the flow of words and phrases that came into his mind spontaneously (cf. Miles 1998: 120ff.). His benzedrine experiences in Vollmer's pad climaxed in December 1945, with a five-day-and-night trip through New York with Ginsberg and Chase. Kerouac collapsed and was taken to Queens VA Hospital, where thrombophlebitis was diagnosed, ending his stay at Vollmer's commune. Kerouac would go on taking Benzedrine occasionally, but soon turned into an alcohol addict (cf. Watson 1998: 63ff.).

In *Memoirs*, di Prima describes some of her roommates in more detail. There is red-haired Lauren, a young man in his mid-twenties, who "delighted in collecting the youngest available specimen of the human race and experimenting on them – physically and psychologically" (87). Jack, a fifteen-year-old teenager, also lives in the apartment. Diane soon starts a liaison with him, even though she goes on having affairs with other bohemians at the same time. Di Prima refers to his sexual abilities, that he "was a good fuck and liked to fuck a lot. […] It was as if he had been born for fucking" (88). Furthermore, there are "Runaway Julie," who has run away from her middle-class Queens neighborhood, and "Henry with the Big Ears," a drop-out from the Electronics Research Lab at Columbia University. His only loves are cocaine and Indian philosophy. Henry "slept wherever he fell out – bed or floor was all one to him – he easily wrapped himself around any of us, and easily fell asleep to the rocking rhythms of our lovemaking" (89). When Henry takes cocaine, his "staying power" in love-making is enormous: He can "literally fuck for hours, past orgasm and the possibility of orgasm, to the point of madness" (90). Other bohemians being mentioned are Little John, who bursts into her apartment – sick and needing a place to stay.

While the last chapters emphasized Beat cultural history of the 1950s – pads, poverty, Village life, and bohemianism – the next chapters focus on the intimate "confessional 1990s," the exploding "memoir-craze," and on the complex author–reader relationship which is a precondition for a successful autobiographical act. Both memoirs, *Minor Characters* and *How I Became Hettie Jones*, can be understood as representational works of individualistic memory, but their aim is also to sustain cultural memory. Furthermore, both life writings will be analyzed according to various autobiographical subcategories.

7.3 Reader Identification with *Minor Characters* and *How I Became Hettie Jones*

> "[…] the bore is someone 'who tells you everything' – more than you need to know and certainly more than you want to know". (Pinsker. *The Landscape of the American Memoir:* 312)

Throughout the 1990s, media experts searched for the right way to characterize the decade. Politically speaking, the 1980s were Reagan, and the 1990s were Clinton. The Clinton era went down in history not only for national prosperity and the birth of the Internet culture, but also for a culture of personal exposure[63]. Clinton's testimony in court appears like a confession. Making the private public to this

---

[63] While working as a paid staffer at the Pentagon, the former White House intern Monica Lewinsky had a sexual relationship with the U.S. president Bill Clinton, which started in 1995. The affair's repercussions are often referred to as the "Lewinsky Scandal" or "Monicagate". It severely affected Clinton's presidency as he was lying under oath about adultery. Clinton's private life was consequently exposed to the American public in every detail: Official investigations of the case reported, for example, that the sexual encounters generally occurred in or near the private study of the Oval Office, most often in the windowless hallway outside the study. It seems absurd that 240 million Americans were informed about the fact that on February 28, 1997, President Bill

kind of degree was even startling in a climate of over-the-top self-revelation. Going back in literary history, the impulse of ask and tell was in no way unique. Yet, what distinguishes the confessional 1990s from other decades when it comes to going public?

The culture of self-revelation and confessional writing is not something new in our times, even though a tendency towards personal exposure has been exploding in literature since the 1990s. In the 1960s, the confessional poets – Theodore Roethke, John Berryman, Sylvia Plath, Robert Lowell, Anne Sexton, to name just a few – were becoming immensely popular. These poets were among the first writers who incorporated their personal experiences in their poetry, who ruptured topical taboos of the time (abortions, alcoholism, mental institutions, suicide attempts), and who did not disguise their personal experience as a source for their poems. This group of poets had the highest number of followers due to the fact that people could relate to what they were writing about. They completely broke with former theories that a "Poetry of Impersonality" should be a poet's major goal. According to T. S. Eliot and New Criticism, or Ezra Pound and the Imagists, poetry should be impersonal, objective, straight, and direct. Furthermore, no metaphors should be used. They wanted poetry to escape from personality and emotion. Agreeing to these views, the Black Mountain poets also appreciated no personal appraisal of a scene. Even though earlier poets and writers have treated personal subject matters before – one might think of Emily Dickinson or Walt Whitman – until then, no group of writers had ever been so direct, revealing, and confessional as the biographical/confessional poets of America's 1960s.

Beat authors Jack Kerouac, Allen Ginsberg, or William Burroughs have also exposed themselves to a sensation-seeking public who was waiting restlessly for new crazy and maniac adventures. Most male Beat authors, however, did not write fully autobiographically. Kerouac's *On the Road* (1957), for example, is only a semi-autobiographical narrative, where Kerouac himself hides behind Sal Paradise and Neal Cassady takes on another personality, namely that of Dean Moriarty. Allen Ginsberg, in contrast, is definitely more confessional than Kerouac. Ginsberg showed a way of exposing himself – "hysterically naked" – through literature. Joyce Johnson noticed that "Allen Ginsberg believed in nakedness as the best defense against the world. A self-exposure so pure and indiscriminate, so total, that no room would be left for interpretation. No legend but in the passing moment's reality" (1999: 78). His most famous poem "Howl" (1955) is different in a way that it centers around an "I" that is similar to Walt Whitman's unified "I". Even though Ginsberg's work is highly autobiographical in general, the idea of an over-soul, a unified persona which speaks from multiple perspectives and to everyone on earth takes over. The Beats wrote both semi-autobiographically and autobiographically in most of their works, and therefore, they were highly influential in smoothing the way for confessional writing, which gained importance in the 1960s and exploded in the 1990s with the publications of uncountable autobiographical works.

Clinton ejaculated on Monica Lewinsky, spilling his semen on her navy blue dress (cf. "A Chronology: Key Moments in the Clinton-Lewinsky Saga". *CNN online*. July 28, 2006. http://www.cnn.com/ALLPOLITICS/1998/resources/lewinsky/timeline/).

The author/reader relationship in memoirs and autobiographical works, in general, is very complex. The autobiographical subject – no matter whether female or not – always requires "a partner in crime". It always takes two to perform an autobiographical act, to make an autobiography: the writing subject and the reader who is gradually drawn towards the story.[64]

Yet, what if the relational mode that can obviously always be found within autobiographical texts is also the model of relation that organizes the experience of *reading* autobiography itself? In order to understand what follows, it seems necessary to reach back to theories devised by Paul de Man. Even Paul de Man, who does not believe in autobiography as a distinct genre, believes: "Autobiography, then, is not a genre but mode, but a figure of reading or of understanding that occurs to some degree, in all texts. The autobiographical moment happens as an alignment between the two subjects involved in the reading in which they determine each other by mutual reflexive substitution" (Miller: 2000: 434). De Man's theory is helpful to analyze the kinds of bonds and desires that connect readers to the memoir. What seems to be going on between memoir writers like Hettie Jones and Joyce Johnson and their readers? How is intimacy created? Why do some readers identify with *How I Became Hettie Jones* or *Minor Characters* more easily than other readers? Which factors create identification and which do not?

By many literary critics, the contemporary memoir is regarded as one of the most important narrative genres of our contemporary culture. The connection between authors of memoirs and their readers is a relational act which forms identifications across a broad spectrum of so-called personal experience. These conscious and unconscious identifications also include disidentifications and cross-identifications. Even though some degree of identification is typically present in reading prose narratives – fiction or nonfiction, memoir reading is not possible without the reader identifying with the author's life story. This heightened process of identification makes memoirs such as *Memoirs of a Geisha* by Arthur Golden, *Not Without my Daughter* by Bettie Mahmoody, *Angela's Ashes* by Frank McCourt, or *Desert Flower* by Waris Dirie popular.

How do you remember your life? How can one even tell it is his/her life and not that of your tribe/family/village in a larger context? In *The Woman Warrior*[65], her classic memoir about growing up Chinese American in postwar California, Maxine Hong Kingston puts the problem this way: "When you try to understand what things in you are Chinese, how do you separate what is peculiar to childhood, to poverty, insanities, one family, your mother who marked your growing with stories, from what is Chinese? What is Chinese tradition and what is the movies?" (1989: 5-6). Referring to this, how can someone separate a life story from that of any nice Jewish girl, like Joyce Johnson,

---

[64] For more information on the author/reader relationship in memoirs, identification, disidentification, cross-identification, and allo-identification, see Miller, Nancy K. (2000). "But Enough About me, What do you Think of my Memoir?" *The Yale Journal of Criticism* 13.2: 421-436. She also includes a discussion of Maxine Hong Kingston's *The Woman Warrior*.

[65] For a discussion of Maxine Hong Kingston's *The Woman Warrior* and the role of autobiographical identification, see Miller, Nancy K. (2000). "But Enough About me, What do you Think of my Memoir?" *The Yale Journal of Criticism* 13.2: 421-436.

growing up middle-class in New York City in the 1950s? Like Kingston's movies, other people's memories can sometimes overwhelm your own, if you are not careful to remember the differences. A female growing up in New York's 1950s might probably identify with *Minor Characters* more easily than somebody born in Austria in the late 1970s. When reading an autobiographical work, one cannot help but remember one's own past: your parents, your family, your love affairs, your circle of friends, your ambitions. This moving back and forth is an effect of what Susan Suleiman has called the "autobiographical imperative," a "strong reading experience that often results in autobiographical writing" (1994: 200). According to Suleiman, the increased identification with the autobiographical subject might motivate the reader to start writing one's own autobiographical work. Suleiman comes to this concept from her own experience of reading autobiographical works of writers whose war experiences of World War II reminded her of her own. "What exactly am I looking for, and finding, in these works? I did not lose a parent during the war – yet I recognize the stories all too well. They could have been my own" (207).

Memoir reading, like memoir writing, participates in an important form of collective memorialization. Since the connections between a reader's life and a writer's text are often more easily seen in the case of memoirs that emerge from the experience of a generation, *Minor Characters* provides a good example of reader identification for females having grown up and having experienced bohemian New York City in the 1950s. This is the reason why it is sometimes difficult for the reader to distinguish details from somebody's own life and details from the memoir – the so-called 'memory bizz'. Readers – most probable female readers – who experienced the 1950s themselves might be lured back into the past by reading *Minor Characters*. This makes the reader's experience more meaningful: One's own experience is therefore not "merely" personal, but part of a bigger picture of cultural memory. When reading a memoir that has already given a life a shape, like the shape of a generation – Manhattan, the 1950s, girls' colleges, Columbia University – the boundaries of the reader's past self may start to blur around the edges. One's own life and experiences as a reader could melt with the text and the author's recollections. This process leads to the creation of a collective cultural memory. The memoir of another person can therefore give back the reader's memory. The reader might start to remember long forgotten places, names, or situations. Seen from this perspective, memoir reading is interactive remembering, helping to construct memory itself.

When the reader tries to find out something about herself while reading a memoir, disidentification is as important as identification. For someone living in the Village in the 1950s, it might be more surprising to find *no* close connections to Jones/Johnson, even if the author and reader went to the same schools, frequented the same bars, or crossed the same streets. A female memoir reader having experienced different teenage days might lose connection with Hettie when Cohen becomes Jones and a mother. However, disidentification turns out to be as important in the self-reconstructive effect of memoir reading as identification.[66]

When reading the memoirs of women of the 1950s, someone being a teenager at that time might feel that the memoir has been written particularly for her, just as Maxine Hong Kingston specifically addresses the Chinese Americans like herself, whom she imagines reading *The Woman Warrior*. Kingston asks the readers sharing her ethnic legacy: "Chinese Americans, when you try to understand what things in you are Chinese […]," how can you distinguish what is you and what is the movies (1989: 5-6)? In fact, the audience for *The Woman Warrior* consists of readers all over the world, but not all share Kingston's Chinese American culture memory, her social history.[67] Yet, this difference does not prevent non-Chinese Americans from enjoying to read about Kingston's memories. Shared experience, it seems, is not the only way a writer can reach the reader. Therefore, the following question arises: What if there are no similarities between the reader's and the writer's life experiences, meaning that both identification and disidentification do not work? What about myself – a twenty-eight-year-old European female reading Beat memoirs in 2007? What do I have to do with a young U.S. teenage girl of the 1950s, who had an affair with Kerouac, who married LeRoi Jones, who spent her life with Neal Cassady? How can an intimate connection between the author and reader of memoirs be established? In other words, can this private contact only be created in relation to memoirs written by contemporary authors living in the same area – in a broader context, meaning, for example, the western capitalist world – having the same age, ethnicity, and gender?

Beside identification and disidentification, the term 'allo-identification' is frequently used to describe the reader's wish to "read yourself across the body or under the skin of *other* selves" (Miller: 2000: 430). By wishing to take part in the writer's life, the reader might indulge in a time travel to experience past scenes from various parts of the world. Similar to the biography boom in earlier decades, nowadays' 'memoir craze' satisfies the yearning for a different, more exciting life through literature, even if the memoirs depict a painful life story characterized by suffering, pain, or physical and mental illness. By revealing intimate personal details, memoirists offer the reader a narrative through which to make sense of one's own past. Reading memoirs is like gazing into somebody else's life: The reader gets intimate confessions and often embarrassing accounts of somebody else's life. Humans are curious by nature, and it is always fun to peep behind somebody's most intimate secrets.

---

[66] Lennard Davis' *My Sense of Silence: Memoirs of a Childhood with Deafness* is a good example to point out the role of reader disidentification. In *The New York Times Book Review*, Margaret Diehl writes, "There are many moments like this – details of a life that effortlessly bring to mind emotionally equivalent details from our own lives. I especially loved his description of his mother's voice. 'It had the quality that a coin has as it spins on a glass table top. It almost squealed, yet beneath was a silver hum.' My mother isn't deaf, but her voice to me as a child was equally distinctive" (Diehl: 2000: 42). Even though the reviewer is not deaf – which indicates disidentification with the author while reading the memoir in the first place – she agrees/identifies with the author's description of a child perceiving a mother.

[67] *The Woman Warrior* was published in 1976 at the height of second wave feminism. The work seems to address that particular emancipated readership, many of whom grew up in the 1950s. In a 1989 interview with Bill Moyers in a show called *World of Ideas*, Kingston pointed out that including the legend of Fa Mu Lan was influenced by the ethos of seventies feminism. Kingston concluded that she would tell a different story in a post-Vietnam and post-feminist perspective (cf. Miller 2000: 435).

Now that the memoirist is openly personal or even confessional, it is easy for the reader to satisfy curiosity. Did Carolyn Cassady really cheat on Neal? How deep was Carolyn and Kerouac's love? Did she feel guilty when she betrayed Neal? Was Joyce Johnson feeling hurt when Kerouac left her? How did they get to know each other? Was it love at first sight? What was living with Kerouac in one crammed apartment like? Did he get home drunk in the middle of the night? Which drugs did he take? Was he a good lover? Did he write at home, in Joyce's apartment? Did he sleep late? How did Hettie Jones feel when LeRoi turned more and more racist? Did he reject his two little baby girls, too? Which incidents led to the rejection of his family? How did Hettie feel when she heard that Diane di Prima was pregnant with LeRoi's baby? Did Hettie suffer a lot when their relationship broke down? Did she manage well to live on her own, or was she desperate for years? What was LeRoi, the person, not the artist, like? Was he a loving father and husband? Was their Beat apartment in the Village messy and cramped? Did they take drugs? Which artist friends came along? Is Diane di Prima really that easy-going and laid-back as she presents herself? Did she have many lovers? Which kinds of sex did she like most?

The reason for the current memoir boom is that autobiography and its subgenres are the only literary forms which seem to give access to the truth. The memoir is a democratic form, letting minority experiences speak which stand apart from 19th century elitist writing; it is a wish to enforce subjectivity after decades of presenting fragmented identities proclaiming the death of the author. Furthermore, it is voyeurism for a declining narcissism.

The memoir boom we are witnessing nowadays should not only be understood as a spreading of self-serving representations of individualistic memory, but its purpose is also to sustain cultural memory. We are experiencing an enormous excitement about memory, about remembering, which was particularly enforced during the nineties and after this fin de millénaire. This concern might also be due to the fact that, especially at present, the testimony of the last living survivors of the Holocaust is being collected[68]. In *Testimony*, Dori Laub puts forward that the "culture of narcissism" could be a "historical diversion, a trivialization [...] a psychological denial of the depth and the subversive power of the Holocaust experience" (1992: 74). Memoir is the record of an experience in search of a community, a broader context, a collective framework in which the individual is protected in a postmodern world. Paradoxically, memoir is the most generous of modern genres. Indeed, the point of memoir is to keep alive the notion that experience can take the form of art and that remembering is a guide to living.

---

[68] Alison Landsberg states that "prosthetic memories" are useful to approximate the memorialization of the Holocaust. In "America, the Holocaust, and the Mass Culture of Memory: Toward a Radical Politics of Empathy" (1997), she asks whether it is possible to create a "bodily memory for those who have not lived through it". This is how she reads, for example, the visit to the Holocaust Museum in Washington, DC. Landsberg tries to foster "mass cultural technologies of memory" and "sites of production of 'feeling'" in order to bring about a greater understanding of the Holocaust (Miller 2000: 436). For more information on Alison Landsberg, see "Allison Landsberg". *Cultural Studies: University of Chicago*. February 12, 2007. http://culturalstudies.gmu.edu/faculty/faculty_bios/landsberg.html

7.4 Categorizing Johnson's and Jones' Memoirs

Minor Characters and *How I Became Hettie Jones* contain characteristics of various autobiographical subgenres. First, they are confessional memoirs according to feminist critic Rita Felski's understanding of confession. Second, one can categorize these two autobiographical works as major documents arising out of second wave feminism, as they discuss feminist issues, such as gender equality, combining work life and motherhood, and women's access to higher education. Third, their development in terms of growth, maturity, and education indicates that both memoirs are modern Bildungsromane or coming-of-age memoirs. The aim of this chapter is to analyze the roles of Jones and Johnson as confessional, feminist writers in the footsteps of Goethe, Dickens, and James Joyce.

What stands in the way of truth? Contemporary autobiographical theory has devised several theories about what it means to present a narrative of life experience. According to Rita Felski: "The goal of confession is to strip away the superficial layers of convention and to expose an authentic core of self, of meaning as fully present to itself. Yet the more frantically this true subjectivity is pursued, the more elusive it appears" (1998: 89). Felski names two goals of feminist confessional narratives: First, to expose and express the truth of oneself and one's experiences, and second, to let others partake to form a bond of intimacy. What fosters attempts to tell the truth, it seems, is the demand for authentic representations that can be shared with others.

Both Joyce Johnson and Hettie Jones appear in Jack Kerouac's or LeRoi Jones' works. Later on in life, when looking back, both had the feeling of being misrepresented. About his wife, LeRoi Jones wrote the following:

> Nellie [Hettie] had something of an inferiority complex. First, she'd been out in Long Island under the heavy sun of gentile suburbia, trying to grow and having to relate to whatever the dominant image and peer pressure was for the Jewish middle-class yearning for American middle-classdom. [...] The black middle-class suffers from the same kind of malady, a lack of self-esteem caused by the great nation chauvinism that is so much a part of American life. (Kristeva. *Revolution in Poetic Language:* 213)

Both Johnson and Jones want to recount their life story from a very personal female point of view. They do not want the reader to only rely on the male Kerouacian or Jonesian version of things, but they clearly state that there is also another perspective worth considering. According to this notion of truth telling, female narrators hope to demystify popular, but problematic discourses and practices by which women come to understand their experiences. They share their discoveries of authenticity with other women who might learn from them and use them to understand their own lives. Through identification, disidentification, and cross-identification, Jones and Johnson hope to be understood and validated by those who regard their stories, establishing a sense of intimacy.

However, how is intimacy in confessional works created? Is intimacy dependent upon truth, and should either be shaped in the way Felski describes? According to Felski, telling the truth is hindered by the functioning of language and the alienating move of reflection which reveals a lack of identity between what is written and the life itself, in short, between experience and its representation. This discrepancy moves the writer to create more texts in order to bridge this gap, leading to a confessional text which is revealed as "infinitely extendible, an endless chain of signifiers that can never encapsulate the fullness of meaning which the author seeks and which would put an end to writing itself". Felski is not alone in this type of analysis. As early as 1956, George Gusdorf argued that "autobiographical selves are constructed through the process of writing and therefore cannot reproduce exactly the selves lived". Terry Eagleton agrees: "Writing perpetually stands in for a reality it can never encompass"[69]. Complicating this sense of writing about one's experiences is the awareness that "the very process of recording intrudes upon that which is being recorded and changes it" (Felski: 1998: 90). The very self that one articulates is itself influenced by the process of articulation. This is also true for Hettie Jones, who invents her own self through articulating and recollecting her marriage with LeRoi Jones. Through her memoir, she invents herself once again. Her narrative self undergoes numerous transformations, which is also indicated by her frequent changing of names.

In offering narratives of their Beat experiences, a slippage between word and experience emerges. Indeed, the process of introspection, as well as the continual interrogation of one's own motives for providing an account of experience, reveals the "impossible ideal of absolute honesty" (91). The desire to bridge the gap between word and thing, the desire for unmediated access to experience, to expose and lay bare the truth, is to be understood as an unrealizable desire. Even though both Johnson and Jones aim at giving a realistic portrayal of their coming-of-age within the Beat circle, memory is distrustful, or as Jones quotes Kay Boyle, "there's no way even the honest among us can be trusted" (1997: 185). Johnson also admits that she had lapses in her memory. She did not consciously invent and sort of recreated, she claims, which is different to her. "There are things you do for the sake of the form," Johnson points out the problem of fabrication in memoir writing (Grace: 2004: 185f.).

Experiences themselves, however, cannot be taken at face value, because they are not 'simply there' to be written down. In her essay "Experience," Joan Scott provocatively asks, "What could be truer, after all, than a subject's own account of what he or she has lived through?" (1998: 59). Joan Scott further observes,

> It is not individuals who have experience, but subjects who are constituted through experience. Experience in this definition then becomes not the origin of our explanation, not the authoritative (because seen or felt) evidence that grounds what is known, but rather that which we seek to explain, that about which knowledge is produced. To think about experience in this way is to historicize it as well as to historicize the identities it produces. (Scott. "Experience": 60)

---

[69] All quotes, see Broin, Valerie E. (2001). "Standing in the Way of Truth: Understanding Narratives of Domestic Violence". *International Journal of Philosophical Practice*. August 29, 2006. http://web.csustan.edu/Philosophy/Data/Broin/Standing.html

It seems that what must accompany Johnson's and Jones' accounts of experience is to ask and explore how they became the texts that they are and how they construct their historicity. Johnson and Jones try to reconstruct and reflect a historical truth in their life writing, yet their recollections are not wholly trustworthy as their own subjective visions are often left aside by the reader. This argument should not indicate that the subjective visions of their male companions are more reliable, as their nature of experience, road adventures, or African American racial issues are also subjectively constructed. The stories Beat memoirists tell are the ones that emerge from negotiating a variety of constructions.

The second goal of confessional narratives that Rita Felski analyzes concerns sharing one's narrative with others to form a bond of intimacy. Both Johnson and Jones create an intimate atmosphere, whereas Jones is even more direct as she sometimes even addresses the reader by using the word "you". In an interview she was asked why she is speaking directly to people, why she is establishing a community with the reader. In her opinion, this is what everything written ought to be: "Why bother to write it down if you don't want to communicate it to others?". She goes on to say that her "impulse is a preachy one – and that requires an audience" (Grace: 2004: 169). Through intimately sharing their life stories, Felski writes, women want to demystify cultural prejudice about women's experiences by offering more authentic accounts. By using the memoir form, for example, female readers assign different meanings to their own lives, get validation and support for their experiences, and encourage personal identification with the author and gender identification among women in order to cause political movement.

Confessional memoirs seek to build up an ideal intimacy between author and reader, whereby the author can expose powerful feelings with the hope of reader validation, recognition, and identification. Felski warns that instead of intimacy, writing often encourages psychological projection and a fantasy of identification. The validation and support that is sought is also undercut: "The yearning for total intimacy, immediacy, and fullness of meaning serves only to underscore the reality of uncertainty and lack, so that attempted self-affirmation (Bekenntnis) can easily revert into anxious self-castigation (Beichte)" (Felski: 1998: 91). By speaking to women's experience *in general*, fictional elements in writing may appear more often, as the narrator seeks to tell her story in ways that are more universally applicable and understandable.

Another question which arises when categorizing Beat memoirs is whether *Minor Characters* and *How I Became Hettie Jones* are feminist memoirs and if yes, to which extent. Nearly all female Beats deny being categorized, being squeezed into a certain schema. Is it then not inappropriate to exactly label them, classify them, push them into certain categories? It seems paradox, but in order to bring female Beat writing to surface, to make female Beats visible in the canon of American literature, one cannot avoid classification.

In the previous argument, it is clearly proved that Johnson's and Jones' memoirs can be categorized as confessional. The following part of the chapter aims at demonstrating the fact that both memoirs are products of second wave feminism, which was influential for the process of daring to write down one's life story from a female perspective. It is also of major importance to analyze Jones and Johnson as protofeminists due to their early cutting the cord from home and following female independence. In order to understand the revolutionary changes of the time better, a brief outline of second wave feminism and Betty Friedan's ground-breaking work *The Feminine Mystique* seems necessary.

Betty Friedan is regarded as one of the founding mothers of feminism's second wave. *The Feminine Mystique*, published in 1963, is often called the most important source of the modern feminist movement in the USA. A postwar wife and mother herself, Friedan spoke directly to women who had lived according to the domestic containment ideology. The book was an instant bestseller and created a national sensation. It seemed to enable discontented women all over the country to find their voices, as hundreds of readers wrote to Friedan, telling their stories. *The Feminine Mystique* stresses the emotional emptiness felt by women trying to live through their husbands' and children's lives and exposes the sexist underpinnings of America's post-World War II conceited prosperity. Friedan argues that millions of American housewives[70] found the destiny of mother and housewife that male society intended for them stifling, repressive, and even dehumanizing. This phenomenon is even given a name: It is called the 'Housewife Syndrome,' which mainly affected middle-class women who had given up pursuit of higher education or a career in exchange for the role of wife and mother (cf. Castro 1990: 11).

Friedan argued that American women, especially suburban women, suffered from deep discontent. In the postwar era, she wrote, journalists, educators, advertisers, and social scientists had pulled women into the home with an ideological stranglehold, the 'feminine mystique'. Women's image of the time was that women could "find fulfillment only in sexual passivity, male domination, and nurturing maternal love" (1963: 37). It denied "women careers or any commitment outside home" and "narrowed woman's world down to the home, cut her role back to housewife" (47). In Friedan's formulation, the editors of women's magazines were the "Frankensteins" who had created this "feminine monster" (58-59). In defense of women, Friedan did not choose a typical liberal feminist language of rights, equality, or justice. Influenced by the new human potential psychology, she argued against full-time domesticity which denied women's "basic human need to grow" (299). Friedan points out that both women and men found personal identity and fulfillment through individual achievement, most notably through careers. Without such growth, she claimed, women would remain unfulfilled and unhappy, and children would suffer at the hands of neurotic mothers.

---

[70] The fact that Friedan's analysis only includes white, middle-class, heterosexual, educated women who found the traditional roles of wife and mother dissatisfying earned her a lot of negative critique. The African American feminist bell hooks, for example, credits Friedan with providing a helpful discussion of the impact of sexist discrimination on a select group of women. Yet, she criticizes that *The Feminine Mystique* represents the sharp limitations of liberal or bourgeois feminism as a theory and as a basis for political action, since Friedan does not discuss who would be called in to take care of the children and maintain the home if more women like herself were freed from their house labor and given equal access with white men to the professions. She does not speak of the needs of women without men, without children, without homes. She ignores the existence of all non-white women and poor white women. She does not tell the reader whether it is more fulfilling to be a maid, a baby-sitter, a factory worker, or a prostitute than to be a leisure-class housewife (cf. hooks 2000: 1-2).

According to Friedan, the 'feminine mystique' emerged in full force in the mass culture of the late 1940s and 1950s. Friedan compared short story fiction in women's magazines of the late 1930s, late 1940s, and late 1950s, and she analyzed both fiction and non-fiction from various magazines of the postwar era. The postwar magazines, she found out, narrowed women's scope to the housewife in the home and adopted Farnham and Lundberg's[71] antifeminist stance. *The Feminine Mystique* was not only a visionary work developing out of the new liberal feminism; it also remained remarkably rooted in America's postwar culture. Friedan did not question women's responsibility for home and children. She also encouraged marriage and femininity, disparaged homosexuality, and feared that neurotic, overbearing mothers ruined their children. A free-lance journalist herself, she adopted terms of the prevailing popular discourse and restated the postwar cultural contradiction between ideals of domesticity and achievement. However, Friedan embraced liberal individualism and validated women's public participation. She saw women's achievements outside the home as a source of both personal fulfillment and public service. Friedan legitimated open protest against "the housewife trap" (325) and presented domesticity as a major problem. She exposed the tension between public achievement and domesticity in ways that affirmed the undeniable anger many middle-class women felt as they increasingly tried to pursue both domestic and non-domestic ideals (cf. Meyerowitz 1994: 251f.).

The Women's Liberation Movement, starting in the mid to late sixties, emphasized women's struggle to free themselves in an autonomous movement. Many ideas appearing in the modern movement can already be found in the past, such as women's claim to control their own bodies, or to protest against inequality at home (cf. Rowbotham 1992: 11). In the late 1960s and early 1970s, divisions began to appear in the Women's Movement. While the Women's Liberation activists focused on the deeply rooted differences between men and women and fought for more radical changes, the Woman's Rights activists focused on the similarities between men and women demanding formal equality. These concepts of equality and difference have been central to feminism and are expressed in the so-called 'equality and difference' debate. Despite these divisions, all second wave feminists achieved many changes in society for the benefit of all women. This awareness that there is not one woman alike, but that class, race, and ethnicity distinguishes one woman from another in the pursuit of her personal needs, led to a "questioning" of nearly everything and a transformation of much of American culture. In this respect, feminism can be defined as "a world view which places [all] women at the centre of analysis and social action" (Ruzek: 1986: 184). But since different women have different opinions on

---

[71] Marynia Farnham and Ferdinand Lundberg described women's proper functions in the household in detail in their 1947 book, *Modern Woman: The Lost Sex*. Farnham points out that modern women who attempted to copy men's lifestyle or expressed discontent with their natural careers as mothers suffered from mental instability, bitterness, and worse. She claims that industrialization had undermined women's productive functions in the home. Women, "frustrated at the inmost core of their beings" (123), attempted tragically to imitate men in the world of work, led "aimlessly idle," "parasitic" lives as frigid housewives, or indulged in "overdoting, overstrict, or rejecting" mothering, with a cumulative outcome of neurotic children, including future Adolf Hitlers (210). Farnham called for a renewed commitment to motherhood, dependence on men, and "natural" sexual passivity.

different subjects, various tendencies in feminism came into existence in the 1960s and 1970s: Liberal or Egalitarian Feminism, Social Feminism, Cultural Feminism, Radical or Dominance Feminism, or Diversity Feminism.

Over the course of time up to today, many female Beat authors have refused the label 'feminist'. Jones herself claims that she is, first of all, a writer and only secondly a feminist, even though she deals with women's issues all the time and likes to write about women. She points out, "In fact, I write largely about women, although a lot of poetry is kind of gender-less" (Grace: 2004: 174). For her, it is quite difficult to define a feminist nowadays. Together with many other female Beats, she shares the attitude of not identifying oneself with any label. Jones has never met women's rights activists such as Gloria Steinem, because the female Beat movement, although incubating feminism, was also complicit with mainstream gender codes of female silence and subordination. Jones' life experiences had already radicalized her before the women's movement texts were published. When the feminists arrived on the scene, Jones was already "feminist-ized" by her circumstances: Having two small children, no money, and no help from anybody anywhere, she did not feel the need to read second wave feminist literature: "Of course, you know, I apologize for that attitude, but there were so many other things that I needed to read" (171). The changes feminist activists made in society by raising the level of attention are certainly extremely valuable for Hettie Jones. The difference between herself and feminists is, however, that in contrast to second wave activists, she was not trying to bring other women along with her, but she was certainly trying to bring herself along (cf. 172).

While Jones was not reading any feminist literature at all, Joyce Johnson was quite involved in second wave feminism. She was "under the influence of those ideas at the time" (202). Through reading many feminist books and partially editing them, she finally found the courage to leave her husband Peter Pinchbeck. As Johnson had an abortion during her teenage years, the abortion movement was particularly meaningful to her. Without the changes in society that occurred due to the feminist movement, Johnson would probably not have written *Minor Characters:* "I think one thing that was an important influence on that book was thinking about the women's movement. Suddenly the recognition that my story was important, and the story of the other women was important" (188).

Women Beats altered and augmented male Beats' revolt for personal freedom, and they were clearly forerunners of women's movements of the post-1968 era.[72] In her novel *Burning Questions* (1978), radical feminist and Beat fellow traveler Alix Kates Shulman states that female Beats were a protofeminist avant-garde. Preceding the women's liberation movement of the 1960s, they were those who advanced "From Silent to Beat to Revolutionary". Suffering a paralysis of expression – "some of us felt we had nothing to say and the rest had no one to say it to" (1990: 8) – this condition finally

---

[72] For more information, see Breines, Wini (1992). *Young, White, and Miserable. Growing up Female in the Fifties.* Boston: Beacon Press. *Young, White, and Miserable* is a critically acclaimed study that shows how the feminist movement of the 1960s found momentum in the seemingly peaceful time of the 1950s. Wini Breines explores white middle class America and argues that mixed messages given to girls during this decade fuelled the 60s feminism.

dissipated with sixties feminism. Focusing on sexual politics and gender difference, the works of di Prima, Jones, Johnson, and other female Beats problematize the gender binary, explaining beginning American feminisms. They prove that second wave feminism and other activist claims for female, sexual agency and subjectivity did not emerge from nowhere in the late 1960s, but were produced by Beat women and others in the vanguard. The bohemian 1950s had so provided a perfect breeding ground for feminist activities to follow decades later. Edward Halsey Foster notes that Beat's concern with self-knowledge and interest in the discovery or recovery of a true mode of perception are "objectives obviously equally important to feminists" (1992: 24). Thus, in spite of its exclusiveness, male Beats' chauvinist, Emersonian insistence on individual truth would paradoxically include feminism in its reach. And it would – even if inconsistently – include and nurture female dissidents and artists who were all too often unseen exemplars of the Beat Generation.

Most women Beats rejected the 1950s 'feminine mystique,' and vice versa, Betty Friedan was no fan of "bearded, undisciplined beatnikery" (1963: 285). She saw Beat not as a movement intervening in mainstream American ideologies of conformity and gender conservatism, but as another product of American culture's sexism: She considered the "retreat into the beat vacuum" as the defeat of a fifties woman by patriarchal culture (74). Disagreeing with Friedan's skepticism, many female Beats already benefited from several advantages of the postwar years, which allowed white bohemian women at least some social freedom. Nearly all second generation writers attended college, although many dropped out. By doing so, they partook of a privilege enjoyed by Beat men. Women's access to secondary education was pivotal for the emergence of a female Beat movement. Nonconformity, noncompliance, mobility, and sexual freedom were made available to them. Sexual freedom – the capacity to choose both male and female lovers – is at the core of Beat female subjectivity. By liberating themselves sexually, they were forerunners to the subsequent era of the sexual revolution in the 1960s. This could not have been achieved without Beat bohemian women who broke down the sexual frontiers in the 1950s. In *Minor Characters* and *How I Became Hettie Jones*, female bohemians are heroically presented in innovative narrative form, a move consistent with women Beats' anticipation of the sexual revolution. Both writers are feminists as they fought for substantive gender equality, an end to workplace discrimination, and reproductive rights that included legal birth control and abortion services.

Beside being confessional and fighting for women's causes, both *How I Became Hettie Jones* and *Minor Characters* contain features of a Bildungsroman, or more specifically, a coming-of-age memoir: "Der Bildungsroman beschreibt die Entwicklung einer Einzelgestalt innerhalb der besitzbürgerlichen Welt. Diese zentrale Person muss lernen, sich in die Gesellschaft einzuordnen" (Rainer: 2002: 242). The Webster's College Dictionary definition of a Bildungsroman is "a novel dealing with the education and development of its protagonist" (2003: 56). The Bildungsroman as a genre has its roots in Germany. Jerome Buckley points out that the word itself has a variety of connotations: "portrait," "picture," "shaping," and "formation," all of which give a sense of development or creation (1974: 13-14). The term 'Bildungsroman' emerged as a description of Goethe's novel *Wilhelm Meisters Lehrjahre*. This was the first Bildungsroman, having been published between 1794 and 1796. Meister's "apprenticeship" mostly deals with work and education.

A Bildungsroman or coming-of-age memoir is, most generally, the story of a person's individual growth and development within the context of a defined social order. It is characterized by the growth, education, and development of a character both in the world and ultimately within himself. The growth process, at its roots a quest story, has been described as both an apprenticeship to life and a search for meaningful existence within society. Very often, the focus of the coming-of-age memoir lies on a young character who, by the end of the story, has developed in some way, through accepting responsibility, or by learning a lesson. Both Jones and Johnson transform from silent, middle-class, burgeois, Jewish girls into mature, self-confident, hard-working women who are independent from men and who are able to live lives of their own. In the traditional coming-of-age memoir, some form of loss or discontent hauls the main character away from the family at an early stage. Aged 16, Johnson moved out of her over-protected home in Upper Manhattan. Aged 17, Jones entered college in 1951. In the classical Bildungsroman, the process of maturity is long, burdensome, and gradual, consisting of repeated clashes between the protagonist's needs and desires and the views and judgments enforced by an unbending social order. However, the two Beat memoirs clearly vary from the 19th century Bildungsroman, in which the spirit and values of the social order finally become manifest in the protagonist. Johnson and Jones are definitely not accommodated to society, even after the end of the Beat era. In this respect, they distinctively differ from Wilhelm Meister, David Copperfield, or Tristram Shandy, as these coming-of-age novels end with an assessment by the protagonist of himself and his new place in that society.

The Bildungsroman can be subcategorized into three specific types, most often found in German literature. First, there is the Entwicklungsroman – or coming-of-age novel – which can be defined as "a chronicle of a young man's general growth rather than his specific quest for self-culture" (13). In other words, it is a story recounting a person's life rather than focusing on the inner changes that contribute to his maturity. Buckley sees the main protagonist as a male person only, as the original Bildungsroman of the 19th century was focused on men's growth and development. Another form within German literature is the Erziehungsroman; this form is primarily concerned with the protagonist's actual educational process. Third, there is the Künstlerroman which describes the development of the artist from childhood until artistic maturity, like, for example, James Joyce's *A Portrait of the Artist as a Young Man*. These categories are strict within German literature, but are more free within English literature.

According to Jerome Buckley, the 19th century classical British Bildungsroman shares three commonalities: It is, first of all, an autobiographical novel with autobiographical elements which contribute to a sense of reality. However, *Great Expectations*, for example, is not Dickens' story, but Pip's; *Jane Eyre*, which is subtitled "An Autobiography," is clearly the autobiography of Jane Eyre, not of Charlotte Bronte. The second common characteristic is the ancestry of the main character. In the classical sense, there is often an orphan who has suffered the loss of a father or mother (cf. 19). This sets the scene for a difficult development, marked by the desire to search for one's own identity. The third aspect Buckley names is the education of the main character. This education is crucial, it is part of the child's maturation, and a preparation for impending adolescence and adulthood. Part of the development is the desire to leave home, which was also crucial for all female Beats. City life and the direct experience of urban surroundings offer new opportunities for the character's development. This urban experience, however, is not always a pleasant one. There is urban squalor and abject poverty in cities like London. But the city, full of opportunity, seems like a perfect destination for Dickens' main characters. What the Beats share with the traditional Bildungsroman is one major aspect city life offers, namely that of love and having love affairs. In the city, no matter if London or New York City, the hero or heroine has first experiences with love and sex. Buckley writes that in the classical tradition, there are "at least two love affairs or sexual encounters, one debasing, one exalting" (17). While the traditional heroes of the Bildungsroman often return home into the country after their urban adventures, Beat women were attracted to the newly-gained opportunities in the city and remained city dwellers.

Similar to the classic hero of the Bildungsroman, many Beat women also experienced love affairs that were positively stimulating – also by fostering literary careers – and love affairs that were devastating. One should, for example, remember the destructive forces of Bonnie and Ray Bremser's relationship, upon which the next chapters focus. Bonnie Bremser, who later on changed her name into Brenda Frazer, is a little-known Beat author. The following chapters seek to place her tragic and shocking memoir *For Love of Ray* in a postwar historical context. In times when globalized problems like workers' exploitation and poverty are a reality in many countries, Frazer's humiliating Mexican experiences have still not lost their relevance.

8   Brenda Frazer's *For Love of Ray*

> I'm thinking I will be whatever he is, whatever he wants me to be. (Frazer quoted in Peabody. *A Different Beat:* 60)

Brenda Frazer's *For Love of Ray*[73] (1971), first published in the U.S. under the title *Troia: Mexican Memoirs* (1969), is a largely unknown text of the Beat movement. The memoir has disappeared from the literary scene and is nearly unavailable nowadays, being out of print for thirty-five years. Through its melting of autobiography and literary construction, it is similar to works of Kerouac, Burroughs, and Ginsberg rather than to those of female writers of the Beat Generation. The memoir presents both a shocking and violent narration of a year Frazer spent in Mexico together with her husband, Beat poet Ray Bremser, and their infant daughter, Rachel. The work is unusual among autobiographic writings by female Beats, because it clearly shows the ambivalence between male sexual and creative freedom, and women who are repressed by economic and bodily realities. *For Love of Ray* is an unbelievable, sad story in many ways: First, the family has to escape across the U.S. border in 1961, because Ray Bremser is charged with armed robbery and bail jumping, and wants to evade the American law; drug-wrenched, Frazer is finally forced into prostitution in order to survive the harsh Mexican life; she is continually degraded by Mexican city authorities, her pimps, and her husband, and she finally has to put up their baby Rachel for adoption to save her own battered life.

Frazer's childhood and young adult life was far from the outlaw world of her memoir. Born in 1939, Brenda (Bonnie) Frazer graduated from Sweet Briar College in 1959, the same year she married poet Ray Bremser. The son of a pianist and a factory worker, Bremser was born in Jersey City on February 22, 1934, and he died in Utica, New York on November 4, 1998. After being discharged from the Air Force, he was arrested for armed robbery and spent six years in the Bordentown, New Jersey Reformatory. During his time in jail, he sent some of his poems to Ginsberg and Gregory Corso, who were in Paris at the time, and, with their help, he was soon included in the New York Beat scene after his release. Bremser, supported by poets like LeRoi Jones, even became one of Kerouac's favorite poets. Bob Dylan was so enthusiastic about Bremser's talent that he sent money to him in the 1970s. Being frantically in love with Bremser, Brenda Frazer was soon familiarized with the world of marijuana, psychedelic mushrooms, and heroin. Frazer recalls her move into the Beat Generation:

> I married Ray Bremser, poet seer, when I was nineteen. He wore an olive drab fatigue jacket and a red hooded sweatshirt to the ceremony. I adored him, even his eccentricities, and justified my existence by typing his poems. I identified with Fidel Castro. His patriotism, presented in lawyer truth, moved me. His actions inspired me to quit school and give thought to the shameful corrupting influence of capitalism.

---

[73] In this work, all quotes are taken from Frazer's British edition *For Love of Ray*, published in 1971 by Universal-Tandem Publishing Co.

> The Beat movement provided me with a husband and a rationale. Ray Bremser's penal/political history began to involve me also. (Knight. *Women of the Beat Generation:* 270)

Six months after their marriage, their daughter Rachel was born prematurely. Frazer's parents, especially her mother, were unhappy about their son-in-law who cast an uncomfortable sadness over the household. In 1959, Bremser was arrested again for violating his parole, because of marrying without permission. He spent six months at Trenton State before lawyers and a letter from William Carlos Williams were successful to quicken his release. When he was additionally accused of robbery, Bremser and Frazer borrowed money from Elaine de Kooning, wife of Willem de Kooning, and other friends, and fled to Mexico. Bremser was arrested in Mexico and sent back to Texas. De Kooning's friends provided bail, and the Bremsers escaped to Mexico again, staying with Beat poet Philip Lamantia. Explaining the situation, Frazer writes:

> The reason the law was after us was because Ray had been accused of an armed robbery he didn't do. It has to do with the way the police department, especially in Jersey City, keeps track of parolees and Ray had grown up there too and was known. A Sergeant Love [ironic] remembered his case and said "That sounds like Ray Bremser". They picked him up for a lineup and he was identified. My testimony and the fact that a fellow parolee was with us that night were both inconsequential. We were desperados because Ray had just served 6 months for violating parole by getting married without permission and talking on the radio about marijuana. We were desperados because we were uncool. We were desperados because we'd just had a baby and couldn't face another separation. (Kurt Hemmer. *Cowboys Crashing:* 44-45)

Back in the United States after the devastating Mexican year, Frazer decided to write down her experiences in 1963, yet the whole work was not published until 1969. Reorganizing her life in New York City, she was totally independent for the first time in her life. Even though the situation was painful, as Ray was in jail once again and she had just stopped using heroin, she enjoyed her new freedom. She had an apartment and space of her own, which she had never had before. In Mexico, there was no privacy at all, because they mostly stayed in hotel rooms, run-down apartments, or other people's houses. For the first time ever, she was now making decisions of her own. Not having ever had a "career" or occupation, she now felt useful when writing (cf. Grace 2004: 122-123). In 1964, Frazer got into contact with Allen Ginsberg and moved to his farm in upstate New York, where she fully regained her health and vigor. Inspired by rural life, she saw in it a lifestyle in harmony with the earth that was capable of revolutionizing culture by getting it back to its roots. Soon, Frazer had transformed the place into a model farm far in advance of its time. She worked, studied, and experimented diligently, earning several master's degrees, including one in biochemistry. She devised a method by which compost and manure were used to manufacture methane, with which the farm was powered. After divorcing Bremser, Frazer raised another daughter, Georgia, also fathered by Bremser. She later on had an unconventional relationship with a married dairy farmer and had two sons with him. In the 1980s, she began a career as a farmer and soil tester. In the 1990s, Frazer moved to Alpena,

Michigan, where she worked as a consultant for the U.S. Department of Agriculture. She is now retired and writes and publishes many technical articles under a different name. Having finally returned to writing, she is expanding her memoir of life in the Beat movement (cf. Knight 2000: 269f.).

Frazer's body of literature is very small: In the early 1960s, she published several texts in the Beat journal *Fuck you: A Magazine of the Arts, Blue Beat, and Intrepid*. *Troia* followed in 1969, her internet memoirs *Poets and Oddfellows* in 1997. Her literary accomplishments were first recognized in the 1990s. In 1992, Ann Charters included her in the *Beat Reader*, which brought her the attention of at least some literary critics she otherwise would not have had. Parts of *Troia/For Love of Ray* have so far appeared in three Beat anthologies. Because of the unabashed sexual explicitness of her memoir, critics have shied away from excerpting her more risqué scenes. Ann Charter's *Beat Reader* includes the opening pages of *For Love of Ray*, Knight's *Women of the Beat Generation* (1996) uses the same piece together with a short part of Frazer's introduction, and Peabody's *A Different Beat: Writings by Women of the Beat Generation* (1997) excerpts a small section from the unpublished work *Poets and Oddfellows*, "Breaking out of D.C.".

Changing her birth name from Brenda Frazer to Bonnie Bremser after her marriage with Ray Bremser was the first of many transformations Frazer would undergo in her lifetime. Bonnie Bremser was the author's name in the 1960s when *Troia/For Love of Ray* was written and published, but after her divorce, she changed her name back to Brenda Frazer. *For Love of Ray* is a significant social and literary document, because the author gives insight into the heart of the male dominated poetry scene around her husband Ray Bremser. Furthermore, despite her seething frustration, she combines romantic and maternal love, enjoyable and exploited sexuality, responsibility for her family, and artistic impulses. Reflecting on her first weeks in Veracruz, Mexico, after their escape from the U.S. legal system, Frazer muses: "In Mexico the sidewalk is a part of the house to be washed every morning with the tile floors – how to be myself in such a different place? Put it all in a sieve and squash your personality through into a new diversified you […]" (1971: 23). No detail of the author's contemplations can be left out if she is to discover her new "diversified" personality.

Like other female writers of the Beat Generation, Brenda Frazer was attracted to the Beat subculture by the hope for sexual independence and intellectual integration. While the postwar years were generally marked by male conformity, female constraint, and the nuclear family as the main buzz word, Frazer tried to connect sexual and intellectual hopes by joining the Beats. When interviewed by Nancy Grace in 1999, Brenda Frazer recalls ignoring "all the stuff that was on the college book lists," and instead, "sneaking out all the sexual literature in the library" (2004: 129). Yet, the male-dominated Beat circle offered women only restricted freedom. *For Love of Ray*, as well as the memoirs of other Beat women, criticizes the fact that women were doubly suppressed: by 'square' society at large, and by their male lovers and husbands who left them behind earning money and caring for the children.

Even though male Beats rejected white, middle-class conformities, Beat men had quite traditional views of women, wanting them to lead ordinary lives as mothers and financial supporters.

8.1 Frazer's Forced Textual Self

In *For Love of Ray*, Brenda Frazer experiences several odysseys from the capital Mexico City, or MexCity, as she calls it, to Veracruz; from Veracruz to Laredo, Texas; back to tiny Mexican mountain villages; and finally, New York City. The memoir is as energetic and attentive concerning descriptions of places and people as Kerouac's *On the Road*, which Frazer used as a model for the text (cf. Grace 2004: 112). Yet, despite sharing Kerouac's heightened consciousness and spontaneous prose, Frazer's work explores a specifically female point of view based on her own style and expression. *For Love of Ray* focuses both on her admiration for the rebellion of the Beats as well as trivial everyday aspects of being a mother and housewife. What might at first seem like a strange mixture of June Cleaver and Jack Kerouac being on the road together, turns out to be a real challenge to form a "new diversified you" (1971: 23). Instead of avoiding contradictions, Brenda Frazer tries to integrate the forces that nearly destroyed her, in order to use them for her literary expression. She is not successful in overcoming the contradictions she has to face, but is successful to stress the complexity of female experience in the Beat movement.

Brenda Frazer constructs the story of her relationship with Beat poet Ray Bremser in true Beat fashion. Escaping across the New Mexican border, the memoir presents one of the most surreal literary discourses of the period. Frazer builds up an enormously powerful and persevering Beat self who does not fear to defy Mexican and U.S. law, as well as obnoxious and violent pimps before returning home to the U.S. Confrontational and confessional, *For Love of Ray* stands apart as a memoir that in form and content may be the most shocking, troubling, horrendous, and provocative of all female Beat life stories.

The work is an important social document of the Beat culture, as the memoir was written closer to the period it portrays than Johnson's and Jones' memoirs. Another crucial difference to these other Beat accounts is the process by which she composed the narrative. *For Love of Ray* was not intended as a book or as a story about the Beat Generation, but rather as a collection of highly personal two-page narratives that Frazer, now back in the United States, wrote to her husband Ray, who was arrested in a New Jersey prison. She wrote down her recollections every day, five days a week, from March to November 1963. Stating that the letters were "literary business," she could side-step the prison regulation of only one one-page letter a week. During the period, Frazer quit her job as a clerk and went into forced isolation to concentrate on communicating with her husband. In this series of letters, Frazer depicts the difficulties the couple had had during their time in Veracruz, Mexcity, Laredo, and other Mexican places. Before, the Bremsers had never talked much about all the troubling experiences, and then, the limitations of jail made communication even more urgent. Frazer's effort was to establish a stage for mutual forgiveness, because so many open wounds were still bothering her and caused her sleepless nights. Through writing, she remembered the happy times, when their daughter Rachel was still with them and Ray was free, but the degrading sex-for-hire-scenes were also constantly present in her mind. Furthermore, her narrations also functioned as a sexual aid for the married couple, as the New Jersey penal system denied them personal meetings and conjugal rights. Through writing, Frazer tried to renew their relation after all the sexual misery she was forced into in Mexico. About her coming-of-age as a writer, she writes:

> I defined myself when I sat down to write. It was a rebellion against my most immediate authority figure, my husband, who was once again in jail. Writing was therapy I could afford. It was exciting then and still is to give myself that freedom. Alone I evolved my personal story. There is no mentor or male muse to be a live-in example for me. I have more faith in my creativity now. Creativity is in the middle, at the turning point of gender, either, neither, nor. (Knight. *Women of the Beat Generation:* 271)

To write was to cope with all the emotional pain, and so the act of composing functioned like therapy. This was a long time before Frazer would allow the need of a therapist to herself. Each day of the week, she would sit at her typewriter and spontaneously compose texts, stimulated by jazz. Frazer could not live the distraught life of being illegal citizens any more, and so she had asked her husband to surrender to the police (cf. Grace 2004: 113). Being on her own now, she would write down a text she had drafted the day before, "reconstructing in [her] mind, going over things, and feeling things evolve about what [she] would write" (114). Similarly to Kerouac's spontaneous prose style[74], she "would just sit down, smoke a joint, sit at a typewriter, and go," she writes about the process of writing her memoirs (113). The letters were then sent to her husband in their spontaneous, original form. Producing a collection of micro-stories, Ray Bremser was enthusiastic about his wife's talent and convinced Michael Perkins to organize a selection of her stories in a four-part book. About her

---

[74] Jack Kerouac designed his 'spontaneous prose' with its run-on sentences, its capitalizations, its eccentric punctuation, and its poetic repetition of sounds, to imitate not only the creative process of jazz – the spontaneity that comes from improvising – but also the sound of jazz, or more specifically, the sound of bebop. In his essay "The Philosophy of the Beat Generation," John Clellon Holmes says that "modern jazz is almost exclusively the music of the Beat Generation," and that it "is primarily the music of inner freedom, of improvisation, of the creative individual rather than the interpretive group. It is the music of a submerged people who feel free, and this is precisely how young people feel today" (Albert: 1988: 16). From the 1950s onward, Jack Kerouac had moved his method of composition closer to the area of music. The improvisatory technique that Kerouac had evolved while revising the long scroll version of *On the Road* – he called it "sketching" – was shaped by his belief that jazz was the essential American art form. He felt that no one before him had seen the potential scope of a jazz prose. Kerouac's model for this new and self-consciously American melody line was adapted from the tenor man, "blowing a phrase on his saxophone till he runs out of breath, and when he does, his statement's been made" (Kerouac: 1991: 64). Kerouac himself "blew" on his typewriter like a jazz musician blew on his instrument. Kerouac could type faster than anyone else, according to the poet Philip Whalen: „The most noise that you heard while he was typing was the carriage return, slamming back again, and again. The little bell would bing-bang, bing-bang, bing-bang! And he'd laugh, and say, 'Look at this!' And he'd type, and he'd laugh. Then he'd make a mistake, and this would lead him off into a possible part of a new paragraph, into a funny riff of some kind" (Foster: 1992: 79).

editor, Frazer says: "He put [the memoir] together. I have notes. I have no idea where those sections were in the original manuscript. He picked and chose among the pieces" (120). Frazer herself was not involved in the construction of her memoir, which was first published by Croton Press as *Troia: Mexican Memoirs* in 1969. Considering this, it becomes obvious that the various stages of the textual process were dictated by Ray Bremser. Seen from this perspective, Frazer was doubly dominated by her husband: On the one hand, she had limited control of her own body, and on the other hand, it seems that she also had limited control of her text. Bremser was even responsible for the title of the book, taking it from a Fellini film. According to Beat critic Ann Charters, "She [Frazer] was angry that the publisher sensationalized her book with the title 'Troia' meaning adventuress or whore" (1992: 465). In 1971, the work was published in Great Britain under the title *For Love of Ray*. This title is perhaps more suitable in consideration of the sacrifices she made to keep her family together. Both the American and British version were "never distributed and slipped into obscurity," Frazer writes, "and then somehow all the books got sold anyway and now are enriching dealerships etc, all independent of me" (Hemmer: 2000: 46). The memoir, largely forgotten outside the world of Beat scholars and enthusiasts, has been advertised as an underground classic. The storytelling process is unusual due to the fact that Frazer's motives for writing her story were radically different from those of most memoirists. The memoir as a whole was not being selected by the author, but by another person – much like the construction of Burroughs' *Naked Lunch*. This aspect challenges analyses on the work's formal techniques.

The narrative voice of *For Love of Ray* immediately sets the memoir apart from *Minor Characters* and *How I Became Hettie Jones*. Frazer turns against the function of life writing to persuade the world of the importance of the self called "I". Memoirists, in general, are always in need of a reader. Johnson and Jones' narrators appear very reliable, because the authors are fundamentally interested in correcting history and creating valuable social documents of the late 1950s and 1960s. Frazer's narrator, in contrast, is a textual self that was created through corresponding with her husband in their own private world, and for their own private purposes. Johnson and Jones claim to reconstruct and reflect a historical truth in their life writing. Both create an intimate atmosphere with the reader, but Jones is even more direct as she sometimes even addresses the reader by using the word "you". Their selves can only emerge through getting into contact with a compassionate audience. Frazer, however, nullifies the author–reader contact through her disregard for conventional readers. Both Ray Bremser, her intended reader, and the text's other readers are dismissed, because they are useless for the creation of the text. The narrative disapproves of the memoir's usual conciliatory offer to readers. Virulently, the narrative self refuses accommodation or compromise.

Already the first pages of *For Love of Ray* clearly show that the author refuses a memoirist's traditional obligation to meet reader expectations. The brief introduction states Frazer's need for expression very concisely. The voice is loud and angry, and the reader is condemned, but also invited on a wild ride. From the first pages onwards, the audience is forced to enter the story with a paralytic feeling of shock and timidity. Expressing the therapeutic purpose of her writing, she makes clear: "Damn the pain; it must be written. Damn reality that all the present infections have to be drained from a stopped hole. Damn the metaphors and the scariness; it is the fever taking over" (43). The preface is outstanding for its transparency and self-revelation, as well as for its declaration of an autonomous identity beyond the claims of others. Frazer's first sentence already foreshadows the disclosure of the reader: "First off, I want to tell you a few really important things about me" (7). Knowing about her chronological disorder and confusion, she agrees that "continuity is necessary," but she also believes in distortion. Rebelliously, she illustrates the primary aim of her writing. She believes that

> [...] if you get to a place where something is taking shape and want badly to comprehend the thing that you have created, supposedly for yourself (since everything is personal anyway), [...] what's important is not the technique or lack of it, but those few minutes when you overcome the frustration, bridge the gap, and hold something incredibly beautiful to you; the point where you don't see yourself anymore but you are there, and that's the way you really are. *(For Love of Ray:* 7)

Explicitly and intensely, Frazer describes the process of transforming her personal experiences into literature. The book's introduction strictly forbids anyone to understand or care about the "I". She disapproves of the reader as an "other" who tries to use worthless philosophy to protect Frazer from herself. On paper, her textual self is hostile towards the reader and declares: "My soul is black to its depth and the heart shines through like a beacon, or that powerful Egyptian self-induced light which moves all material things effortlessly. The pacified ghost roams at leisure within the pyramid, takes on the countenance of its own sphinx, expresses inwardly and that pretty much excludes everyone else" (10). By excluding the audience, the narrator gets rid of the guilt and shame she feels, because moralists may accuse and reject her for sexual promiscuity, open prostitution, and rejection of her child. By breaking all normative 1950s/1960s gender codes, she clearly violates the patriarchal restrictions towards women. She straightens out that the writing of her memoir is an exclusionary and selfish clearing process for herself, and not an act for the reader. Not surprisingly, her openness and aggressive assertiveness are not sustained until the end of the book. Frazer continues being conscience-stricken and restless: she feels guilty, because she cannot fulfill the duties of being a good wife and mother, and restless, because she cannot grasp the exotic Mexican context and surreal events. For Frazer, writing is a transformative process, and she playfully invents her textual self: "I can hardly believe that what I write is me. So it's all confusing if you stop to think about it seriously – better to make it a game, maybe even revel in it" (131). She suggests that literary categories are inadequate to describe both the self and the process of writing. She rejects creating a historical context, which would only distance herself from the truth. For Frazer, experience is a present tense reality:

> Sometimes I wonder what people think; not people reading this, but people who saw us in that time. Usually I start out thinking of the general beauty of the things we undertake, […] reworking conversations we have had with friends, or interesting conversations I have had with johns […] and then from that I start considering, though briefly, what the other participants feel. But I usually prefer to have faith in what we personally have done, said and felt, and if the opposite reaction was not good, then it is they who have missed out, somehow. *(For Love of Ray:* 131)

The scene clearly shows that other people, apart from herself, are insignificant. These other individuals appearing in the book are only secondary to Frazer's creative processes. She hardly leaves space for others and takes on a very selfish position, in which the "I" is enormously powerful. Frazer is only interested in her own linguistic journey. The "me" about which she writes and wonders allows her to transcend herself. Through avoiding all form or design, she paradoxically creates a textual self which is freed to be confessional.

Frazer's most confessional voice appears in Book One titled "Mexico City to Veracruz and Back to Texas". The angry and confrontational tone of the preface gives way to a voice which intends to reveal the most intimate details to her confessor. The self that Frazer creates speaks as both a reporter and confidant for Ray Bremser, who is her audience. "I was trying to get at the truth," she explains: "I had this huge burden of guilt because I'd told him that […] I couldn't live that way anymore. I couldn't live the desperate life anymore. So then he was in jail. […] I was just weepingly trying to make things okay between us" (Grace: 2004: 121). Frazer's text is immensely important for the Bremsers, because it protects them from breaking off the relationship. The end of writing would be the end of their relationship, which would mean the loss of Ray Bremser, initiator of her textual self. As a consequence, Frazer is unwilling to move forward too quickly or complete her story too fast. Her aim is to keep their relationship alive through a narrator who appears extremely interesting, eloquent, and challenging to Bremser. Most of the time in the book, this self being presented is a prostitute and a sexual deviant.

8.2 The Outlaw Prostitute

Much of Frazer's story reveals her experiences as a prostitute in Mexico, a brutal life she entered at her husband's urging that she should support the family financially. Poet Ray Bremser sometimes even served as her pimp or was watching while she was having sexual intercourse with other men. Frazer's descriptions are detailed, shocking, and make the reader shiver, but she is not as explicitly focused on the body as Diane di Prima in *Memoirs of a Beatnik*[75]. Even if it soon becomes clear that

---

[75] By many literary critics, *Memoirs of a Beatnik* is often devalued as mere pornography. Di Prima seems orgasm-seeking and independent, has sex with multiple partners who are both male and female, and is focused on what she calls her "sexual power" (1998: 33). For more information on di Prima's explicit sexual details in many of her works, see Quinn, Roseanne Giannini (2003). "'The Willingness to Speak': Diane di Prima and Italian American Feminist Body Politics". *MELUS* 28.3: 175-193.

Frazer cannot break through the dominant gender codes of the time, her memoir is generally even more subversive than Kerouac's *On the Road*.

Influential factors which drive Frazer into prostitution are poverty, the Bremsers' shared acceptance of normative gender roles, and responsibility for their baby Rachel. When she confesses her affair with their landlord N to Ray, "I was called a pig – a thing I well believed by the time this argument was through […]. Whew, that cleared the air – after that point it was fully believed that I was capable of walking the streets. I began to know what was expected of me". She adds, "This was one of the few times in our marriage I was not forgiven". Frazer does not dare to oppose her husband. Fugitive outlaws and without any money, Rachel is the final reason why Frazer becomes a prostitute. Caring for her family is more important for her than personal freedom. Her first hustling experiences are depressing. She admits that "I have been a little too lyrical in parts perhaps, but it was not at all for fun or experience that I was forced to be a con artist – pure necessity sent me into town to try my luck". Justifying her decision, she points out, "don't forget in my head also that we are fugitives" (33). From the beginning of her prostitution onwards, Frazer both revolts against and embraces sex for hire. On the front page of the British version *For Love of Ray*, it says "She had to be a whore. But she also liked it. And hated it." This quote taken from the *Times Literary Supplement* hits the point: At first, she despises her new job and spends her days haunted by what she will have to do in the evening. Yet, in several other passages, Frazer sees her prostitution also as liberating, because she enjoys the feeling of being admired or sometimes even worshipped by her customers. Not knowing what to wear the first evening she is out in the streets, she describes her clothes as "pitiful":

> I had only a very short corduroy skirt I had purchased at a bargain store in Hoboken and it was no bargain – and a gift from one of our neighbors nearby, who it seems to me were conspiring for me to go out and get some money too, a blouse of limp rayon which hung very low on straps that wouldn't hold so that sometimes it wasn't even hanging – what a farce that whole evening was – of course there was the afternoon headache, trying to get out of it, and pleading with Ray, who answers me reasonably with our broke and hungry situation – so I go, walk, how did I make it through the streets with my shame and everybody staring at my outrageous outfit? *(For Love of Ray:* 33)

Frazer is ashamed of having to go that far, but when she resists walking the streets in search for customers, Ray reminds her of their economic destitution and her obligation to Rachel and himself. Sitting miserably in the plaza park in Veracruz, "I guess it began to shine from my face," she remembers. Suddenly, "some little punk sympathizes with me, admired me, and I talk him into coming home with me". This very first experience leaves its mark on her self-confidence: It "almost finished me, the circumstances, Ray watching, the fact that the little punk never delivered the money, and no doubt spread the news to all of his friends about me. From then on I felt hunted, furtive" (34). Selling her body to Mexican men is extremely humiliating, and she is often disgusted by the men she sleeps with. One of the most shocking scenes in the book is a "gangbang," as the narrator calls it. She spends an evening out with three men, two Mexicans and a "blond husky Canadian" (65). When they are sitting in a coffee house, she is "reluctant to talk the money over with all of them". She admits, "I had never been involved in one of these gangbang scenes before and I was not the only one who was self-conscious". They finally drive to a waiting house in Colonia. Then, she is "ushered self-consciously to the waiting cot next to the ping pong table and [...] laid in sequence by the three of them, the others carousing in adjoining long rooms of empty space". Frazer depicts the scene with disgust and unemotionality: "I am frantic with being treated so casually and not enjoyed, the tall dark guy fucks me twice making like he enjoyed it a great deal, and wants me not to continue with the others after I finish him". She is also nauseated by the Canadian who follows: "the fat Canadian disgusts me with his empty conception of up and down, athletic notions of making love and checks with me if I have had any disease even before he will venture in". The passage is abhorrent not only because she is paid half of the 600 pesos she has been promised, but also because the men are crude and repulsive, and come to her one at a time while she lies on a cot beside a ping pong table. Frazer is "totally disgusted with the scene long before it ends; we all shower together and I do not talk" (all quotes page 66).

Feminist theorists have triggered a discussion about whether prostitution, or "sex work," is liberating or degrading for women or not. Julia O'Connell Davidson writes about both positions: "Where 'radical feminists' think prostitution is fundamentally wrong because it commodities something that cannot be detached from the self, the 'sex work' feminists [...] think it is fundamentally right because it provides clients with access to something they require to fulfill their human needs and express their true selves" (2002: 90). For Frazer, both interpretations work, as she sometimes also insists on her own sexual gratification as well as money from her sexual partners. For example, she is suspicious the first time she works in a Mexico City brothel, wants to ''get it over with'', and collect her pay. Yet, her need for money is not always a barrier to enjoyment: Once, she even confesses, "I embrace my prostitution" (51). This attitude is also manifested in the fact that she feels attracted to several customers: ''[...] it is a hot afternoon and all I am thinking of is myself, within reason, got to get the money, but it is natural pleasure and this cat is O.K.'' (129). In several scenes, she sees her prostitution as liberating, honest, and spiritually motivated. She, for example asks, "Is this not God's honest clean sweaty labor and pleasure of good wholesome things?" (39). In another early scene, she describes the positive sides of her work:

> I am the deity being worshipped, this is something I cannot cope with, my dress is pushed upward and then dispensed with – o hot afternoon – I know I am better off without clothes, sandy legs being caressed, no manual labor this, I am completely relaxed, except an occasional thought of the unpocketed money causes me tremor. *(For Love of Ray:* 46)

Frazer equates herself with a deity. Her worries about the pesos make clear, however, that she is not as relaxed as it seems. Even though she sometimes enjoys being admired and worshipped, her primary reaction to her job is one of revulsion, feeling like a "heifer to the slaughter" (34). It soon becomes obvious for the reader that Frazer does not have control over her own body. Her hustling is not a celebration of her true self. The detailed depictions of sexual intercourse in *For Love of Ray* are more clinical or sociological than prurient. Frazer explicitly rejects conventional female passivity, but at a closer look, she is subservient to the U.S. containment culture of the time. Frazer's conflicting attitude about sexuality and the ambivalence of her descriptions of sex in *For Love of Ray* mirror the postwar discussion about gender roles. Several sociological studies, such as Lundberg and Farnham's *Modern woman: The Lost Sex* (1947), were published after the war. These publications aimed at pushing women back into the household after they had been successful war industry workers a decade before. Lundberg's antifeminist bestseller argues that modern American women have abandoned their traditional roles as wives and mothers to the disadvantage of society and their own happiness.

Another passage in which the narrator is presented as a conflicted woman in a desperate situation who, on the one side, resists, but on the other hand appreciates sex for hire, is the following. Frazer is sitting in a patio parlor, when a young man approaches and asks to sit down next to her:

> His youth is a motivation for me to set the price as soon as I can. I am nervous, he tells me how impressed he was by my entire profile in silhouette, like a queen, a young queen I think he specified. [...] He is short of money and reluctant at first to pay the 300 pesos I ask for, but when we get to his room [...] I lay the whole story on him of the baby sleeping back in the hotel and Ray across the river [...]. We somehow achieve a good enough fuck and unity through conversation, that when it is done it is a clearing away of the day's cares, good healthy boy and girl fuck. He wants me to sleep there and give him more [...]. The second was an aftermath and reluctant for me, for I never want to do twice what I am getting paid for once [...].
> (*For Love of Ray:* 95-96)

In this scene, Frazer is flattered by the young man's compliments. Usually, she overcomes her disgust by allowing her body to respond to the physical pleasure, similar to the reaction of the narrator in *Memoirs of a Beatnik* who is raped by a friend's father. This intimate confession of enjoying the sexual pleasures of hired sex, but of being at the same time disgusted by the emotional pain may have appealed to both Ray Bremser and Brenda Frazer. They may have been aroused by the idea of simultaneous pleasure and pain. This hypothesis is fortified by the fact that while in Mexico, they were both reading *Juliette* by the Marquis de Sade, a book which impressed them immensely.

Juliette was among the few possessions Frazer had brought to Mexico. "I had taken along a de Sade book," Frazer writes, "and read a little of it before sleep each night; it is *Juliette*, a story of a whore, like me" (57). *Juliette* was included in the third version of *Justine*, published in 1797. While Justine, Juliette's sister, was a virtuous woman who consequently encountered nothing but despair and abuse in life, Juliette is an amoral nymphomaniac who ends up successful and happy. Both works, *Justine* and *Juliette,* were published anonymously. Due to their scandalous contents, Napoleon ordered the arrest of the author, and as a result, de Sade was incarcerated without trial for the last 13 years of his life. The 20th century French poet Guillaume Apollinaire appreciates de Sade's work in comparison to the 19th century French courts which found it scandalous and immoral. In the preface of *Juliette*, Apollinaire calls the Marquis de Sade the "freest of spirits to have lived so far". He

> [...] had ideas of his own on the subject of woman: he wanted her to be as free as man. Out of these ideas – they will come through some day – grew a dual novel, *Justine* and *Juliette*. It was not by accident the Marquis chose heroines and not heroes. Justine is a woman as she has been hitherto, enslaved, miserable and less than human; her opposite, Juliette represents the woman whose advent he anticipated, a figure of whom minds have as yet no conception, who is arising out of mankind, who shall have wings, and who shall renew the world. (Hemmer. *Cowboys Crashing*: 40-41)

Probably, Brenda Frazer did not know about Apollinaire's radical views of de Sade's *Juliette* when she compares herself with the heroic main protagonist. The equation is inappropriate, however. For the emancipated female reader, de Sade's sadomasochistic position makes it difficult to accept Frazer's claim of female liberation. De Sade, who took pleasure in torturing women, hardly seems a role model for female empowerment. By embedding her philosophy of sexual freedom and pleasure in the conflicting discourse of prostitution, she ultimately works against the emancipation of women. Her particular position as a woman selling her body does not demonstrate female liberation, but male exploitation. As Frazer becomes more self-assertive and independent as a prostitute, or more "fully woman," as she calls it, her Beat effort to free herself from middle-class sexual mores consequently leads to a costly drug addiction, life-threatening abortions, the devastating loss of her daughter Rachel, and the humiliating beatings by her husband and various pimps. Bremser's beatings become more intense throughout the memoir. When Frazer does not light a cigarette for him, but just offers him the cigarette pack, he brutally attacks her. She writes that he "belted me one right there on the street and then when I try to protest he gave me another one and then when I got mad and tried to hit him, he hit me again, and each blow was a resounding slap that cleared my head for new comprehension. No, I told him 'I'm through,' and he hit me again as if to say goodby[e]" (141-142). Frazer leaves hurt and frustrated, but when Ray does not follow, she decides to see where he is: "He had still be standing in the same place and when I walked back slowly with my head lowered, it started all over again, and as soon as I said something out of place and unforgiving, he hit me again – pow!". Subserviently, she justifies his behavior: "He maintains it is good for a chick to get pounded on once and awhile for it increases the circulation and makes her pretty". She also confesses that she "didn't love him any less" (142). Helen McNeil claims that masochistic behavior patterns were "part of the definition of the chick who follows her man on the road" (1996: 194). To a large extent, this is also true for Frazer. She seems to like her masochist role for Ray's sadism despite her simultaneous rebellion to the dominant male expectations of female subordination. Even if Frazer herself might call the times in Mexico and the following months after having arrived back in the U.S. liberating, this does not seem so for the reader. The truth that she confesses is contradictory. Her attempt to shake off the guilty conscience associated with purchasable sex finally destroys the independent self she is yearning for.

Being the creator of Frazer's textual self, as he convinced her to write down her memories, Ray Bremser places himself in a very dominant position in both Frazer's real life and *For Love of Ray*. He points out that Frazer relies on him, and it is not he who relies on her. Bremser's 1960 prose poem "Angel," written in only one night in Trenton State Prison, gives a unique impression of his views about his wife, to whom it is dedicated. In the poem, published in 1967, he writes, "I shaped her, limned her, limbed her, trimmed her, blued her, grew & sylphed & hoped to God & prophecied her nightly & by darkness everywhere" (Hemmer: 2000: 55). Because he is a poet and his wife is not, he has the feeling that the suffering he experiences can never be fully understood by her: "Angel thinks she knows how horrible it all is! I know she has a fantastic capacity to get into the pain & torture of that which is all around her [...] but she don't know this to its sharp core, her dreams are as flying wonders compared to my waking walks through the stygian stinking vomited halls of dolorous sprang & crong muck". Bremser denies her the possibility to have sympathy with him. He creates a barrier between them by banning her to the world of fiction and dreams, while his sphere is that of a harsh reality. Later on in the poem, he elevates the poet into the position of a seer: "Nobody knows anything [...] only the poets". Because he is a poet, he sees himself in a privileged position as both creator and seer of the world. "Still," he writes, "angels aren't always worthy of what love a man can sometimes offer up to them" (56). Bremser is convinced that only men can be gifted poets, while women are passive muses who can never satisfy the men's needs. This attitude was common among male writers of the Beat scene. Even Ginsberg, who was generally considered open-minded and liberal, stated that Beat women were not capable to be good writers: "Yes, it's alright to blame the men for exploiting the women – or, I think the point is, the men didn't push the women literally or celebrate them. [...] But then, among the group of people we knew at the time, who were the writers of such power as Kerouac and Burroughs? Were there any? I don't think so" (Peabody: 1997: 1).

Even though Frazer cannot free herself from the burdens of male domination and exploitation, she is fighting against the oppressive constraints of postwar sexual mores. Like Juliette, Frazer threatens the culture from which she emerges. American popular culture of the time insisted on women sacrificing their desires for the stability of the household. Even though Frazer imitates Juliette in many ways, they only share some similarities. Both, for example, reject moral codes. It is ironic that Frazer does everything for Ray rather than for herself – For Love of Ray, but to such an extent that her unselfishness is as harmful as Juliette's selfishness.

Throughout *For Love of Ray*, Frazer conforms to the typical acquiescent, quiet Beat chick who is pliable and docile. In a 1959 excerpt from an early manuscript she wrote before their escape to Mexico, Ray tells her, "I like your quietness, you know". He goes on,

> "Other women talk too much and it's meaningless. I can hear things in your silence".
> And later he said, "Quiet people are usually writers". I'm thinking I will be whatever he is, whatever he wants me to be. Mortal practice, a life/death pact to come of this spontaneous knowledge. (Peabody. *A Different Beat*: 60)

Even though she devotes her life to her husband, Ray is mostly excluded from Frazer's sexual adventures. He tries to involve himself into her experiences and gives orders with whom she should sleep. Additionally, he wants his wife to bring her customers home at the beginning and sometimes even watches the scenes from the patio. Later on in the story, he operates as her pimp, asking men in the streets and cafés if they would pay for hired sex with his wife. But Bremser is also jealous and furious at times and acts as Frazer's protector. When his wife tells him she has been beaten by a man who did not pay, Bremser "takes a knife from the kitchen and goes downtown to find him" and kill him: "Ray comes back later, unsuccessful, questions me further and the incident ends there" (42). Bremser wants to know every single detail about his wife's sexual encounters, especially later on in the story when he is in prison again. Driven by jealousy, Bremser desires to gain access to Frazer's secret, shameful life. In a letter to her, written from the Webb County Jail in Laredo, Texas, Ray demands: "… tell me some sexual items … draw up a plan, a plot, a sequence! Start alone, self-sex, then me, then he, the he or she and so on! Your limits? Define yourself, time yourself, breaking point-weary? Write me information, so I know […] Make your flesh delirious for me, but unperformed without me!" (73). This order makes clear that *For Love of Ray* is a narrative-on-demand. Ray Bremser commissions the narrative he wants to hear. Frazer tells her story for patriarchal amusement only. She has to report rather than merely depict how she sees the world. The book is therefore paradoxical, because Frazer, on the one hand, wants to be recognized as a Beat writer, but on the other hand, she herself negates this by taking orders from Ray.

Bremser is inquiring thoroughly, but the more he knows, the more jealous he gets. Even though he forces her to sell her body, he sees the 1950s Anglo-Saxon domestic ideal in danger. Bremser's urge to control his wife is connected to the patriarchy in their relationship. He is intrusive, wants to watch his wife with her customers, keeps the pesos she delivers to himself, and hits her when she tries to rebel. Superficially, Frazer is not disturbed by his dominant position. But as the story continues, she starts acting more confidently – also because Ray is in a U.S. jail across the border again. The reader enjoys Frazer's new emancipation, but unfortunately, her freedom is only short-lived.

Throughout the book, Frazer is ambivalent about being a hustler and a mother at the same time. For her, the line between her two roles blurs. Frazer can therefore be compared to the Tijuana prostitutes who were interviewed by sociologists in the 1980s. In an article written by Castillo, Gomez, and Delgado in 1999, the results showed that most of the Tijuana prostitutes were also mothers and wives who were, on the one hand, family-loving and domestic, often providing the only income, but on the other hand, societal outsiders due to their profession (cf. Anderson 2003: 259). Frazer becomes a hard-working businesswoman, leaving for Mexico City by bus on her own to earn money. Every day, she writes passionate letters to Ray who has stayed in Veracruz. Now, the money stays in her own pockets. She has "succeeded in taking care of business" (1971: 96). When she comes back home, she disappointedly realizes that her husband has been arrested and is in jail in Laredo, on the American side of the border. Frazer is now responsible for all three lives. Being afraid of the American police, she feels safer in Nuevo Laredo on the Mexican side of the border. The weeks she spends there living in various hotels are desperate. With the baby in her arms, she crosses the border every day to talk to her husband through the window of his cell. She writes, "I am in a perpetual state of sweat […] I do not look or wish for pleasant weather, have no prospects of pleasure and so continue this soul drive in the withering heat, but do not wither" (87).

Frazer fights to survive physically and psychically while getting Bremser out of jail. She frantically challenges the Laredo police; they threaten to imprison her too, but she stays stubborn and refuses any discipline. Desperately, she risks looking for customers in Nuevo Laredo, but she is careful, because the police are constantly observing her. For her husband's release, she even offers her services to city officials who use and humiliate her. She does not earn much, but enough to buy Bremser peaches and pay the nickel toll to cross the bridge to Texas:

> Oh it is good to eat after several days of nothing but worry, and good to know that in the morning I will go the jail across the bridge, not problem with the nickel toll; I will probably even ignore the tollkeeper as I pass and hitch the baby higher on my hip, and buy peaches for Ray, enormous ones that make a whole meal for our shrunken stomachs, and sit square down on the sidewalk between the courthouse and Ray's jail window [...]. *(For Love of Ray:* 96)

Living in Nuevo Laredo with the baby, she now has to carry the burden of shame and guilt all by herself. "Sure," she writes, "I have to take care of the baby, and I am proud that I can do it independently of American law, but the light and the dark still haunts me, I am so close to the brink of being ashamed, maybe because I liked it" (97). When Bremser is finally released on bail, her financial and individual independence end abruptly: "Ray is in control I discover later, and I am just a useless wife who was so tired out that I did not dare to enjoy anything any more, the very dress that I wear is a badge and I know that everyone knows what I have been through to keep things going" (106). The Bremsers have to stay in Fort Worth, Texas, while he is on bail. In the U.S., they try to get money from patrons of literature, but they remain poverty-stricken: "I had thought that it was my devotion, that my sacrifice in Mexico had kept us alive, and now in Texas it became clearly dependence on poetry, and poetry has lofty words to describe a purity I had a long time been on vacation from. So where was I to turn for sympathy?". At the end of Book Two – "Mexico to Laredo: Getting Ray out of Jail," rich friends of Bremser offer to help them escape to Mexico again and to adopt Rachel: "when they offer us money to leave, when they offer through Ray this possibility of the baby being taken care of by some rich people where she will be safe and I will not have the immediate worry that my investigations will be tampering with anyone else's life but my own, I am relieved" (108).

In Book Three titled "Mexico City and Rural Excursion: Losing Rachel," Frazer is only shortly relieved to be able to free herself from all restricting factors that oppressed not only her, but also numerous suburban U.S. women suffering from Friedan's "problem that has no name". The loss of Rachel eventually destroys the Bremsers as a nuclear family. Nevertheless, without Rachel with them on the road, they can escape to Mexico again. For a short time, she enjoys living out her new freedom, having no one to care for except herself. Traveling around aimlessly, the Bremsers "indulged in a new kind of tourism". They "hunted out the most ideal places, every once and awhile returning to the hub Mexcity, oh Mexico time snake, where I have to exert myself to raise as much money as possible quickly so we can get away and be safe again". She continues, "I found out later that this is a cycle many Mexican prostitutes do with their boyfriends: fierce work, extended vacations, though I know none who got so elemental as us" (119).

Drugs seem to be a substitute for Rachel now that the baby is lost forever. The Bremsers get high on hallucinogenic magic mushrooms every day and stay with the "magic mushrooms people in the hills (mountains) of Oaxaca" for several weeks (117). In the mountain village Huatla, they worship the mushrooms' effects now instead of the "beautiful blond American baby". They smoke pot, indulge in "cocaine rages of numbness" (113), and Frazer starts feeling alive again: "the mushrooms start to tell me something of life: whole other conception of living, again" (120-121). For Ray Bremser, however, the split-up of the family means depending on his wife's income again. Once again, he keeps the money his wife brings home, but he is aware that he, too, is in a destitute situation. In former times, Rachel was Frazer's burden, but mentally, it was Ray who restricted her mobility. As an outlaw in Mexico, he is dependent on Frazer's money, and therefore tries to regain his patriarchal position.

In Book Three, after losing Rachel, Frazer gradually loses her confessional role, and the memoir becomes more reflective, but also fictitious at times. Her personal reflections concerning the country and their drug experiences are intersected with several sex-for-hire stories in Mexcity. Similar to other female Beat authors like Joyce Johnson, Frazer skillfully includes letters written to or received from Ray to appear more trustworthy as a memoirist. The letters are important documents for Frazer in order to confront Bremser with the pain he had caused her. Here, she also addresses herself in order to contemplate who she was and who she had become: a young woman who had left her middle-class family in Washington, D.C. and who had become a street hustler. Both Book Three and Book Four – titled "Mexico City and back to New York" – are confusing, unchronological, and drug-inspired. Frazer's narrative self reflects on how worn out and conflicted she feels, how the Beat myths of romance and freedom have been shattered by Ray Bremser's behavior. She is brooding about how salvation can still be possible for her, and how she and Ray have deceived themselves by believing that a rebel lifestyle on the margins might lead to a real cultural change.

When she finally abandons Bremser after several angry beatings and controversies, she tries to become fully independent. Still frantically in love with her husband, she tells him to leave, and he returns to New York City alone. Her love of Ray remains as strong as ever, but she feels she cannot go back to the U.S. Regretfully, she states, "Ray, don't you think I can get along by myself, I have to prove something" (170). She thinks it is best for her husband to be reintegrated in New York's Beat scene: "I thought that Ray would want to go back, and I wasn't ready to go, but I thought it would be good for him, so when I said goodbye to him I thought I was being kind" (183). Ray Bremser returned to New York on the word of a reporter who said the city is safe for him. This turns out to be a lie and he is incarcerated once again for drug and flight charges. Frazer remains in Mexico with her two main lovers, Ernesto, a rich man, who "was the better ball," and Pedrito, aged 23 like herself :

> So I was being influenced on two sides, and took both seriously: Pedrito, who was living the life with me, and Ernesto, actually doing the same, though it was different. [...] I lied to both of them, forgetting the other when I was with one, and a voice in my head told me to go ahead and be savage with all men if I want. *(For Love of Ray:* 179)

After Ray left, Frazer also becomes involved with Mexican lesbians at the S café: "The blond chick would sit next to me, or stand behind me and look over my shoulder, her hand so soft, and hypnotize me with her eyes. I let her kiss me, wondering, and her lips were the softest-sweet kiss [...]" (179-180). In a moment of insight, she yearns to end her prostitution and lead a normal life. Grasping that her life is characterized by lack of love in all of her relationships, she now clearly understands that her "faith in life had begun to fail" (178).

Without Bremser, she is independent. Yet, in comparison to her desperate love efforts in Laredo to see her husband in jail every day, Frazer is now even more wrecked than before. Her hustling and drug addiction have become destructive powers. Being all alone in the huge capital of Mexico, she has no one to protect her. Once, she even uses a switchblade to defend herself after being attacked by a customer who wants to rape her (cf. 182-183). When Frazer's two steady lovers depart, she is left back all alone. "Ernesto Z was saying goodby to me again, and for the last time. [...] just one last fuck Brenda, he said; he couldn't resist me" (185). Her second lover Pedrito departs for Nicaragua. Meanwhile, Ray Bremser writes a threatening letter "demanding that I send him some pot, and for me to follow it immediately or we were through forever; he said this was my last chance". He orders: "You have not got the right to hang me up with your indecision like you did before in Trenton. You must write an immediate and direct note or letter telling me you'll be back in three weeks, on April such-and-such [...]" (183).

Being unsure of whether Ray, who was totally addicted to heroine and cocaine now, was free of law or not, Frazer finally travels back to the United States. She is relieved to be dressed "in blue jeans, going to the village. It felt good to just walk the street again and not worry about who was looking at me or where I was going" (190). Back home, she does not have to change her appearance. Her return to the U.S. is promising, and she vows to make it on her own. Normalcy, however, ends abruptly again. First, she returns to her father's house, then to New York City, where she takes on a more conventional female role. *For Love of Ray* ends like a fairy tale romance. Frazer, walking alone in the Village, sees Bremser magically appearing before her: "I heard my name (I had been walking with my head down, thinking) behind me, hesitantly, sounding familiar. I turned and saw Ray there, as natural as if it were meant to be" (191). Immediately, they are together again. They return to his apartment and there "was not much need to talk, the world was all full of beautiful things to see, I had Ray beside me and I was not lonesome any more" (192). Together, they look at old photographs and new poems he has written. In the original 1969 U.S. version *Troia*, they both get high on amphetamines. Romantically, they come together in "a perfect fuck" (209), and the great love begins anew:

> First we fucked, and I reserved this here out of respect mainly for girls who might get envious and discontented, and say to someone: if they went through that, and the result was that she achieved such a perfect fuck, just that one time (but it didn't stop! oh be cool) then I say it's worth it. It was. *(Troia:* 209)

The British 1971 version *For Love of Ray* leaves out their love making, but the end is also similar to a modern fairy tale in which everything turns out beautifully. Once more, drugs, love, and sex are evoked as a holy trinity, and the two lovers renew their spiritual, seemingly never-ending love. The book's ending represents the classic subordination of the female to the sexual prowess of the male and the promise of eternal love. The narrative self who concludes by finding the perfect "fuck" – like the "Holy Grail" for which the male Beats were questing – has destroyed Frazer's voice of anger that had promised revolution. Frazer eventually gives in, and does not leave the Beat subculture that is so destructive to her. The book's conventional ending is shocking for the reader. After she had survived the miserable time in Mexico, many readers might have been relieved that Bremser finally disappears from the scene. When he reemerges at the end of the book, all illusions are once more shattered. Frazer seems to reflect on her Mexican year from the point of view of other Beat girls and points out that all misery was justified, because she was included in real Beat life. The shocked and confused reader, however, questions her freedom and rebellion.

The strange effects of the memoir's conclusion represent a good example for the immense tension produced in the text by the fact that Ray Bremser is both its first audience and a participant in the events she describes. He treated Frazer much as other Beat men treated women. Even though most male Beat authors had old-fashioned attitudes towards gender roles, they sometimes also offered women insight into life they otherwise would not have gained. Joyce Johnson, for example, is grateful that Kerouac showed her parts of New York's hidden nightlife:

> I remember walking with you at night through the Brooklyn docks and seeing the white steam rising from the ships against the black sky and how beautiful it was and I'd never seen it before – imagine!. [...] You don't know what narrow lives girls have, how few real adventures there are for them; misadventures, yes, like abortions and little men following them in subways, but seldom anything like seeing ships at night. (Johnson. *Door Wide Open:* 42)

Kerouac was influential for Johnson, because she felt safe and free when he was around. Ray Bremser did not represent safety for Brenda Frazer, but – sarcastically speaking and overlooking all the misery he caused her – he did open a door to possibilities she otherwise did not have. Whether her experiences were that enlightening is open to discussion. What cannot be denied is that Bremser is of importance for her coming-of-age as a writer, because as an audience for the book, he also gave her an excuse to write. Anger which would have dissolved their relationship disappears at the end of the memoir. Finally, this costs her not only their romantic attachment, but also the freedom to create.

8.3 Baby Rach

From the beginning onwards, Frazer is over-concerned to negotiate her outlaw status as a U.S. citizen prostituting herself in Mexico with her responsibilities to care for her little baby. She soon sees that it is difficult to fulfill both – being a good mother and "grooving" like males at the same time. Frazer entered the poetry circle around her husband Ray and was fascinated that this particular subculture offered a substitute for the repressive gender codes of the time. Yet, being on the road with an infant on one's lap was more difficult than Frazer might have imagined. Her worries about the health and welfare of "baby Rach" are dominating the first part of the book. Her "Love of Ray," in contrast, only comes second. Apparently, Rachel is Frazer's "handicap," always accompanying her on the road adventure. It is the story of Rachel that best expresses the shifting nature of the book. The first part of the book is reflective history, but further on, Frazer moves from non-fiction to redemptive fiction. Her daughter is an eerie presence throughout the memoir, always the baby Rach, who is uncorrupted and open to natural wonders. The baby is constructed as an innocent version of her mother, a shadow of Frazer herself. The infant is a symbol of her yearnings to create a perfect mother, who she wishes she had been. As long as the baby is part of the story, the Bremsers' survival is guaranteed: "Rachel was one of the keys to our survival in this destitute period – everyone loved her and all we had to say, or not say, to our hosts was, what will happen to the baby – and we were allowed to stay" (32). As Rachel gets skinnier and skinnier from week to week, neighbors also come by to offer food to help support the family: the "[…] poor baby got as skinny as we did almost, pitiful to see" (34), and therefore "Little Mexican chicks knock on our door with plates of some kind of tortilla concoction with tomatoes and onions, they all have different names, depending on how they are cooked, *Panuchos* and *gordas* were the best though" (34-35). Frazer's "head is threatened by the hopelessness of trying to keep alive under these conditions". She is frustrated because naively, she had expected a new world of love with Ray, romance, happiness, and modest wealth after having escaped the U.S. law. Angrily, she shouts out, "Hang on! Where is my romance – where is the total image?" (23).

Rachel's story is tragic, as it also condemns Ray Bremser for eventually convincing Frazer to give up their daughter for adoption, as they are not able to look after her any more. This was an act that Frazer could never forgive him.[76] At the same time, Frazer realizes that she also carries the burden of guilt, because she cannot even cope with her own life, let alone with that of the baby: "Ray is in control I discover later, and I am just a useless wife […]. The baby Rach sleeps next to us on the seat and I am unable to take care of her anymore. Say this is the end" (106). In Book Three, Rachel will be forever lost, and guilt and shame is all that is left for the rest of the book.

---

[76] After having put up Rachel for adoption, Frazer eventually found Rachel years later with the help of a private detective. Their relationship, though, is still strained.

Throughout the memoir, the discrepancy between Frazer's hope for freedom and responsibility towards her child is clearly visible. In her own words, she leads a double/triple life which includes prostitution, being a mother/wife, and poetry:

> The double life I am leading and the two parts yearning toward each other, I wonder, is everything about to fall? Ray tells me to fuck with as much sweetness as he did in Laredo when he was in jail there and I had no money [...] He told me not to be afraid and that I must take care of myself: "so go and get some money to do it" and I did. Or should I say a triple life; there is the life of letters too – those letters in Laredo between us: courage, hope and a dawning of poetry too. *(For Love of Ray:* 55)

When taking the bus to Mexico City, she complains that she is "constantly with the baby on my lap, broken hearted at every spell of crying, the frustration of not being a good mother really – trying to groove, trying to groove under the circumstances" (13). Frazer's language conveys the burdens of the road for bohemian women who are mothers. For many Beat women, pregnancy and motherhood were the consequences of free sex. Despite the many complications of having a baby with her, crossing the border between the U.S. and Mexico brought a new kind of independence from conservative postwar America. *For Love of Ray* enriches the male-centered Beat road tale with domestic aspects and shows how Beat relationships were enemies of women's liberation and sexual independence. Frazer experiences adventures in existential and sexual danger, which deviate from the male road tale by the presence of baby Rach. Having arrived in the glory country, she hopes for tempting new experiences. Yet, she would have never suspected that her road tale would exclude her from the male version of having fun and "kicks". After their daring escape across the border, Ray is the only familiar person Frazer knows. Trying to keep the baby healthy is a crucial factor for Frazer's mental sanity and physical health. When the baby finally breaks away from the family, things deteriorate rapidly.

Even though *For Love of Ray* tries to imitate Kerouac's *On the Road* in language and contents, Frazer clearly wants to break down the prevailing gender roles of the time. She sees being on the road as a chance to do so. In most works by male Beats, the typical road girl was presented as a "chick," an attractive, young, sexually available and, above all, silent ("dumb") female. Throughout *On the Road*, women are often presented as dumb or dull, however, they do not lose attraction for Sal and Dean as sex objects for at least one night: "We picked up two girls, a pretty young blonde and a fat brunette. They were dumb and sullen, but we wanted to make them" (1991: 34). Remi Boncoeur's girl Lee Ann is presented as having "a bad tongue and gave him a calldown every day" (61). According to Sal Paradise, her only intention was to marry a rich man, and there was "hate in her eyes for both of us" (62). Even safer for Sal and Dean Moriarty are Mexican fellahin women, with a few expectations lower on the social scale than the two hobos Sal, who is a college boy, and Dean, who is working class. Rebellious Beat women are soon sent home: Marylou, for example, joins one mad trip with Dean and Sal. Her willingness to break the gendered behavior codes concerning women of the time is not credited, and, indeed, she is dismissed as little more than a sexually attractive, but occasionally dangerous nuisance. In *On the Road*, two completely contrary images of family are being shown. Both

Sal and Dean yearn for domestic emotionality. For the two of them, family means the short-lived moments of closeness and real affection that they are missing when they are having their road kicks. Dean's efforts to care for his family cannot be fulfilled, because responsibility objects to experience. Sal imagines Beat women "spending months of loneliness and womanliness together with, chattering about the madness of the men" (187). But for Camille (Carolyn Cassady), Dean's wife, family is more concrete than Kerouac's clichés. She has to pay the bills, look after the children, and send her husband money by mail.

In *For Love of Ray*, Frazer connects both responsibility and experience. As long as Rachel is part of the family unity, Frazer is able to combine both idealized and practical concepts of family life. Frazer's prostitutional adventures and miseries in MexCity and Veracruz are getting more and more complicated due to Rachel's needs to be fed and taken care of. Diving into the new Veracruz landscape, the sugar fields, "this beautiful land of Veracruz," Frazer imagines to settle down forever, but she also tries to make Rachel comfortable and washes the diapers on the patio. Veracruz represents a hard time for the baby, and Rachel's "sweet little cherub face" soon gets thinner and thinner (20). The Bremsers are not used to the rough Del Norte wind which blows rain under their doors every time it is raining. As a consequence, the "baby sneezes, coughs, gets sick all over every day" (22). In this uncomfortable situation, Frazer dreams of "the stove in Hoboken sending off warmth and expectation of endless comforts" (22). Sleeping on a summertime cot on a tile floor, everything can be heard through the walls of the run-down house where they stay – "including Rachel crying, twenty times in the night, heard but unseen. I go to her in the absence of lights at Ray's orders to shut her up, or alone worried to bother our host and hostess so, I walk up and down for hours – the vigil with Rachel until dawn" (23).

Getting appropriate baby nutrition is a grave problem for the Bremsers, and Rachel's weight loss is wearing them down immensely. Yet, the author also delights in interludes of family togetherness and envies couples who can be both "hip" and "normal". In an interview, she remembers looking up to the lifestyle of Hettie and LeRoi Jones, who were "the mother and father of the literary scene at the time" (Grace: 2000: 125). They managed to combine their Beat life with an everyday life full of normalities: "[…] they were married, they had kids, they were living a normal life; they were very hip, and yet they were paying the bills, which was incomprehensible to me, how could you do both at once?" (126).

Middle class family life according to the Anglo-American domestic ideal of the 1950s is incompatible with the Bremsers' main goals of individual liberation and an alternative rebel lifestyle modeled on the lives of Che Guevara and Fidel Castro. In fact, the 'square' nuclear family was the enemy of experience. No wonder Ray disappears for hours under the pretext of getting money from the post office or stays away for days to write poetry and find new personal kicks. Being on the bus from Mexico City to Veracruz with the baby on her lap, she muses:

> Ah bitter, I was not about to accept with grace my maidenly burdened-by-baby responsibility at this particular time [...] But I go — midway between holding the baby on the eight hour bus trip, the night quickly sets in and I decide to try my seductive powers on N, and [...] did indeed entice his hand where it should have by any standards stayed away from, the baby on my lap. *(For Love of Ray:* 18-19)

Frazer's disappointment about Ray's prevailing gender prejudice is obvious throughout the memoir, but remembering the days in Mexico, the author forgives Bremser and thinks that her frustration towards her husband was unjustified, that he was not alone responsible for the gender restrictions she had to face in their relationship. Despite the anger and frustration she had to go through, Frazer's forgiveness of Ray can be interpreted as an indication of female sacrifice and self-blame, which was typical for the acquiescent subordinate 1950s woman.

Similar to her two contemporaries Joyce Johnson and Hettie Jones, Brenda Frazer creates powerful, eternal images around life, which are dissolved from time and place. Similar to Kerouac's method of sketching, she skillfully visualizes particular Mexican places and people in present tense. "Can you visualize it?," Frazer asks the reader at the beginning of Book Three when telling "we return to our cabin security T.V. dinners and beer and a haphazard Indian blanket to warm up the dream a little chilled from cocaine rages of numbness in the back of my head" (113). Like *Minor Characters*, *For Love of Ray* is like flicking through a photo album; the author zooms in past moments and presents them in present tense. This writing technique of alternating between past Mexican and present New York scenes, of creating powerful images, of zooming in photograph-like recollections is surprisingly similar to other Beat memoirists' writings. Child-care and domestic life are burdensome, but they are not always presented as tiring and shattering. One of the most striking of these zoomed-in passages is Frazer's depiction of a photograph taken on the beach when she is walking sea-shore with baby Rach in her arms.

> We call a photographer to get her and me together at the side of the eastern sea, wash over our feet, and as he focuses a wave comes unexpectedly high to kiss her feet and gets her pure little cunt in a wash of foamy come, the diapers fall about her feet discarded and she looks at the camera man with a grimace of double purity, picture of her infant womanhood. Always pure my muse Rachel [...]. *(For Love of Ray:* 54)

Caring for her child is difficult and exhausting in such a destitute situation. She is aware of being responsible for a helpless infant and tries her best, but she is at the same time unable to care for the child properly, because of her life circumstances full of poverty, violence, and prostitution. In another photo taken on the beach, "Rachel and I sit in a beach chair smiling at each other's smiles, growing smilier with smiling". Defending herself, she asks, "Who says we weren't happy?" (44-45). Frazer's love of Rachel, the act of changing diapers, getting food for the child, or everyday worries about the baby's state of health are examples for her conception of motherhood. In Book One and Two, the family is still united, and so baby Rach's physical presence is in the foreground of the text. When they are finally separated in Book Three, her daughter – "my hip little adventuress so deserving of love and fun" (29) – stays a ghostly presence until the end of the memoir, mirroring Frazer's wish to reunite.

In contrast to Jack Kerouac's clichéd, conservative, and negative conception of family life, Frazer's portrayal of the pleasures of early parenthood correspond to the contemporary suburban, Anglo-American family ideal of the postwar years. Romantically, the author tells about details of their family life after the Bremsers have settled down in a house in Veracruz and have thus created a nuclear family themselves. "It is morning now on Calle Revillagigedo and though the whole of Veracruz is awake, on the move, we in our house emerge into our own self-made world" (35). The baby would greet the morning with "her gurgling goos in the crib alongside us" and spends the next hour "looking at the picture gallery we have made for her out of classical paintings collected from Classicos match boxes". Meanwhile, Frazer goes back "to sleep, next to Ray, oh sweetness of his hand touching my head now, the sun softly rising behind the clouds" (36). This passage is one of the few optimistic scenes in the book. Wanting a perfectly harmonious family life, she envies the Mexican families she sees in Veracruz. She muses about the Mexican way of coping with fear and loss: "Loss of something dear is not a vague unreality that the police will take care of if it is found to be illegal, but something you gotta watch out for yourself […]. Fear and loss causes people to care "for what is most close to them – somehow very real to me – somehow very much more than just the direction of responsibilities" (29). Her "Veracruz mama" (32), mostly called J in the book, which stands for Jovita, becomes Frazer's best friend and Rachel's foster mother. However, when she finds out that J is in contact with a Native Mexican witch who wants to use baby Rach for her Native customs, she ends their relationship. In an interview, she remembers, "When I left Rachel with Jovita and then came back and they had this smoke-filled room and were doing the rituals – that was a different kind of blackness. That was my paranoia against black magic" (Grace: 2004: 125).

Frazer admits that her response is rooted in the general Western prejudice towards dark-skinned exotic people. Actually, the general point of view was that the 1950s isolated nuclear family had to be protected from various political and societal threats, like communism, homosexuals, and other sexual deviants. U.S. postwar society, in general, was characterized by a grave racism against people who looked non-American. In numerous passages throughout the memoir, Frazer's subservience to the dominant U.S. containment culture of the time can be seen. Her female self-sacrifice for the love of her husband, her prejudice and disapproval of homosexuality, and her reinscription of the narrative of whiteness show that she is – even though rebelling against it – a victim of that oppressive culture. In the following part, Frazer's affinity to the containment culture's metanarrative of white supremacy will be discussed in more detail.

8.4 Racism in *For Love of Ray:* Frazer's Kerouacian 'Romantic Primitivism'

For Love of Ray clearly reinscribes the containment narrative of whiteness.[77] The Bremsers' conflicting attitude concerning racial prejudice is shown in several passages throughout the book. In one scene while hiding from the police in Veracruz, the Bremsers enjoy ice cream sodas on a sidewalk café of the Hotel D. "Ray is wearing white trousers and a blue shirt with tails out and tucks and puckers in front of it, he does not look jive like a Mexican," Frazer writes about her husband, "though dressed as they do, he looks like a movie star, and I no doubt too, in the skirt with slits up the side I have premeditatively fashioned to entice eyes, the tightness of it shows the bikini I wear underneath, still wet and full of sand" (45). The Bremsers sees themselves as white expatriate Hollywood movie stars. Life in Mexico is like playing parts in a film where the magnificent film stars are white, surrounded by the dark Mexican fellahin population. Native Mexicans are depicted as "jive" (38, 76) or "phoney" (98, 99); the Bremsers, however, are real white American movie stars. They decide to see *Tarzan and Jane* in the cinema, and – similar to the main protagonists of the film – they have to live far away from home in an exotic jungle of hostile darkness. Just as U.S. popular culture of the time equated white skin with security and dark skin with disorder and chaos, Frazer equates her own image and that of her white, immaculate child with the concept of purity. As the story continues, Frazer frantically tries to maintain Rachel's outstanding whiteness, while the author herself metaphorically loses her whiteness/purity to join the outlaws populating the streets of Veracruz and Mexcity. She realizes that the child's pale skin gives Rachel cultural capital in Mexico: "Rachel greets the morning light squinty-eyed, the babe in all its encompassing beauty and complete expression draws all open hearts to it, an object of worship, our white baby. Moreso later, to my circumstantial chagrin, I find that intrigues of stealth surround the worship of this white baby". Fearing about the baby's security due to its skin color, the author swears, "oh my soul, my Rachel, I will turn black to get you back" (22). Often, Mexican mothers offer to look after the baby in the afternoon or evening, "they had begged to be allowed to take care of her, a thing I couldn't understand yet". According to Frazer's opinion, Mexicans were totally drawn towards the child and "worshipped her because she was so white" (32). Rachel gradually develops into Frazer's "the little me" (19). The baby stands for everything Frazer cannot be or reach herself. In contrast to the pure, untouched child, Frazer loses her symbolic whiteness to hustling and her literal whiteness to the burning Mexican sun. In one scene of the book, Frazer holds Rachel in her hands and they sit down on the beach, but suddenly, a wave reaches the baby's feet and "gets her little pure cunt in a wash of foamy come" (54). Here, Frazer implies that the baby is so pure that even nature is over-enthusiastic about Rachel. Moreover, in

---

[77] See Hemmer, Kurt Richard (2000). „Cowboys Crashing: The Beat Generation and the American Western Outlaw". *Dissertation* Washington State University. 58ff. for a close analysis of the Bremsers' hidden racist attitude towards Mexicans.

Frazer's words, the baby even brings nature to orgasm. Rachel represents everything natural, white, and pure, while her mother gets darker and darker by offering her sexual services under the fiery Mexican sun. She borrows the neighbor's sewing machine and sews a dress that will clearly identify her as a prostitute. Her "suntan is getting very fine and voluptuous which is a help also," because now everyone in the streets clearly sees that she sells her body for money. Ray also likes her dark appearance and says she looks "melon colored" (43). She is shockingly frank about her destitute situation, and even acknowledges that her dark sunburned skin is "impressive in contrast to the yellow sheets" (153). Darkness becomes a symbol for her plight and misery, but through entering the dark, she can experience both kicks and misery. Frazer contradicts herself by, on the one hand, favoring, but on the other hand, refusing the idea of white supremacy that the conservative U.S. containment culture of the time suggested. The paradox is that for her, darkness is indispensable in her dreadful adult world where purity has long been lost, but this darkness has to be kept from "the beautiful blonde American baby" (113). Rachel's whiteness is depicted in an over-romanticized way, and Frazer eventually loses her own whiteness to maintain that of the baby.

Even if Frazer has open prejudice against the Mexican people, she is at the same time wishing to be closely connected with the oppressed indigenous population. In her so-called 'romantic primitivism,' Frazer shares many ideas with Jack Kerouac[78] and the circle around him, who totally overlooked the misery and poverty of the Mexican 'fellahins' by depicting them in an over-romanticized way as authentic, primitive, truly happy, and nature-loving. By bridging the gap between herself and the Native Mexicans, Frazer writes in true Kerouacian tradition. Kerouac embraced Oswald Spengler's notion of the 'fellahin' he described in *The Decline of the West* (1926), and thought he found it realized in Mexico. What had captured his imagination was Spengler's controversial theory that all civilizations inevitably decline and that the apocalypse of Western civilization was close. Spengler talks of three groups in his historical "morphology of peoples": The first stage, the primitive, refers to early stages of culture; the second category includes those imperial cultures that rise to control the historical stage. The 'fellahin' is the third term, and refers to those largely "primitive" groups who are marginalized by "civilization" because of Western predominance, and who remain little changed when the empire is finally completely destroyed (cf. Holton 1999: 57). This new, to his mind better world, however, would finally have to give way to a new emerging civilization which will replace the cultureless fellahin. Spengler builds up an opposition between the "historical peoples, the peoples

---

[78] Similar to her father, Kerouac's daughter Jan also felt a close affinity to Mexico and its people. She went to Mexico in 1967 after visiting her famous father for only the second and last time in her life. There, her child was stillborn. Like her father, she immediately identified with the Native Mexican population. In her autobiographical novel *Baby Driver*, published in 1981, she writes, "A tourist couple had mistaken me for a native. I was flattered" (1998: 4). Even though she was not a criminal fleeing across the border, Jan Kerouac lived as an outlaw much of her life. She joined society's outsiders and happily reports that she worked in a restaurant in Santa Fe, New Mexico, where "Billy the Kid had once washed dishes" (67). Similar to Frazer, she wanted to "groove" with the outlaw men in her life and copy their lifestyle, and like Frazer, she finally became a prostitute in Mexico.

whose existence is world history" and the fellahin, whose lives are post-historical and post-civilization. Whereas the lives of the "civilized" people are full of meaning and depth, legitimated and guaranteed by the imperial culture, "Life as experienced by fellaheen peoples is just a planless happening without a goal wherein occurrences are many, but, in the last analysis, devoid of signification" (Spengler: 1991: 170).

Spengler's pessimistic vision of the world was enormously influential and can be found echoed in many cultural documents of the first half of the 20th century. After the trauma of the Second World War, Kerouac and other Beat writers felt civilization would finally come to an end. This posture manifests itself in his spontaneous prose style and the emphasis on the here and now. Jack Kerouac uses the term 'fellahin' very generally meaning all peoples – in North America and throughout the world – who he thought to be situated outside the structures and categories of modern Western life. Throughout his works, his fellahin presentations are out of touch with reality. For example, Kerouac writes of the fellahin as the "basic primitive, wailing humanity that stretches in a belt around the equatorial belly of the world from Malaya to India to Arabia to Morocco to Mexico to Polynesia to Thailand, and so on" (1991: 280). He also speaks of the music of the fellahin as "the world beat" (287). Kerouac began thinking of Mexico as the land of the fellahin that would survive the collapse of Western civilization. William Burroughs was worried about his friend, who was romanticizing the country too naively according to his opinion. He reminded Kerouac that "Mexico is not simple or gay or idyllic. It is nothing like a French Canadian naborhood [sic]. [...] Mexico is sinister and gloomy and chaotic with the special chaos of a dream. I like it myself, but it isn't everybody's taste, and don't expect to find anything like Lowell down here" (Burroughs: 1994: 91). Influenced by Burroughs and Ginsberg, Kerouac also traveled to Mexico several times. Enthusiastic about the "dark, barefoot Native Mexicans who walked the streets, their heads hung down, in silent prayer, as they walked into the churches of Roman Catholicism," many novels and short stories depict the lives of Mexico's fellahin people (Olvera: 1991: 12).

Similar to Brenda Frazer in *For Love of Ray*, Sal Paradise also has identification problems while he is in Mexico. Both Frazer and Kerouac share implied racist attitudes concerning Mexicans, who are seen as inferior due to their skin color. In *On the Road*, a balance is achieved by Sal's being perceived as "Mexican" in the United States, but as "white" in Mexico. When in California picking cotton with his "Mexican girl" Terry, Sal does not see the unromantic reality of a life in poverty. He is convinced that he is Mexican, but in Mexico such an approach is not useful. To identify with the marginalized Mexican people is no longer necessary for Sal, because in a fellahin nation, Americans have to demonstrate strength in order to show their request to conquer the Wild West.

Frazer's 'primitive romanticism,' her supremacist attitude towards racial minorities, and her racial prejudice are amazingly similar to Kerouac's attitudes. Frazer, who regretfully faces the Americanization of Mexico, is comforted by her belief in an eventual "final revolution in Mexico City, the Indian overthrow" (186). Her wish to be part of this breakdown of established orders mirrors

Kerouac's assumption that the Beat Generation is definitely an "Indian Uprising" (Kerouac: 1993: 51). For both authors, it is important to be part of the indigenous population, which survives in the end. Both Sal Paradise and Brenda Frazer imagine themselves as Mexicans. "They thought I was a Mexican, of course, and in a way I am," Sal says in *On the Road*. Feeling to be part of the fellahin, he imagines, "I was a man of the earth, precisely as I had dreamed I would be" (1991: 97). The similarity to Frazer's accounts is striking: She aims "to make some claim to Indian heritage" (187). "I know that I am as much Mexican as I am New Yorker or even spade, Negro, Veracruzana, I have undergone the metamorphosis complete and my heart is warm and happy," she writes about her transformation from white to dark (40).

Sal Paradise's and Brenda Frazer's ways cross in a border city called Laredo. Frazer comes there, because her husband is imprisoned. In Laredo, "the end of America," Sal gets the feeling that rules and order are totally falling away; the country is free of authoritarian and hierarchical structures, and every person is free to choose one's own fate. Yet, Sal's exploration of Mexico is safe, because as an American, he finds himself in social and financial security. Brenda Frazer, in contrast, is not safe in Mexico, because she has no money, a baby on her lap, and she is a woman. She cannot call her mother to send money, because she gets no support from her side of her family. Sal comes to the conclusion: "For when destruction comes to the world of 'history' and the Apocalypse of the Fellahin returns once more as so many times before, people will stare with the same eyes from the caves of Mexico as well as from the caves of Bali, where it all began and where Adam was suckled and taught to know" (280-281). Similarly, Brenda Frazer is also convinced that only the Native fellahin peoples will eventually survive when Western civilization declines. For her, Mexico City is a terrible "place of germ nurture". The only ones who are immune against various germs are the Native Mexicans: "Flu germs once set loose into that air spread in hopelessness of complete take over, and everybody gets sick and stays that way, except for the Indians, who have some built in resistance – that had become traditional by killing off the unfit" (1971: 180). In true male Beats' fashion, Frazer believes that the fellahin will survive destruction.

While Kerouac talks of Indians' "primitive, wailing humanity," Frazer uses similar words to describe the Native Mexicans in Acapulco, where she visits her sister.

> I delight in the Indians must live somewhere and I find them though the way is tortured and hidden on secret hillside entrances. I walk up gutters of rainflow from impoverished backyards over someone living above to another chicken-coop up higher – a troop of little boys follows me – the gringa is better known here than any other city in the country [...]. *(For Love of Ray:* 51)

Frazer does not only copy Kerouac's style, but she also ignores the social realities of many poverty-stricken Mexicans. She writes: "I feel a great compassion and want to live in one of those hillside houses of wicker branches propping someone precariously on his neighbor – and once or twice I see a house so ghettoed isolate that it would be like a Chinese puzzle to gain entrance" (51). The reality of living in a wicker branch shack is probably not as romantic as it might seem. Furthermore, Frazer compares the Native fellahin Mexicans, whom she adores, with the American Spanish, whom she detests: "I delight in glee in the Indians all around the hill […] give it back to yourselves Indians! It is as easy as that – how I hate the American Spanish" (51-52). Several times throughout the book, she speaks of the incorruptness and beauty of the "barefoot Indians," who are the only ones who know about the essence of life. Immersing in stereotyped assumptions, the narrator in *On the Road* shares Frazer's views:

> What a contrast between the well-clad, reading, writing, thinking American, with a watch, a pencil, and a bill of exchange in his pocket, and the naked New Zealander, whose property is a club, a spear, a mat, and an undivided twentieth of a shed to sleep under! But compare the health of the two men, and you shall see that the white man has lost his aboriginal strength. If the travelers tell us truly, strike the savage with a broad axe, and in a day or two the flesh shall unite and heal as if you struck the blow into soft pitch, and the same blow shall send the white to his grave. *(On the Road:* 279)

Being black and savage are uncorrupted human conditions, but being white finally leads to decline and a breakdown of the established order.

In *For Love of Ray*, Native Mexicans and Americans are similarly presented in stark contrast to each other. For Frazer, the fellahin population is natural and authentic, while she gradually starts to hate all Americans and the United States. Frazer does not want to sell her body to Americans on Mexican streets and states, "everyone on the streets is busy hustling the Americans and I am not interested or able to try them yet, (my prejudices)" (95). While her husband Ray is in jail on the U.S. side of a town called Laredo, Texas, Frazer feels safer to stay in a hotel on the Mexican side called Nuevo Laredo, because she fears the American police and legal system. For her, "Texas is the most vicious atmosphere I have ever suffered" (98). Frazer's views are that whites and especially the United States are decadent, whereas Native Mexicans stand for "the Indian continuation of life" (97). The author also distinguishes between the Native Mexicans and the Spanish Mexicans who are a dying society for her. She confesses, "how I hate the American Spanish" (52). In the past, "Mexcity is a nightmare of the dream it must have been of lakes and straight solid standing rock houses simple with the primal worshipping fervor". However, "it has now become Spanish trash and dust and shame" (61). Additionally, she gets angry about Mexicans who "are almost Americans," who have "sold out to the States, and retain none of their heritage" (97). Another scene in which she angrily shows her affinity towards Native Mexicans is how she reacts towards an arrogant Spanish Mexican customer named Ernesto Z: "[…] one Indian footstep on those hills out there was worth more than all his Spano-Mexican properties multiplied by years of tradition" (185).

When reading the works of Kerouac and Frazer, it becomes clear that both are companions in their outlaw status. Both escaped the American white middle class in search of a non-conformity, which included drugs, adventures, and sexual deviation. To join the fellahin population of Mexico, the two authors have to become outlaws. They are able to imagine an alliance with oppressed natives living in poverty by putting themselves into positions that are scorned by the dominant containment culture. So,

Frazer literally becomes an outlaw by joining her criminal husband when escaping the U.S., while Sal Paradise only imagines himself to be one. "This road," he tells Dean, "is also the route of old American outlaws who used to skip over the border and go down to old Monterey, so if you'll look out on that graying desert and picture the ghost of old Tombstone hellcat making his lonely exile gallop into the unknown" (1991: 276-277). Sal ponders over his connection with American outlaws, while he is driving "beyond where the outlaws went" (279) with Dean. Together, both Sal and Frazer disappointedly realize that their status as outlaws is not merely pleasant, but hard and shattering. Sal, as a male hedonistic macho, is much better off than Frazer, even though he is left behind sick and lonely by Dean Moriarty. With the help of his aunt, he gets home safely. Frazer, in contrast, does not have the chance to call her mother for help and money. Her family falls apart, and prostitution and hallucinogenics almost drive her into suicide.

In a 1999 interview, Frazer reflects on the ambiguities of her views of dark-skinned Mexicans. She believed she had achieved empathy, first, because as a light-skinned U.S. citizen, she was part of a minority, and second, because she lived a life in poverty. She was linked to the Mexican people who "are so open to their poverty, or so open to the oppression of being down-trodden". She identified with the poverty in the country and points out that she had gradually become Mexican and black: "That's what I was identifying with, that darkness in myself, as, okay, now the worst has happened to me, yet these people can accept me. And being a prostitute in Mexico, I was accepted" (Grace: 2004: 124). On the one hand, Frazer was closely connected to the Mexican people by sharing their oppression. On the other hand, unlike white, male Beat writers who saw both the oppression of African Americans and women only as a mirror for their own sense of alienation, Frazer is much more honest and sensitive about her own prejudice. Even though Frazer yearns to spiritually unite with the Native Mexican population, she is unsuccessful in the end. She cannot bridge the gap between herself and the fellahin, due to the Kerouacian 'romantic primitivism' she embraces.

8.5 Narrative Devices, Language, and Categorization

For Love of Ray is a personal and highly confessional memoir that records Frazer's shattering experiences in Mexico. The title of the American version, *Troia: Mexican Memoirs*, is misleading, because Frazer obviously confuses her 'memoirs' with 'the memoir'. This is probably due to the fact that in the 1960s, the literary memoir was not that popular as it is today. According to Judith Barrington, the term 'memoirs' is used to describe autobiographical writings which are more extensive in time and text than the shorter literary 'memoir'. These 'memoirs,' generally depicting the lives of famous people, deal with several different aspects of a life story and do not only choose one particular topic, as the 'memoir' does. The boundaries between these two genres, however, have not been clearly delineated so far. Frequently, a book might be subtitled 'a memoir' when it would rather fit under the heading of 'memoirs' or 'autobiography,' if one strictly considers the boundaries of autobiographical genres (cf. 2002: 32ff.). Nancy Grace points out that "The memoir [...] is a fitting form for narratives about Beat women's associations with particular men or participation in the Beat historical moment. [...] The memoir, focused on a slice of one's life rather than the full sweep, provides a manageable temporal space within which to reflect" (2002: 142). Frazer's open and honest memoir consists of intimate, confessional "books" that shift between past tense scenes being zoomed in, flashbacks, and retrospective insight. She tells her story like it is, without covering up the truth. She frankly depicts the hunger and poverty she had to suffer not to arouse pity, but to represent an accurate experience.

Frazer's distressing story is told with little conventional narrative structure and context. The text is uneven, chaotic, elliptical, and shockingly confessional. As historicity is completely missing, the reader cannot identify the text's validity. Frazer does not mention the exact year/s she writes about. The story does not place the self in a historical setting, and so it is difficult for the reader to find a context and perspective for the story. In the text, there are only tracks of linearity. The narrative relies on the free movement of mind through Frazer's memory and ambiguous feelings, which result in surrealism and fragmentation. Her chapters, called "books," but also singular paragraphs, begin in medias res: The author leads the reader immediately into the center of the story. The narrative starts in the middle of what is happening instead of from its beginning. Frazer consciously uses this method in order to take away emotionality:

> "Isn't it funny how unemotional it all becomes if you tell the ending first, and then tell it again? Actually I have done no more than set it all up so that I can knock it down at my will. I am a great believer in self-determination, so if I sometimes seem flippant it is because I ascribe little importance any more to external events for I am involved in the personal handling of them – these experiences, as my life, have heightened my abilities of calculation. *(For Love of Ray:* 53)

In the story, time shifts are frequent even within paragraphs and sentences, just as memory moves from one moment to the other. Frazer's narrative voice frequently repositions itself, breaking the illusion of permanence, reliability, narrative consistency, and character development. Especially in Book Three and Four, the reader is hardly able to follow Frazer's quick moves from one memory to the other. Memories seem to pop up in her mind, and she is unable to categorize them in terms of time and place. One passage in the book which clearly illustrates Frazer's non-linearity is when she runs back home after having been hit by a customer. Ray grabs a knife and goes looking for the man. She writes, "so it was only another day, a bad one, I tell myself that this is a tough business, and should have expected as much". What follows is confusing for the reader. Without linking the scenes, she continues,

> Play me a danzon – flute lighted thump the Indian heart trip light across the snake-veiled dance floor. An Indian whore, her hair braided with ribbons and runs in her stockings, red shoes – the taxi cab drivers loves her – she only costs five pesos.
> But I am getting ahead of my story and run the risk of telling various endings first and never getting back to the middle, leaving it like that. Excuse my timeless

> sentences, I want to experience it all over again, so take it on me to flash back again as necessary. *(For Love of Ray:* 42)

Another timeless, strange, and endless scene happens in a hotel in Fort Worth, Texas. Frazer tells that Rachel is sleeping on the floor while the Bremsers "arranged pornographic sessions of getting together again". Suddenly, she changes the topic abruptly: "Go back. We both immediately want to go back. My urge is to go back without delay and my first words to Ray when he is out of the Webb Country jail are that I would like to take him to Nuevo Laredo and show him what a real border town is" (107). The reader is left uncertain about the chronology of the events. Throughout the book, Ray Bremser appears as a ghost-like, transparent figure, sliding between reality and the shadowy world of fiction. He fulfills two roles: He is, on the one hand, the present tense, second-person "you" that Frazer addresses, and on the other hand, a companion of the past. Like Bremser, figures are continuously floating in and out of the text without explanation. Short-lived, seemingly unimportant "apparitions" are her sister, mother, father, and numerous other people identified only by their first name or an initial letter. Using the first name only, however, is often typical for life writing in order to protect both the referent and the author. Frazer depicts short interactions with these persons, but as fast as they have turned up, they vanish forever. After their arrival, they, for example, stay with N and his wife B for a while. Other people are B, the cop, and M, a non-identified woman. The reader is often confused due to the many initial letters which occur: "One day N went down to the Museum to see R, (his regular jaunt,) and comes back with news of a crazy redheaded Mexican who speaks English and is great. Later to be known as L, he arrives minutes behind N, and we see him coming from blocks away" (25). Frazer is secretive about all these people, and the reader is even more confused, as L and R turn up for the first time in the book. The only longer relationship Frazer develops is with her "Veracruz Mama" J. She, too, only gets an initial letter which hides her identity. For Frazer, her American family is unimportant. The only purpose of including her parents and sister is their role of historical referents. They are responsible for anchoring her story in history, and they are to confirm that her story is a truthful account. But ironically, they are given no narrative attention.

The narrative devices used in the text in order to manipulate time result in a dehistoricized memoir. The story gradually becomes a dreamlike reality in which temporality does not exist or is even erased. Frazer's memoir is subversive, because life writing claims serving history as its major function. *For Love of Ray* is a memoir by its own definition, but Frazer breaks the categorizations of "memoir" as a subgenre of autobiography. For her, time, space, and people are mixed up and spiral away from the events the book records. Frazer's account is not an easy read as her long, complex, contorted sentences with their distorted syntax remind the reader of time travel. Her Kerouacian spontaneous style and the immediacy of her memory leave the reader breathless, as in the following example:

> The trip – maroon bus awaits us beside the low immigration building, near the broken-down bridge – beer cans clatter in the dusty road; afternoon no sunlight but the approaching lowering clouds of a thunderstorm spreading out over the sky into gray vastness of a depressing standstill underneath any tree; lonely your reality here

in Matamoros, the streets which carry through the center of town growing in importance to the four central parallels which cut out the square of the plaza, where afternoon bistek eaters and shoe-shine boys eye each other from across the unpaved streets [...]. *(For Love of Ray:* 14)

Frazer's imagination is so enormous that she can easily leave aside the daily drudgery and misery by integrating nature and the beauty of the landscape into her own vision of the cosmos. Driving through innumerous Mexican towns – Padilla, Guemez, Ciudad Victoria – they approach Mexico City: "I look out and God drops from his hand the myriad stars and constellations I have never seen before, plumb to the horizon flat landed out beneath the giant horoscopic screen of Mexican heaven" (15). Her visionary power enables her to focus on the smallest details of our world. She does not only focus on metaphysical elements (myriad stars, the giant screen of Mexican heaven), but is also very skillful in depicting mundane, every-day details, like diapers or leg cramps. Several times throughout the book, she asks Ray, as her primary audience: "Can you visualize it?" (113). Without knowing it at the beginning, she was intentionally copying Jack Kerouac's method of sketching: He set an object before the mind and drew it with words through concentration and visualization. Like Kerouac, she is an expert in zooming in and visualizing certain objects, but her expression is female experience. In an interview, she analyzes her own way of writing:

> It was copying, but it's different from sitting down and copy book copying. It's more like what you hear changes the way you think and the way you speak. The way he, Kerouac, fits words together – the sweetness of it, the way things expand when you look at it. I tried to keep those things in mind [...] If I sound like Kerouac, it's because I tried to. I read him while I was writing, just like I listened to Bessie Smith. I think it is in Dr. Sax that he talks about looking at the grain of the wood in the stairway of a porch of the house where he grew up. A way of concentrating, visualizing [...] I obeyed him. (Grace. *Breaking the Rule of Cool:* 129)

Frazer's world is full of surreal and strange images: She talks of jade earrings, gaucho pants, Coca-Cola, chicken sandwiches, waterfalls, baby food, and wet diapers. Her prose implies that she comprehends the essence and meaning of life. Similarly to Kerouac, her language moves toward the sublime, and constantly links two worlds, the existential and the eternal. Through life writing, she aims to record and reflect on her experiences, but at the same time she moves beyond history and removes time. Frazer follows the Beat aesthetics of immersion in memory and imagination. This exemplifies her intention to use language to connect, to escape, and to transform – ambitions that evolved from her imitation of Kerouac's methods for composing prose and poetry.

For Love of Ray is a grotesque, horrifying story that has the effects of a surreal horror trip. Frazer's nightmare is a useful tool in order to confront the events and emotions of this particular time, especially when she tries to describe how she must use her body to trigger her self-emancipation. One of the most shocking scenes of the book, which is also among the most surreal ones, is her account of an abortion she was forced to undergo. When she realizes she is pregnant, she has already made up her mind: "I didn't want anything growing in me that might threaten to bring another beauty such as

Rachel into a sordid no-hope scene of life such as this we were going through". The surrealism of the passage is achieved by the placement of the scene in the midst of a series of tiresome and bored descriptions of having sex with her customers. The abortion is successful, but while she is still under anesthetic, Frazer has feverish nightmares, feeling the impact of her decision in full force. She gets lost in frightening dreams and is about to vomit: "I woke through horrifying dreams later, through memories of retching and trying not to. I cried, pleaded the nurse to tell me it was done. Yes, she said, and pulled ten yards of bloody gauze out of my cramping womb". When the doctor shows her a piece of the baby's vertebra to demonstrate that the fetus was already well developed, Frazer is so shocked that she runs screaming out of the room: "He started being very erudite, and held a section of vertebrate up in front of my face to indicate to me by size that the baby was two months developed". Back home in the hotel, when she wants to talk about the abortion, she writes, "Ray taught me to forget about it" (156). Frazer's surreal play of images shows what is going on in her most intimate, emotional, and interior world.

In terms of defining autobiographical subgenres, *For Love of Ray* contains features of a therapeutic memoir. Second, the memoir is a Beat outlaw road tale with an "escape-to-Mexico" theme in its center. Third, the work also echoes issues of second wave feminism through its critique of patriarchy and its degrading effects on women. Forth, Frazer clearly disfigures the codes of traditional pornographic writings.

Writing has a therapeutic purpose for Frazer's fragmented "I" that suffers from many cracks on different levels. Even though writer Dick Francis used the famous saying "Writing for therapy is usually bad writing," writing becomes synonymous with healing within Frazer's tragic context. Certainly the act of writing autobiography is a road to self-discovery, but the road does not end there. Wendy Rawlings describes the therapeutic effects of life writing as follows:

> The therapeutic effects of writing might indeed be a welcome by-product of writing memoir, but that personal catharsis should never be the primary intent. Therapeutic effects are the side trips off the main road. The destination that must always be kept in mind, however, is the reader. (Rawlings. "Just Beneath my Skin: Autobiography and Self-Discovery": 184)

For Frazer, writing down her misery leads to a personal catharsis, which is her primary aim, while the reader is being rejected. Literary critic Judith Herman analyzes the effects of trauma on the process of writing. The writer who has experienced traumatic events must come to terms with how the trauma has fragmented her/his life. The memoirist gradually starts to create meaning-making schemas which help to articulate what has happened. In trauma research, it is generally acknowledged that symptoms like numbing, dissociation, denial, or intrusive images, thoughts, and emotions complicate the process of remembering and reconstructing the past. The traumatized writer tries to analyze the fragmentation that results from the trauma, and to give meaning to what happened, but the responses often gravely influence the skill to reconstruct the past. When writing down their experiences, the traumatized person – especially when being abused – might

> [...] experience *confusion* concerning how to make sense of abusive treatment from a loved one, *surprise* at her own coping strategies which may include acquiescence, retaliation, manipulation, or substance abuse, *shame and guilt* over perceptions of "participating" in the abusive relationship, *lack of confidence in her perceptions of reality* which are often called into question by the abuser and others, and a *shattering of fundamental beliefs* about herself, loved ones, security, meaningfulness of life, personal autonomy, physical integrity, predictability of the world, and the ability to have some control over herself.[79]

Taking into consideration these categorizations, *For Love of Ray* can clearly be called a therapeutic memoir. Frazer experiences confusion, which also manifests itself in her chaotic, unchronological writing, and surprise about her strength and will to survive ("I have succeeded in taking care of business," 96). She also feels shame and guilt about both her profession as a prostitute and not being able to provide a good life for her family ("I am so close to the brink of being ashamed," 97). Her perceptions of reality are often doubted by Ray and others, and finally, her fundamental beliefs in love, freedom, and independence are totally shattered.

Even though Frazer sees herself as a revolutionary, her rebel stance is limited in what she desires to change. She identifies with revolutionaries and is enthusiastic when she learns that one of her customers knew Pancho Villa, a Mexican Robin Hood figure, personally. She is also influenced by David Alfaro Siqueiros, a painter and anti-fascist revolutionary, or Fidel Castro and Che Guevara. Despite her being affiliated with the revolutionary cause, today's reader does not consider her a revolutionary. Being in favor of political anarchy, she clearly achieves anarchy in her own life, but she loses the fight to gain independence and control over herself. Nevertheless, her book is rebellious and subversive if seen in the face of the repressing U.S. containment culture of the time.

For Love of Ray is a road tale, or rather road memoir, written from a uniquely female perspective. The work is a Beat outlaw memoir with an "escape-to-Mexico" theme at its center. Almost four decades after the book was published, Frazer remembers, "the exact term we used in describing our alienated condition in Mexico was 'fugitives from justice' or 'desperados'" (Hemmer: 2000: 45). By describing her life as an outlaw in Mexico, Frazer follows the tradition of leaving the American legal system behind. Fleeing the country, many Beat icons remained in Mexico until they were safe again. Frazer's theme of escaping to Mexico is omnipresent in U.S. popular culture. Even though the United States are often referred to as the "land of the free," Mexico has always been a destination promising independence and kicks. In popular media, particularly in Hollywood, Mexico is often presented as the ideal destination for U.S. fugitives from justice. In Jim McBride's *Breathless* (1983), for example, the

---

[79] Broin, Valerie E. (2001). "Standing in the Way of Truth: Understanding Narratives of Domestic Violence". *International Journal of Philosophical Practice.* August 29, 2006. http://web.csustan.edu/Philosophy/Data/Broin/Standing.html

main protagonist is an outsider, Jesse Lujack (Richard Gere), who tries to flee across the border to Mexico with a girl named Monica (Valérie Kaprisky), after having killed a cop. In *Thelma and Louise* (1991), directed by Ridley Scott, Susan Sarandon and Geena Davis escape to Mexico, after Louise killed a man who had tried to rape Thelma. In *The Shawshank Redemption* (1994), Andy Dufresne (Tim Robbins) flees across the border after breaking out of jail by crawling through a tunnel dug by himself over the years.

Literary critic Drewey Wayne Gunn argues that the writers of the Beat Generation formed the only noteworthy group of English speaking writers who lived and worked together in Mexico (cf. 1974: 229). Yet Mexico has always attracted writers and artist from all over the world. Same as D. H. Lawrence, Hart Crane was enthusiastic about the country. He was portrayed by the famous Mexican muralist David Alfaro Siqueiros and committed suicide while returning from Mexico. In *Another Mexico* (1939), Graham Greene wrote about the differences when crossing the border:

> Over there everything is going to be different; life is never going to be quite the same again after your passport has been stamped and you find yourself speechless among the money changers. The man seeking scenery imagines strange woods and unheard-of mountains; the romantic believes that the women over the border will be more beautiful and complaisant than those at home; the unhappy man imagines at least a different hell; the suicidal traveler expects the death he never finds. The atmosphere of the border – it is like starting over again [...]. (Hemmer. *Cowboys Crashing:* 38)

In his short biographical abstract of Frazer, editor Michael Perkins euphemistically writes the following about Frazer's road tale: "In it, she places herself on the side of the outlaw, not simply because her husband was an outlaw, but because – through her own daily adventures – she learned the hard way that living outside the law was the only honesty that was left to her, the only grace" (1983: 35). Frazer's road story explores the possibilities a road adventure can represent for women: laws are made by men, and women are mainly regarded as sexual objects. In *For Love of Ray*, Frazer criticizes the conservative sexual politics which is also prevalent in her circle of friends. Being married with Bremser differs only little from being a prostitute: Both Bremser and her customers exchange sexual service for material support. The memoir suggests that for female Beats who enjoy their sexual freedom, the road is not synonymous with sexual kicks, but stands for exploitation, degradation, and abortions. With its critique of the hipster marriage and its deconstruction of sexual politics of the road, the narrative modifies traditional Beat literature enormously. Seen from this perspective, *For Love of Ray* is clearly a forerunner of second wave feminism, which tried to foster a common female identity. At a closer look, the work echoes the most uncompromising manifestos of second wave feminism, such as The S.C.U.M. Manifesto of 1967[80], W.I.T.C.H. of 1968[81], or THE FEMINISTS v. THE

---

[80] Valerie Solanas' "SCUM Manifesto" (Society for Cutting Up Men Manifesto) was written in 1967 and published in 1968. In it, a violent anarchic revolution is propagated in order to create an all-female society. Solanas was also charged with the attempted murder of Andy Warhol in the same year (charges of attempted murder, assault, and illegal possession of a firearm). See Solanas, Valerie "The SCUM Manifesto". *Gifts of Speech*. September 3, 2006. http://gos.sbc.edu/s/solanas.html

MARRIAGE LICENCE[82], which sparked off controversies throughout Western Europe and the U.S. *Troia/For Love of Ray* was published in the midst of the hippie-counterculture, a period characterized by increased feminist activity.

Summarizing, the work is a road memoir, written for therapeutic purposes in the wake of second wave feminism. Yet, some literary critics might also argue that *For Love of Ray* is clearly a pornographic memoir, as it includes masses of explicit sex scenes which are depicted in rich detail. Etymologically, 'pornography' comes from the Greek word *pornographos*, literally "writing about prostitutes". To devalue the book simply as pornography, however, would be to overlook the text's cultural struggles, which openly denounce the dominant containment culture.

According to Robin West, pornography as a literary genre has three major aims. First, pornography is an aid to sexual pleasure and satisfies a sexual interest. Second, pornography has a commercial nature, as it is a commercial product which is produced, bought, and sold on the market. Third, pornography is offensive and an assault on traditionally accepted values of sexual virtue (cf. 1987: 682). Two of West's categories can be applied to Frazer's memoir: First, the narrative satisfies Ray Bremser's sexual interests when the married couple is separated from each other while he is in jail. And second, the work assaults all sexual virtues of America's postwar containment culture that implicated female sexual sacrifice and domestic security. In her memoir, Frazer manipulates the codes of pornography. By doing so, the book becomes a commentary on discourses of containment culture that she tries to resist, even if they influence her behavior. Throughout the memoir, Frazer's style is openly pornographic when describing sex acts with her clients. The following passage illustrates Frazer's explicitness. She writes, "I am prone on the bed caught in my own snares,"

> – big daddy (no, little daddy in this case) wants to do well by me, instructs me to relax on the bed while he goes over me, wants to bring it all out it is apparent – he is beside me feeling my drunkenness in every direction, no more mutual contact at first than a reassuring kiss, then I am to be aroused, I am felt and played with, tantalized, my movements do not yet betray what I am thinking as I try to keep still, it is not right that I should give in quick or easy, stem the flood rising, he goes down on me finally and I give way, the true me comes out and we are in it, fucking uncontrollably. I outdo myself and in the end it is drawn between us excelling the other – then having let go too much of what I am, I am called upon (surely discreetly) to go down on him, guess what is beckoning, I am ready to stop and leave at this point, but what I am being paid for after all, 300 pesos is enough and I have certainly been courted, besides in fucking I guess I always give away my true nature, once having let go completely I am somewhat ashamed at enjoying what I am paid for, enjoying it immensely at times and when I don't I put on a good enough show so that none would ever know – I am able to close my eyes and dream myself alone – so I do it, but not for long – he finds it unbearably pleasurable and we go to take a shower – he hangs ecstatically from the shower knobs – then for a cool refreshed fuck, the last one obviously, he is exhausted, he sleeps while I clean up alone in the bathroom [...]. *(For Love of Ray:* 48-49)

---

[81] W.I.T.C.H. is an American socialist feminist organization formed in 1968.
[82] 'The Feminists' was a group of radical feminists in the late 1960s and early 1970s who protested against the marriage contract, which would only strengthen patriarchal systems. Inequalities between men and women could only be cleared away if marriages are dissolved. For more information see Echols, Alice (1989). *Daring to Be Bad: Radical Feminism in America, 1967–1975.* Minneapolis: University of Minnesota Press.

Describing this sexually explicit experience, Frazer quite frankly includes her feeling of shame over finding pleasure in her work. In *Sade/Fourier/Loyola*, Roland Barthes argues, "there is no language site outside bourgeois ideology: our language comes from it, returns to it, remains closed up in it. The only possible rejoinder is neither confrontation nor destruction, but only theft: fragment the old text of culture, science, literature, and change its features according to formulae of disguise, as one disguises stolen goods" (Hemmer: 2000: 48). Frazer tries to oppose bourgeois ideology and therefore uses the language of pornography. Similar to the Marquis de Sade, she hides the rebellious aims of her book. Barthes asks, "Does the best of subversions not consist in disfiguring codes, not in destroying them?" (49). *For Love of Ray* is a good example of how the code of pornographic writing is disfigured. By doing so, Frazer can now express her conflicting attitude concerning U.S. popular culture of the time. The memoir's explicit sexual scenes should not be read as obscene pornography, but as attempts to affirm her female sexuality. Even though Frazer is abused, battered, and cannot liberate herself as a woman, she tries to break down the burdens of sexual constraint and patriarchy.

In *For Love of Ray*, Frazer employs various languages: Often, her depictions of places and landscapes are beautifully poetic. When writing about having sex with customers, however, her words are unreserved, licentious, and pornographic. Her language use also shows her roots in the dominant U.S. containment culture of the time: First, Frazer is often openly racist. Whiteness is superior to darkness/blackness for her. While Mexicans are often depicted as phony and hostile due to their skin color, her white baby is worshipped because of its pure, pale body. Second, Frazer's language reveals that her fear of homosexuality is deeply rooted. She is openly discriminating homosexuals. Her homophobia is only one of her reinscriptions of the contemporary American containment culture. Frazer is drawn towards her husband because of her heterosexuality. In contrast, dark-skinned Mexicans are often referred to as "fags". She clearly shows her aversion through her pejorative language. By calling Mexican men homosexuals, she adjusts herself to the typical containment rhetoric of the time: Heterosexuality was associated with order and discipline, whereas homosexuality was frowned upon as it stood for deviance, instability, and weakness. This 'homosexual degeneracy' was seen as a threat of national security in the times of the Cold War. "Armed with this questionable logic, anticommunists turned their wrath on homosexuals," Elaine Tyler May writes (1988: 94). Similar to the McCarthyist rhetoric, Frazer views heterosexuality as superior to homosexuality. Being openly homophobic, she calls the men who laugh at her when she loses her wedding ring "Mexican faggots" (44), observes "faggots wrestling in their sandy suntan" (44), and says that two men who were involved in the "gangbang" scene "looked to be a little faggish" (64). For her, a police man customer who likes anal stimulation has "a definite streak of what I immediately term as fag" (75). She refers to a male secretary of one of her pimps as a "faggot" (91), and about an older-looking client she writes, "I remember he was a creepy fifty odd short old man fag-looking type who fucked like a satyr" (99). In a letter to her husband, she writes that a police man she sees in front of the prison is "obviously a repressed homosexual" (103), and a client is described as "a small faggish forty year old who was up on some social hip I didn't understand" (133). Ernesto, her lover, "had escaped the threatening fag element by throwing himself so fully into degeneracy that it didn't do much good to suspect him of anything" (179). Frazer also uses the stigma of homosexuality against her sister[83] who she thinks "is frigid to a point bordering lesbianism" (149) – despite the fact that she admits being captivated when a lesbian gives her "the softest-sweet kiss" (179). Her pejorative homosexual references can be found everywhere in the memoir. One revealing scene that might be useful to understand her fear of homosexuality is when she refuses to have anal sex with a man. "Later with my pimp O," she writes, "I got so I dug it, pretending I was getting back at Ray for his homosexual jail experiences" (148). Her inability to contain Ray's sexuality leaves her frustrated: Ray "gets curious and bugs me with questions regarding his untested homosexuality – which I start to think has something to do with why we aren't fucking any more" (159). Frantically trying to please Bremser, Frazer paradoxically violates and embraces the containment culture simultaneously: She affirms her female sexuality while sacrificing it for the benefit of her husband.

8.6 Drugs, Sex, and the Bremsers' Spiritual Love

It is no secret that drugs were a hallmark of both female and male Beat experience. Diane di Prima and Hettie Jones enjoyed smoking marijuana in huge quantities, but only sometimes immersed themselves in artificial drugs. Joyce Johnson, in contrast, was only involved with drugs during her affair with Kerouac. While these female Beats rejected hard drugs, Brenda Frazer succumbed to the temptations of everything the market had to offer: Heroin, peyote, marijuana, magic mushrooms, amphetamines, and later on LSD and cocaine.

Generally, the Beats used a huge variety of mind and mood altering substances which symbolized rebellion and disassociation. They turned to drugs because they saw them as a means of fleeing the banality of conservative American cultural life and gaining access to a new level of spiritual insight. Drugs promised spiritual effects like the broadening of their consciousness, increased interconnection, and the comprehending that suffering is necessary for the final salvation. The problem was that these illegal substances also brought with them addiction, desperation, legal difficulties, and individual destruction. For hipsters and beatniks, drugs were another means by which they could express their 'beatness,' which included both being beaten down and feeling beatific. The extensive drug use among Beats has become a well known fact, but its causes have often been interpreted as fleeing from reality and yearning for more and more kicks. Most times, however, drugs were important to show their rejection of the prevailing modes of meaning-making. When the Beat culture

---

[83] When her sister Chris visits her in Mexico, Frazer takes the opportunity to sing the praises of love for Ray. She writes, "I feel sorry for Chris and always have; she has never known a love as I do and never will, incapable of it, and yet she lives her life" (50). Contemplating her sister's loveless and therefore sad life, she adds, "Thank the poets I have been saved from such a fate and better all my exile than to tempt that loveless life" (54). Frazer seems to deny the harsh Mexican reality of getting love only in exchange for her sexual services.

disappeared and blurred with the hippie counterculture of the 1960s and early 1970s, drug experimenter Timothy Leary, merry prankster Ken Kesey, or acid jam bands like The Grateful Dead influenced many more young people to experiment with drugs. In his extensive study on the Beats, John Lardas refers to the connection between drugs and the search for spirituality:

> Like William James a half-century earlier, they [the Beats] preferred a religious praxis that was not a "dull habit" but rather induced an "acute fever". Drugs helped them experience a holistic and immediate sensitivity to the cosmos, even moments of synaesthesia whereby natural facts became social ones and previous conceptions of self were rendered fraudulent. By enhancing immediate sense perceptions, drugs also enabled the Beats to transcend the limits imposed by well-worn ideas, even those of space and time. (van Slooten. *Amen the Thunderbolt:* 80)

Kerouac, Ginsberg, and other writers wanted to create a new, enlightened reality outside of the self, but were also interested in how to gain insight into the most hidden parts of the self. In many works of the Beat canon, drugs and their influence on the body and mind are at least part of the story. The works of Brenda Frazer and William Burroughs, however, are particularly drug-infused. Both authors depict the potentials and limitations of drugs in great detail[84]. The two autobiographical works of Frazer written in the 1960s, *Troia/For Love of Ray* and *Poets and Oddfellows*, depict numerous drug experiences. The Bremsers frequently tried out both non-hallucinogenics, like heroin and cocaine, and hallucinogenics, like peyote, magic mushrooms, or marijuana, which are supposed to help them to experience spiritual insight. Page after page, Frazer describes their physical and psychic effects. For them, taking both non-hallucinogenic and hallucinogenic drugs were ways to transcend their bodily existence. In *For Love of Ray*, the Bremsers mostly smoke marijuana in Books One and Two, but after their daughter Rachel is left behind with a rich U.S. family, the text becomes more and more surreal due to their increased use of magic mushrooms.

Burroughs' journalistic narrative *Junky* (1953) and his correspondence with Ginsberg while searching for the drug yage, *The Yage Letters*[85] (1963), give insight into his hopes and expectations while frantically looking for drug kicks. Burroughs differentiates between junk and hallucinogenic drugs. For him, heroin is an aid to escape reality, and he uses it when there is nothing else to be done. Hallucinogenic substances, however, have increased value, because they heighten the consciousness

---

[84] In chapter 2 of her 2003 dissertation, Jessica Lyn van Slooten dedicates one whole chapter to the drug experiences of the Beats. See van Slooten, Jessica Lyn (2003). "Amen the Thunderbolt and the Dark Void: Spirituality and Gender in the Works of Female and Male Writers of the Beat Generation". *Dissertation* Auburn University.

[85] One of Burroughs' motivations to explore South America was his search for the new product yage, also called Ayahuasca, a drug with fabled power and telepathic qualities, which can be found in the Amazon rainforests. Fictionalized in *Queer* (1985), which was written in 1957, but not published until 1985, he desperately tries to find this miracle hallucinogen. For him, yage signified the ideal drug: non-absorbing, portable, requiring no civic responsibility or membership to enjoy its privileges. Eventually, Burroughs is disappointed with his yage experiments. *The Yage Letters*, first published in 1963, are an exchange of letters between Burroughs and Ginsberg, and record their complementary quests for the plant. Burroughs' letters guide Ginsberg's later quest for yage, including both practical details for the trip as well as facts about the drug's effects. Throughout the text, Burroughs' ambivalence towards yage is clearly shown.

and lead to spiritual insight. He describes the use of both substances in his works, while Frazer's drug experiences are more strictly confined to hallucinogenics. In many Middle and South American countries, the legal system was less restrictive regarding the use and selling of drugs. Therefore, many beatniks flocked to Mexico in order to flee the anti-drug law enforcement of the U.S. Moreover, in their opinion, these suppressed fellahin societies understood that drugs served important spiritual and heightening purposes. Disappointingly, Mexico often failed to offer complete independence and insight the Beats were seeking.

Brenda Frazer's two autobiographical texts, *Poets and Oddfellows*, published on the internet in 1997, but written in 1959, and *Troia: Mexican Memoirs/For Love of Ray*, depict the ups and downs of a drug life in full detail. Similar to Burroughs, drugs influence her social contacts, her family life, her job as a prostitute, and finally her perception of reality, which becomes more confusing from page to page. Both writers see drugs as spiritual aids that might lead to final salvation. Burroughs' drug-wrecked life, focused on telepathy and gnosis, is a means to escape from the conflicting attitude towards his own body. Trying to cope with his homosexuality, Burroughs denies sexual difference. He finally becomes a heroin addict, because so he temporarily transcends his own body (cf. van Slooten 2003: 75f.). Similarly to Burroughs, Brenda Frazer also feels trapped within her body. Her quest for spirituality, caused by her endless devotion to her husband Ray, imprisons her body. Frazer defines herself through her female body, and her hustling to support the family financially is just a further degradation caused by Bremser's patriarchal attitudes.

In her first autobiographical text, *Poets and Oddfellows*, Frazer remembers her first meeting with poet Ray Bremser and the following first months of their relationship. The events depicted in *Poets and Oddfellows* can be considered the pre-story to *For Love of Ray*. The autobiographical essay consists of nine chapters: Chapter 1 is titled "Poets and Oddfellows"[86], chapter 2 "Do you Believe?"[87], chapter 3 "Breaking out of D.C."[88], chapter 4 "Changes (May 1959)"[89], chapter 5 "The Village Scene"[90], chapter 6 "Triptych USA"[91], chapter 7 "California Come-Down"[92], chapter 8 "How to be a Poet's Wife"[93], and

---

[86] See Frazer, Brenda (1997). "Poets and Oddfellows". *The Blacklisted Journalist*. August 14, 2006. http://www.bigmagic.com/pages/blackj/column74d1.html
[87] See Frazer, Brenda (1997). "Do you Believe?". *The Blacklisted Journalist*. August 14, 2006. http://www.bigmagic.com/pages/blackj/column74d2.html
[88] See Frazer, Brenda (1997). "Breaking out of D.C.". *The Blacklisted Journalist*. August 14, 2006. http://www.bigmagic.com/pages/blackj/column74d3.html
[89] See Frazer, Brenda (1997). "Changes (May 1959)". *The Blacklisted Journalist*. August 14, 2006. http://www.bigmagic.com/pages/blackj/column74d4.html
[90] See Frazer, Brenda (1997). "The Village Scene". *The Blacklisted Journalist*. August 14, 2006. http://www.bigmagic.com/pages/blackj/column74d5.html
[91] See Frazer, Brenda (1997). "Triptych USA". *The Blacklisted Journalist*. August 14, 2006. http://www.bigmagic.com/pages/blackj/column74d6.html
[92] See Frazer, Brenda (1997). "California Come-Down". *The Blacklisted Journalist*. August 14, 2006. http://www.bigmagic.com/pages/blackj/column74d7.html
[93] See Frazer, Brenda (1997). "How to be a Poet's Wife". *The Blacklisted Journalist*. August 14, 2006. http://www.bigmagic.com/pages/blackj/column74d8.html

chapter 9 "Hoboken"[94]. In this work, Frazer sees her husband as a Christ-like person promising spiritual salvation. They try to reach a unifying spiritual state through marijuana and hallucinogens. Peyote, magic mushrooms, and marijuana strengthen her conviction that her dedication to Ray is never-ending. Their common drug use solidifies their relation, however, also consecrates her downfall into prostitution as spiritual love. In both *Poets and Oddfellows* and *For Love of Ray*, drugs, dedication, and sex become Frazer's spiritual trinity through which she definitely knows that "THERE IS SALVATION" (chapter 5).

Already during their first encounter at a poetry reading in her hometown, Frazer is fascinated by Bremser's religious outward appearance: "He looked like a monk". Soon after their first sexual intercourse, she again depicts him in religious terms, "his long body looked like a naked Jesus, stretched out in undershorts". Frazer's assumption that Ray is Christ-like may derive from his experiences in various prisons. She considers his prison times as "spiritual redemption" and calls him a poet, seer, and prophet: "[…] but in actuality Ray was a poet, with all the saintly stature of his beautiful work. Ray was no longer a criminal, poetry had redeemed him" (all quotes chapter 1). Yet, this redemptive love is not crisis-proof. Bremser tells her that he is also in love with another girl in New York City, who wants to marry him. Frazer's dreams of a shared future shatter: "It feels like suicide. A death leap away from him, away from the love that could save me, more faith now in gibbering beer cans as I threw them around, enjoying the noise". To show his superiority, Bremser gives her "a quick slap in the kisser". This passage "made it obvious to us both, as sure as any words, that it was real, this love". In both *Poets and Oddfellows* and *For Love of Ray,* it soon becomes obvious for the reader that their love is doomed and that Frazer is the one who will lose the game in the end. Amazingly soon, the Bremsers marry in a Presbyterian church, sanctifying their marriage within the Christian tradition. When they are back at home, listening to some jazz records after the marriage ceremony, they discuss love and religion: "'I find it impossible not to believe in God', he said, as we sat looking at each other. 'Do you believe in God?' All of my intellectual reservations dissolved in that moment, wanting to be wholly with him, in him. 'I believe in love'," Frazer replies (all quotes chapter 2). Her love object and supreme deity is her husband. Frazer later on points out, "Our isolation was a privilege, a pact against the outside world. Perhaps there was something more for him, fame, poetry, but not for me" (chapter 4).

The Bremsers' spiritual love is furthermore intensified by their frequent use of marijuana. While smoking dope with his Beat circle, Bremser makes clear, "Love's our religion, it's holy, man". To his mind, the establishment tries to prevent their holy love: "But our system kills it, you know. Kills it and eats it for lunch like sandwich meat, our wounded heart" (chapter 3). Marijuana is an intimate connector for the married couple: "I am probably over loaded with bronchial nicotine and marijuana

---

[94] See Frazer, Brenda (1997). "Hoboken". *The Blacklisted Journalist*. August 14, 2006. http://www.bigmagic.com/pages/blackj/column74d9.html

alkaloids. There is the feeling of him around me, a comfortable adoration. I am grateful for it. It redeems me. […] A physical euphoria, not just from the weed, but from having found him, the poet" (chapter 4). Marijuana is not only important, because it intensifies their passion for each other, but also their friendship with numerous other Beat artists and writers.

Frazer soon realizes that being the wife of a Beat poet is not always easy. When Bremser leaves for several weeks to spend some time in New York City, Frazer has to stay in Washington D.C. She follows, but Ray is disappointed about her behavior, because the police must not know he is married. When Frazer hears that Bremser slept with his former girlfriend, she justifies his betrayal: "It was his spirituality, it was the Jesus figure that his skinny body and ravaged face so resembled. I had been betrayed by the very essence of him that I loved, compassion, understanding, the poet. But his feet on the coffee table, so intimate! 'I had to do it,' he explained" (chapter 4). The Bremsers reconcile over and over again, building up a pattern which is repeated in both *Poets and Oddfellows* and *For Love of Ray:* pain, deceit, reconciliation. After Ray admits his infidelity, they reconcile while visiting the Museum of Natural History after having smoked marijuana. Bremser starts to fantasize about being in the middle of a scene of Egypt's ancient mythology. Frazer writes, "At every turn he reminded me, the philosophy of our love, of our beatness, or even smoking pot and the whole rebellion. 'It's our identity, Babe!' I could hear him say, challenging me to believe. 'Have trust and faith in the goodness of what is happening'" (all quotes chapter 5). Love is their philosophy, something they can depend on. For her, love is "a way out of yourself and the counterbalance to a hundred ills. It can be the reason to overcome hardship. It can make things easy" (chapter 6).

Even though Frazer does not always explicitly talk about marijuana or magic mushrooms, she does refer to the fact that she and Ray experienced "day to-day drug adventures," meaning their drug use seven days a week. They experiment with peyote, a small cactus which can be found in the Southwest of the U.S. through to central Mexico. The buttons of the plants can be chewed or boiled as a tea and have psychedelic effects that supposedly trigger states of deep introspection and insight. Frazer is afraid at the beginning, but wants to make her husband happy, and so they "chewed it up" on countless afternoons. Peyote's mind altering effects strengthen their unity and their conviction of a final salvation: For her, it was "kind of spooky at first," because the drug does not only taste disgusting, but "when it hit my stomach there was an uneasiness like nausea, something green and indigestible residing, palpable in the stomach". She cannot tell if she is high and asks Ray what it is supposed to be like. Just then, however, her focus is drawn to the flame of the candle: "Look, Ray, there's a man in the candle," she whispers. Going through their drug madness together, she continues,

> "The wick is one with the flame, the wax feeding it." By that time I was crying. "That's what it is, oneness. Everything fits tight together, material and energy. The wax, the wick and the flame consuming!" It was joy – a vision as well as an answer, a cleansing sight! Then there were changes, just like a key or tempo shift though for once we were not listening to music. Ray took the candle and wrote on the white ceiling, low enough for him to reach standing. The flame smoking, the black letters THERE IS SALVATION. (Frazer. "The Village Scene")

In the 1960s, Timothy Leary's Harvard experiments attracted the public's attention, and numerous experiments were made in order to analyze the effects of hallucinogens. For Frazer, the use of hallucinogenic drugs does not always lead to positive trips. A later peyote adventure does not lead to dreamy perceptions of harmony and unity, but into deadly fear of Bremser. In front of her, she suddenly envisions a shadow that "looked like Ray's arm raised WITH A KNIFE!". Her drug haze further increases her fear, but Ray apologizes that it is only a paintbrush in his hand and that she should not take him too seriously. This episode makes Frazer "wonder if I really knew him" (chapter 7).

Soon after the Bremsers settle down in New Jersey, their seemingly redemptive love is at the brink of being destroyed. Bremser is imprisoned once again for "parole violation, for being out of state without permission, for getting married without permission, for talking on the radio about marijuana". Frazer is destitute and left alone. As a protest, she does not read his daily letters and finds herself new lovers, something Bremser had suggested before. Ray Bremser's behavior is similar to Neal Cassady, who wanted his wife Carolyn to share his own male lovers, but also to find new ones while he was away on his road trips. Frazer does not trust in their relationship any more. She confesses, "My guilt was obvious, because I had given up on him. As soon as I had lost everything in the swoop of separation. Love, trust, belief in providence, belief in him and in myself, all gone in a moment. I had been a victim of despair. His guilt was his irresponsibility, but could jail resolve that?" (all quotes chapter 9). Due to the fact that her faith is depending on the unity with her Christ-like husband, she gets completely lost while he is in prison. Consequently, Frazer spends numerous nights out with different men, enjoying her sudden freedom: "There was always a lot of really good marijuana and beer, and I began to lose memory of the days or who I was balling". She is shocked when she finds out that she is pregnant, and immediately stops her frantic sexual activity, as her "womb was feeling abuse from all this balling, but no joy" (all quotes chapter 8). After half a year, Bremser gets out of jail, they move together again, and look forward to a more domestic life of child care. Soon after Rachel was born, they agree that Ray will jump bail, and they will escape to Mexico. They will be together, "Mexico would be good for the baby," and "Mexico would be our dream" (chapter 9).

For Love of Ray continues where *Poets and Oddfellows* ends, with the Bremsers' flight to Mexico. In Mexico, they re-immerse themselves in the drugs, sex, and love philosophy they had already followed in the U. S. For Frazer, marijuana has spiritual qualities: "God praise marijuana, yes, my baby, I will never put you down. A few things stay close to our hearts, definitive, a happy to have habit thing with no pain, no remorse, no sickness [...]. Sweet marijuana lotus blossom I am entitled to call you now, being thoroughly a member of the club (1971: 18). Like marijuana, Mexico also has the properties of a drug: "There is no indecision, Mexico blacks out slowly the hurtsome parts of the brain" (20). Disappointedly, Frazer soon realizes that the holy trinity of drugs, sex, and love is challenged when she becomes a prostitute. Every time Frazer is selling her body, drugs play a particularly crucial role. When she, for example, depicts a meeting with one of her customers,

Humberto, "the coach at The University, fat, plump with Falstaffian belly, therefore always good for a blow job," they get totally high on drugs (59). After usually talking for a while, they would smoke dope: "[…] he would just taste it and I would inundate my head with it, cooling, allowing myself to be as much in illusions' light as pot will allow" (59-60). Later on, the story gets more and more drug-infused. Living in a hotel in Mexico City, she writes, "Everything is designed to make life as palatable as it can be with so many bad things happening that can't be helped". Therefore, "the object is to stay high and out of it and still operate to keep the money coming in and us fed and Ray writing poems frantically" (144). Through marijuana, she can distance herself from what she is doing. Financially, the Bremsers get into deeper troubles, because of their constant use of marijuana, and so, she has to earn more pesos. Pot is responsible for keeping Frazer in a situation similar to William Burroughs' "Algebra of Need" – with the difference that Burroughs was addicted to heroin.

After having put up Rachel for adoption, the Bremsers start experimenting with various hallucinogenic drugs as a way to gain access to the most hidden parts of the consciousness and to see the true nature of things. Experimenting with peyote, magic mushrooms, cocaine, and marijuana, she can escape the cruel reality of her degrading hustling, her violent relationship with Ray, and life without baby Rachel. Probably the most shocking drug experience of the memoir happens when Rachel drops out of the narrative. High on drugs, they decide to take the bus, and stay with the magic mushroom people in Oaxaca and Huatla, wishing "to have stayed there forever". They buy mushrooms from the village people, but also try to find them in the woods: "We walk up sides of adjoining mountains, searching through meadow grasses to find fresh mushrooms growing. They have to grow somewhere" (123). "Ever find it hard to accept that a dream place exists, like the peyote church in Brooklyn?", Frazer asks: "That's how I felt about Huatla […]" (119). Frazer worships the mushrooms' religious effects after her first mushroom experience: "I ate a lot, immediately, having great faith (all of these organic highs are religious, don't ask me chemical effects), and immediately the bright day hotel window draws sounds of saxophones, clarinets, flutes and danzon drums of the Indian hillside road top" (120). The Bremsers buy a kilo for eighty pesos, and they spend a couple of hours tearing the stems off them. Frazer eats masses of them, while "Ray is timid of them (too organic) but eats enough to get high". The mushrooms fill Frazer with powerful emotions, new strength, and enthusiasm:

> I go crazy and eat about a pound of them while we are in Huatla, knowing that I will worship the effects, the taste is something to be ignored, I keep eating, every time we return to the room I eat mushrooms. I ate so many mushrooms I was never able to describe or remember the immediate feeling of their effect coming on, but know looking back that I was high for months (this is the way peyote hit me too – I can say a few beautiful high experiences, but the effect is a large time cycle change of life: how I get my religions) and the stomach gurgles in digesting these rinds of pure clean hilltop earth. *(For Love of Ray:* 124)

Frazer's drug use is a dead-end street, because hallucinogenics do not help to achieve spiritual liberation. Drugs fail, because her life becomes even more surreal and alienated. Alix Kates Shulman points out, "Bonnie Bremser's memoir, for all its Beat syntax, language, and rhythm, tells a story of a woman less Beat than beaten" (1989: 19). She is "beaten down" in the extreme. *For Love of Ray* shows Beat men from their worst side and Beat women in their most oppressed state. Frazer's holy trinity of drugs, sex, and love is ultimately a deceptive trinity; it does not lead to Frazer's final liberation, but fortifies her personal entrapment in her humiliated female body.

9 Conclusion

When asked whether women played an important role in Beat literature, most literary critics would have answered with a resounding NO fifteen years ago. Despite the advent of second wave feminism in the late 1960s it took more than twenty years before feminist literary criticism started to pay attention to the complex role of women Beat writers. Since the first literary attempts of the movement's iconic male figures – Jack Kerouac, Allen Ginsberg, and William S. Burroughs – most critical discussion has excluded female Beats. They have not been absent, but elided, and their denied presence has left substantial traces in Beat literature and discourse.

Autobiography and its subgenre, the memoir, have historically been dominated by the life stories of great men, and it is somewhat ironic that life writing has become the vehicle which has brought public attention to the presence of women writers in the Beat movement. The memoir has become the most commonly used literary genre by female Beats. At the height of the Beat movement, Brenda Frazer published *Troia, Mexican Memoirs* in 1969, the same year that saw the publication of Diane di Prima's *Memoirs of a Beatnik*. Most female Beat voices, however, remained astonishingly silent until 1983, when Joyce Johnson published *Minor Characters: A Young Woman's Coming of Age in the Beat Generation*, which won the National Book Critics Award in the same year. Johnson's longtime friend Hettie Jones followed with *How I Became Hettie Jones* in 1990. All four memoirs draw upon the genre's social authority derived from the author's privileged relation to real life. All four memoirs benefit from the genre's close connection to discourses of truth-telling. The life writing of Beat women chronicles their intimate relationships with icons of the time: Jack Kerouac, Allen Ginsberg, LeRoi Jones/Amiri Baraka, and Ray Bremser. Being there at a crucial moment in history validates female Beats' stories as "different" and "unusual". Thus, the authority from which and with which they write is guaranteed. Most likely, their presence during the Beat era compelled them to write memoirs which by definition focus on a short period in one's life, rather than lengthier autobiographies. The memoir form serves to achieve the directive that life writing should be intimately exploring the inner and emotional life, thus distinguishing the form from mere historical documentation (cf. Jelinek 1980: 10).

Yet why has a considerable number of female Beats chosen to communicate through life writing, a form often marginalized, trivialized, and considered inferior and pseudo-historic? For female Beats who have effectively been erased as legitimate artists from the historical Beat movement, autobiographical writing heightens the importance of their self-validation, self-expression, and authority as writers. While the memoir stresses the first-person pronoun "I," putting one's own life into the center of writing, fiction, poetry, and other literary forms cannot provide similar verifiable historical referents who present themselves as believable truth-tellers. For the four memoirists, the memoir genre serves different purposes. Di Prima's *Memoirs of a Beatnik,* often disregarded as "for hire" pornography, was mainly written in order to financially support her San Francisco hippie commune; Johnson's *Minor Characters* manifests the development of Johnson as a woman and a writer during the fifties and sixties, trying to depict the Beat years from a female point of view. While Joyce Johnson omits the discussion about whether she is a talented writer or not, *How I Became Hettie Jones* focuses on the author's assumed "poetry of lack," questioning whether she is a gifted writer or not. Both Johnson and Jones see themselves as advocates for a whole generation of silenced women, making their female friends visible in their memoirs and giving them a voice to speak for themselves. *For Love of Ray* was written for therapeutic reasons, yet also to obey Beat poet Ray Bremser's order to entertain him while in prison, urging his wife Frazer to write down the devastating humiliations she had to bear in Mexico.

For all of them, self-representation finally emerges as self-creation, yet often the past remains beyond their grasp. Through the construction of personal and cultural history, they write themselves into being. Johnson's and Jones' memoirs represent a form of autobiographical writing which identifies more explicitly with history. Anchoring themselves in a historical setting is crucial for them, even though they try hard to simultaneously depict their personal coming-of-age as writers. *Minor Characters* and *How I Became Hettie Jones* assert that their narrators serve as reliable historical referents who try to retell the Beat story, adding a dimension to Beat literature men could not offer – a woman's perspective. Yearning to be intimately connected with the female reader, Johnson and Jones try to satisfy reader expectations circling around identification and sympathy. However, in comparison to other Beat works, such as *For Love of Ray*, they refuse to use Beat style in their works. While Johnson and Jones are directly linked to history, di Prima's *Memoirs of a Beatnik* and Frazer's *For Love of Ray* approve of autobiograpy's claim to historical veracity, but both are not interested in accounting for the 1950s as a historical period or social movement. They allow their memoirs to be more fictive, imaginative, and playful concerning both form and content. Both works distort reality and repeatedly slip from fiction to history, from novel to memoir. Untypical for traditional woman's autobiography, di Prima, for example, over-embellishes scenes which were unspectacular in reality, and adds various options and endings about erotic or un-erotic events, leaving the reader unsure about the truthfulness of the accounts. Through writing an inventive pornography, di Prima departs from the fidelity that is a precondition for the prevalent author/reader contract in memoir writing, and thus challenges common characteristics of autobiography. Similar to Diane di Prima, Brenda Frazer also skillfully merges truth and fact and puts the author/reader relationship at stake by nullifying affective bonds with the audience. Originally, the personal letters she sent to her husband in jail were not intended to be published, yet upon Ray Bremser's suggestion, editor Michael Perkins rearranged the letters and organized them in a book. Di Prima's and Frazer's textual subversions indicate a certain affinity towards male Beat writings because formal devices of life writing are clearly neglected. Both fuse various literary genres and destroy the necessary author/reader contract in life writing. What all

Conclusion

four memoirs share, however, is their attempt to construct an alternative, corrective history of Beat culture, Beat art, and female Beat subjectivity.

Beside having explored specific ways in which each of the four Beat writers has approached and used the memoir genre for her own individual purposes, this study also tried to categorize the four memoirs at hand in terms of autobiographical subgenres. Confession and feminism are two buzz words which are crucial for all four memoirists. Since the beginning of second wave feminism, a large number of confessional texts have been published. Feminist critic Rita Felski sees the confession as a distinctive subgenre of autobiography which has become prominent especially since the beginning of the 1980s (cf. 1989: 83). As Francis Hart states: "'Confession' is personal history that seeks to communicate or express the essential nature, the truth of the self" (1970: 491). Confession makes public what has been private for a long time, typically claiming to avoid filtering mechanisms of objectivity and detachment in its pursuit of the truth of subjective experience. Sharing an explicit rhetorical foregrounding of the relationship between a female author and a female reader, confessional texts cannot live without reader identification. Coming clean, like confessing abortions, infidelities, or drug use, allows all four female Beat writers to "step into the light". Forthrightness is liberating, especially because telling the truth allows the memoirist integrity.

Writing themselves into Beat history through including strongly confessional streaks, di Prima's, Johnson's, Jones', and Frazer's writings are also protofeminist acts of subjectivity which connect twentieth-century first and second wave feminism. All four writers are protofeminists, leaving home during their teenage years, and following female independence. The communal personae speaking in Johnson's and Jones' works avoid attachment, refuse victimization, and absolutely resist confinement to traditional gender roles. For di Prima, the non-conformist 'Rule of Cool,' which oppresses the open display of feelings and emotions, but also prohibits the feminine in both sexes, is a revolt for personal freedom, finally leading to her participation in second wave feminism. She is confessional and among the first women memoirists who openly talk about taboos like lesbian sex, pornographic jobs, or abortion. For Johnson and Jones, feminism means discussing feminist issues in their works, such as gender equality, combining work life and motherhood, and women's access to higher education. *Minor Characters* and *How I Became Hettie Jones* are products of second wave feminism, which was influential for the process of daring to write down one's life story from a female perspective. For Brenda Frazer, feminism includes different meanings: Influenced by the women's liberation movement in the late 1960s, she finally takes courage to leave her patriarchal and sexist husband Ray Bremser, and starts a new life. With its critique of the hipster marriage and its deconstruction of the sexual politics of the road, *For Love of Ray* radically modifies traditional Beat literature. Even though Frazer lives through a surreal nightmare which nearly destroys her, her work is clearly a forerunner of second wave feminism, which tried to foster a common female identity.

Trying to create categorizations for *Memoirs of a Beatnik, Minor Characters, How I Became Hettie Jones,* and *For Love of Ray* was a complex task, as female Beats, in general, mostly resist labels and categorizations. Beside being confessional and feminist – categories which fit all four memoirs being discussed – each singular memoir contains features of several other literary subgenres.

In *Memoirs of a Beatnik*, di Prima skillfully reinvents the masculine genre of pornography to present a woman's coming-of-age from a very personal point of view. She embraces heterosexual intercourse and homoerotic affairs, rejects patriarchy and sexism, and tells square U.S. society that women are free to choose their own sexual identity. Yet, *Memoirs of a Beatnik* can also be called a quest narrative. Similar to the main protagonists in Jack Kerouac's *On the Road,* di Prima embarks in a quest for experience and kicks, breaking down barriers of sexual confinement, shocking America's rigid and paranoid postwar culture.

The main protagonist's development in terms of growth, maturity, and education in *Minor Characters* and *How I Became Hettie Jones* indicates that both memoirs are modern "Bildungsromane," or, more narrowly defined, coming-of-age memoirs. In the classical "Bildungsroman," the process of maturity is long, burdensome, and gradual, consisting of repeated clashes between the protagonist's needs and desires and the views and judgments enforced by an unbending social order. Through the course of a decade both Johnson and Jones transform from silent, middle-class, burgeois, Jewish girls into mature, self-confident, independent women living lives of their own.

In contrast to di Prima, Johnson, and Jones, writing *For Love of Ray* has a therapeutic purpose for Brenda Frazer's fragmented "I" that suffers from many cracks on different levels. For Frazer, writing down her misery leads to a personal catharsis, which is her primary aim, while the reader is being rejected. Frazer, who has experienced numerous traumatic events in Mexico must come to terms with how prostitution and patriarchal oppression have fragmented her life. In retrospect, she gradually starts to create meaningful strategies which help to articulate what has happened. Beside being a therapeutic memoir, Frazer's text is an autobiographical road tale or, rather, road memoir, depicted from a uniquely female perspective. The problem of being on the road, however, is the patriarchal context: For her, the road is not synonymous for sexual kicks but stands for exploitation, degradation, and abortions.

Through their autobiographical writings, all four memoirists have found a vehicle by which they escape the shadow of famous Beat men and participate in the creation of their own history and subjectivity. By refusing to let others talk for them, women take their responsibility to assert their place in a pivotal period in American history. They were there, creating niches of resistance, and their life stories both alter and sustain cultural memory. Through writing their own histories, they become both subject and creator, and by presenting themselves publicly, women Beat writers have joined the males as fellow travelers and innovative artists, because "merely being there is not enough".

Works Cited

Primary Literature

Bremser, Bonnie (1971). *For Love of Ray*. London: London Magazine Editions.

di Prima, Diane (1998). *Memoirs of Beatnik*. New York: Penguin Books.

Johnson, Joyce (1999). *Minor Characters. A Beat Memoir.* New York: Penguin Books.

Jones, Hettie (1997). *How I Became Hettie Jones*. New York: Grove Press.

Secondary Literature

Albert, Richard N. (1988). "Jazz and the Beat Generation. John Clellon Holmes's *The Horn*." *Moody Street Irregulars* 20: 16-19.

Alther, Lisa (1999). *Kinflicks*. London: Virago Press.

Anderson, Linda R. (1997). *Women and Autobiography in the Twentieth Century: Remembered Futures.* London: Prentice Hall/ Harvester Wheatsheaf.

Anderson, M. Christine (2003). "Women's Place in the Beat Movement: Bonnie Bremser Frazer's Troia: Mexican Memoirs". *Women's Studies International Forum* 26.3: 253-263.

Bailey, Beth (1988). *From Front Porch to Back Seat: Courtship in the Twentieth Century*. Baltimore: Johns Hopkins University Press.

Baldwin, James (1962). „The Black Boy looks at the White Boy". In: *Nobody Knows my Name: More Notes of a Native Son*. New York: Delta. 214-235.

Baraka, Amiri (1966). *Home: Social Essays.* New York: Morrow.

Baraka, Imamu Amiri (1984). *The Autobiography of LeRoi Jones*. Chicago: Lawrence Hill Books.

Baraka, Imamu Amiri (1991). The LeRoi Jones/Amiri Baraka Reader. New York: Thunder's Mouth Press.

Barrington, Judith (2002). *Writing the Memoir*. Portland: Eight Mountain Press.

Barthel, Diane (1988). *Putting on Appearances: Gender and Advertising*. Philadelphia: Temple University Press.

Bataille, Georges (1986). *Erotism: Death & Sensuality.* San Francisco: City Lights.

Bendel, Larissa (2005). *The Requirements of our Life is the Form of our Art: Autobiographik von Frauen der Beat Generation*. Frankfurt: Peter Lang.

Berriault, Gina (1972, Oct. 12). "Neal's Ashes". *Rolling Stone Magazine*. 32-36.

Works Cited

Bjorklund Diane (1998). *Interpreting the Self: Two Hundred Years of American Autobiography.* Chicago: Chicago University Press.

Brée, Germaine (1988). "Autogynography". In: *Studies in Autobiography.* Ed. James Olney. New York: Oxford University Press. 171-189.

Breines, Wini (1994). "Not June Cleaver: Women and Gender in Postwar America. 1945-1960." In: *Not June Cleaver*. Ed. Joanne Meyerowitz. Philadelphia: Temple University Press. 382-408.

Breines, Wini (1992). *Young, White, and Miserable. Growing up Female in the Fifties.* Boston: Beacon Press.

Bremser, Bonnie (1969). *Troia: Mexican Memoirs.* New York: Croton Press.

Brossard, Chandler (1987). "Tentative Visits to the Cemetery: Reflections on my Beat Generation". *Review of Contemporary Literature* 7: 11-15.

Broyard, Anatole (1948). "Portrait of a Hipster". *Partisan Review* 15.6: 720-723.

Buckley, Jerome Hamilton (1974). *Season of Youth: The Bildungsroman from Dickens to Golding.* Cambridge: Harvard University Press.

Burroughs, William (1994). *Letters of William S. Burroughs, 1945- 1959.* Ed. Oliver Harris. New York: Penguin.

Burroughs, William (1992). *Naked Lunch.* New York: Grove Weidenfeld.

Burroughs, William and Allen Ginsberg (1963). *The Yage Letters.* San Francisco: City Lights.

Bush, Clive (1996). "'Why do we always say angel?' Herbert Huncke and Neal Cassady". In: *The Beat Generation Writers*. Ed. A. Robert Lee. London: Pluto Press. 128- 157.

Cassady, Carolyn (1990). *Off the Road: My Years with Kerouac, Cassady, and Ginsberg.* New York: Morrow.

Cassady, Neal (1981). *The First Third and Other Writings.* San Francisco: City Lights.

Castro, Ginette (1990). *American Feminism. A Contemporary History.* Feminist Crosscurrents. Transl. from the French by Elizabeth Loverde-Bagwell. New York: New York UP.

Chafe, William (1986). *The Unfinished Journey: America since World War II.* New York: Oxford University Press.

Charters, Ann, ed. (2001). *Beat Down to Your Soul.* New York: Penguin Books.

Charters, Ann, ed. (1983). *The Beats: Literary Bohemians in Postwar America.* Dictionary of Literary Biography, vol. 16. Detroit: Gale Research.

Charters, Ann (1994). *Kerouac. A Biography.* New York: St. Martin's Press.

Charters, Ann, ed. (1992). *The Portable Beat Reader.* New York: Penguin.

Clark, Tom (1990). *Jack Kerouac.* New York: Paragon House.

Works Cited

Corber, Robert J. (1997). *Homosexuality in Cold War America. Resistance and the Crisis of Masculinity*. London: Duke University Press.

Corbett, Mary Jean (1998). „Literary Domesticity and Women Writers' Subjectivities." In: *Women, Autobiography, Theory: A Reader*. Edited by Sidonie Smith and Julia Watson. Madison: University of Wisconsin Press. 243-259.

Cowie, Elizabeth (2003). „'Representation vs. Communication'. No Turning Back : Writings from the Women's Liberation Movement 1975-80". In: *Feminist Literary Theory*. Ed. Mary Eggleton. Oxford: Blackwell Publishing. 156-174.

Crossman, Richard, ed. (2001). *The God that Failed*. New York: Columbia University Press.

Cuddon, John A. (1991). *A Dictionary of Literary Terms and Literary Theory*. Cambridge: Blackwell Reference.

Culley, Margo (1985). *Introduction to A Day at a Time: Diary Literature of American Women, from 1764 to 1985*. New York: Feminist Press at the City University of New York.

Davidson, Julia O'Connell (2002). "The Rights and Wrongs of Prostitution". *Hypatia* 17.2 : 84-98.

Davidson, Michael (1989). *The San Francisco Renaissance: Poetics and Community at Mid-Century*. Cambridge: Cambridge University Press.

D'Emilio, John and Estelle Freedman (1988). *Intimate Matters: A History of Sexuality in America*. New York: Harper and Row.

Diehl, Margaret (2000, March 5). "Pounding at the Door. Review of Lennard Davis' My Sense of Silence: Memoirs of a Childhood with Deafness." *The New York Times Book Review*. 42.

Dinesen, Isak (1985). "The Blank Page". In: *The Norton Anthology of Literature by Women*. Ed. Sandra M. Gilbert and Susan Gubar. New York: W.W. Norton. 1416-1420.

Dinnerstein, Myra (1992). *Between Two Worlds: Midlife Reflections on Work and Family*. Philadelphia: Temple University Press.

di Prima, Diane (1961). *Dinners and Nightmares*. New York: Corinth Books. Expanded ed. San Francisco: Last Gasp Press, 1998.

di Prima, Diane (1999). "The Tapestry of Possibility". Interview with Diane di Prima. *Whole Earth* (Fall 1999): 20.

di Prima, Diane (1958). *This Kind of Bird Flies Backward*. New York: Totem Press.

Doherty, Thomas (1988). *Teenagers and Teenpics: The Juvenilization of American Movies in the 1950s*. Boston: Unwin Hyman.

Duberman, Martin Bauml (1989). *Hidden from History: Reclaiming the Gay and Lesbian Past*. New York: New American Library.

Eagleton, Terry (1982). *The Rape of Clarissa: Writing, Sexuality, and Class Struggle in Samuel Richardson*. Oxford: Basil Blackwell.

Echols, Alice. (1989). *Daring to Be Bad: Radical Feminism in America, 1967–1975*. Minneapolis: University of Minnesota Press.

Works Cited

Ehrenhalt, Alan (1995). *The Lost City: Discovering the Forgotten Virtues of Community in the Chicago of the 1950's.* HarperCollins Publishers: New York.

Ehrenreich, Barbara, Elizabeth Hess, and Gloria Jacobs (1986). *Remaking Love: The Feminization of Love.* Garden City, N.Y.: Doubleday.

Ehrenreich, Barbara (1983). *The Hearts of Men. American Dreams and the Flight for Commitment.* New York: Anchor.

Ehrmann, Winston (1959). *Premarital Dating Behavior.* New York: Henry Holt.

Eisler, Benita (1986). *Private Lives: Men and Women of the Fifties.* New York: Franklin Watts.

Evans, Judith (1995). *Feminist Theory Today. An Introduction to Second-Wave Feminism.* London, Thousand Oaks and New Delhi: SAGE Publications.

Fallows, Randall (2004). "Gentlemen's Games & Witches' Brews: Lillian Hellman's 'Another Part of the Forest' and the Emergence of the Cold War Culture". *American Drama* Summer 2004: 43-60.

Farnham, Marynia F. and Ferdinand Lundberg (1947). *Modern Woman: The Lost Sex.* New York: Harper and Brothers.

Felman, Shoshana (1993). *What Does a Woman Want?: Reading and Sexual Difference.* Baltimore and London: Johns Hopkins University Press.

Felski, Rita (1989). *Beyond Feminist Aesthetics: Feminist Literature and Social Change.* Cambridge: Harvard University Press.

Felski, Rita (1998). "On Confession". In: *Women, Autobiography, Theory: A Reader.* Ed. Sidonie Smith and Julia Watson. Madison: University of Wisconsin Press. 67-89.

Foster, Edward Halsey (1992). *Understanding the Beats.* Columbia: University of Southern Carolina Press.

Foucault, Michel (1980). *The History of Sexuality.* Vol. 1. New York: Vintage Books.

Frazer, Brenda (1997). "Breaking out of D.C." In: *A Different Beat: Writings by Women of the Beat Generation.* Ed. Richard Peabody. New York: High Risk. 60-64.

Friedan, Betty (1963). *The Feminine Mystique.* New York: Dell.

Friedman, Susan Stanford (1998). "Women's Autobiographical Selves: Theory and Practice". In: *Women, Autobiography, Theory.* Ed. Sidonie Smith and Julia Watson. Madison: The University of Wisconsin Press. 64-85.

Gifford, Barry, ed. (1977). *As Ever: The Collected Correspondence of Allen Ginsberg and Neal Cassady.* Berkeley: Creative Arts Book Company.

Gifford, Barry, and Lawrence Lee (1978). *Jack's Book.* New York: St. Martin's Press.

Gilmore, Leigh (1994). *Autobiographics: A Feminist Theory of Women's Self-Representation.* Ithaka: Cornell University Press.

Ginsberg, Allen (2006). *Howl and Other Poems.* San Francisco: City Lights Books.

Works Cited

Ginsberg, Allen (1984). "Howl". *Collected Poems: 1947 – 80*. New York: Harper and Row.

Ginsberg, Allen (1984). *Collected Poems: 1947 – 80*. New York: Harper and Row.

Ginsberg, Allen (1966). "The Art of Poetry VII". *The Paris Review*. 10. 37: 36.

Ginsburg, Faye D. (1998). *Contested Lives: The Abortion Debate in an American Community.* Berkeley: University of California Press.

Goodman, Paul (1960). *Growing Up Absurd. Problems of Youth in the Organized System.* New York: Random House.

Gordon, Linda (1977). *Woman's Body, Woman's Right: A Social History of Birth Control in America.* New York: Penguin.

Grace Nancy (1999). "Women of the Beat Generation: Conversations with Joyce Johnson and Hettie Jones." *Artful Dodge* 36/37: 106-133.

Grace, Nancy M. and Ronna C. Johnson (2004). *Breaking the Rule of Cool. Interviewing and Reading Women Beat Writers.* Jackson: University Press of Mississippi.

Grace, Nancy M. (2002). "Snapshots, Sand Paintings, and Celluloid". In: *Girls Who Wore Black. Women Writing the Beat Generation.* Ed. Ronna C. Johnson and Nancy Grace. New Brunswick: Rutgers University Press. 141-177.

Graebner, William (1990). *Coming of Age in Buffalo: Youth and Authority in the Postwar Era.* Philadelphia: Temple University Press.

Gubar, Susan (1981). "'The Blank Page' and Issues of Female Creativity". *Critical Inquiry* 8.2: 243-264.

Gunn, Drewey Wayne (1974). *American and British Writers in Mexico, 1556-1973.* Austin: University of Texas Press.

Gusdorf, Georges (1980). „Conditions and Limits of Autobiography." In: *Autobiography: Theoretical and Critical Essays.* Ed. James Olney. Princeton: Princeton UP. 28-48.

Hampl, Patricia (1996). "Memory and Imagination". In: *The Anatomy of Memory*. Ed. James McConkey. Oxford: Oxford University Press.

Harris, William J. (1999). *The LeRoi Jones/Amiri Baraka Reader.* New York: Thunder's Mouth Press.

Hart, Francis (1970). "Notes for an Anatomy of Modern Autobiography". *New Literary History* 1: 481-492.

Hartman, Susan M. (1982). *The Homefront and Beyond: American Women in the 1940s.* Boston, MA: Twayne.

Heilbrun, Carolyn G. (1999). "Contemporary Memoirs: Or, Who Cares Who Did What to Whom?" *The American Scholar Summer* 1999: 41.

Heilbrun, Carolyn G. (1989). *Writing a Woman's Life*. New York: W.W. Norton.

Works Cited

Hemmer, Kurt Richard (2000). "Cowboys Crashing: The Beat Generation and the American Western Outlaw". *Dissertation* Washington State University.

Hepworth, Mike and Brian S. Turner (1982). *Confession: Studies in Deviance and Religion*. London: Routledge and Kegan Paul.

Holmes, John Clellon (1952). "This is the Beat Generation". *New York Times* Magazine 16. Nov. 1952 10-22.

Holton, Robert (2004). "Beat Culture and the Folds of Heterogeneity". In: *Reconstructing the Beats*. Ed. Jennie Skerl. New York: Palgrave. 11-26.

Holton, Robert (1999). *On the Road. Kerouac's Ragged American Journey*. New York: Twayne Publishers.

hooks, bell (2000). *Feminist Theory: From Margin to Center*. Boston: South End Press.

hooks, bell (1989). *Talking Back, Thinking Feminist, Thinking Black*. Boston: South End Press.

Horemans, Rudi, ed. (1985). *Beat Indeed!* Antwerp: EXA.

Hornung, Alfred and Ernstpeter Ruhe, ed. (1998). "Preface". In: *Postcolonialism and Autobiography*. Amsterdam: Rodopi BV. 1-6.

James, Henry (1948). *The Art of Fiction and Other Essays*. New York: Oxford University Press.

Jelinek, Estelle C. (1980). "Introduction: Women's Autobiography and the Male Tradition." In: *Women's Autobiography: Essays in Criticism*. Ed. Estelle Jelinek. Bloomington: Indiana University Press. 1-20.

Jelinek, Estelle C., ed. (1980). *Women's Autobiography: Essays in Criticism*. Bloomington: Indiana University Press.

Jezer, Mary (1982). *The Dark Ages: Life in the United States, 1945-1960*. Boston: South End Press.

Johnson, Joyce and Jack Kerouac (2001). *Door Wide Open: A Beat Love Affair in Letters, 1957-1958*. New York: Penguin.

Johnson, Ronna C. and Nancy M. Grace (2002). *Girls who Wore Black. Women Writing the Beat Generation*. New Brunswick: Rutgers.

Jones, Hettie (2003). *All Told*. New York: Hanging Loose Press.

Jones, Hettie (1998). *Drive. Poems*. New York: Hanging Loose Press.

Jones, LeRoi (1964). *Dutchman and The Slave*. New York: Morrow.

Jones, LeRoi (1960). "How You Sound". In: *The New American Poetry*. Ed. Donald Allen. New York: Grove Press. 424-445.

Jones, LeRoi (1997). *The Autobiography of LeRoi Jones/Amiri Baraka*. Chicago: Lawrence Hill Books.

Keitel, Evelyne (1983). "Verständigungstexte – Form, Funktion, Wirkung". *German Quarterly* 56 (3): 430-449.

Works Cited

Kerouac, Jack (1978). *Desolation Angels*. New York: Capricorn Books.

Kerouac, Jack (1993). *Old Angel Midnight*. San Francisco: Grey Fox.

Kerouac, Jack (1991). *On the Road*. London: Penguin.

Kerouac, Jack (1990). *Mexico City Blues*. New York: Grove Weidenfeld.

Kerouac, Jack (1995). *Selected Letters 1940-1956*. Ed. Ann Charters. New York: Viking.

Kerouac, Jack (1958). *The Dharma Bums*. New York: Viking Press.

Kerouac, Jack (1979). "The Origins of the Beat Generation". In: *On the Road: Text and Criticism*. Ed. Scott Donaldson. New York: Viking Press.

Kerouac, Jack (1981). *The Subterraneans*. New York: Grove Press.

Kerouac, Jack (1993). *Visions of Cody*. New York: Penguin.

Kerouac, Jan (1998). *Baby Driver*. New York: Thunder's Mouth.

Kingston, Maxine Hong (1989). *The Woman Warrior: Memoirs of a Girlhood among Ghosts*. New York: Vintage Books.

Knight, Arthur and Kit Knight, ed. (1988). *Kerouac and the Beats*. New York: Paragon House.

Knight, Arthur and Kit Knight (1982). *Beat Angels*. California: Unspeakable Visions of the Individual.

Knight, Brenda (2000). *Women of the Beat Generation. The Writers, Artists and Muses at the Heart of a Revolution.* Berkeley: Conari Press.

Kornbluth, Jesse (1968). *Notes from the New Underground*. New York: Viking Press.

Kristeva, Julia (1981). "Oscillation between Power and Denial". Interview. Trans. Marilyn A. August. In: *New French Feminisms*. Ed. Elaine Marks and Isabelle de Courtivron. New York: Schocken. 165-167.

Kristeva, Julia (1984). *Revolution in Poetic Language*. New York: Columbia University Press.

Kroeger, Rebecca Lynn (2001). "'Why were the Most Gifted of People also the Most Barren?' Sterilities and Fertilities in Twentieth-Century Subcultures". *Dissertation* University of Virginia.

Landau, Ellen G. (1989). *Jackson Pollock*. New York: Abrams.

Laub, Dori and Shoshana Felman (1992). *Testimony: Crises of Witnessing in Literature, Psychoanalysis, and History.* New York: Routledge.

Lauber, Lynn (1990). *White Girls*. New York: W.W. Norton.

Leavitt, Craig (2001). "On the Road: Cassady, Kerouac, and Images of Late Western Masculinity". In: *Across the Great Divide: Cultures of Manhood in the American West*. Ed. Matthew Basso. New York: Routledge. 112-131.

Lewis, George (1972). Side-Saddle on the Golden Calf: Social Structure and Popular Culture in America. Pacific Palisades, CA: Goodyear Publishing.

Works Cited

Lionnet, Francoise and Ronnie Scharfman, ed. (1993). *Post/Colonial Conditions: Exiles, Migrations, and Nomadisms*. New Haven: Yale University Press.

Lipsitz, George (1982). *Class and Culture in Cold War America*. South Hadley, Mass.: J.F. Bergin.

Mailer, Norman (1959). *Advertisements for Myself*. London: Transworld Publishers.

Mailer, Norman (1957). *The White Negro: Superficial Reflections on the Hipster*. San Francisco: City Lights.

Marcus, Laura (1995). "Theories of Autobiography: The Face of Autobiography" (Part 1). In: *The Uses of Autobiography*. Ed. Julia Swindells. London: Taylor and Francis. 13-23.

Marmor, Marcel T. (1980). *Homosexual Behavior*. New York: Basic Books.

Martin, Biddy (1998). "Lesbian Identity and Autobiographical Difference". In: *Women, Autobiography, Theory: A Reader*. Ed. Sidonie Smith and Julia Watson. Madison: University of Wisconsin Press. 380-392.

Martinez, Manuel Luis (1998). "'With Imperious Eye': Kerouac, Burroughs, and Ginsberg on the Road in South America". *Aztlan* 23.1: 33-53.

Mason, Mary G. and Carol Hurd Green, ed. (1979). *Journeys: Autobiographical Writings for Women*. Boston: G. K. Hall.

May, Elaine Tyler (1988). *Homeward Bound: American Families in the Cold War Era*. New York: Basic.

May, Elaine Tyler (1994). *Pushing the Limits: American Women 1940-1961, Volume Nine*. Oxford University Press: New York.

McCormick, Donald (1992). *Erotic Literature: A Connoisseur's Guide*. New York: Continuum.

McDarrah, Fred, ed. (1985). *Kerouac and Friends*. New York: Morrow.

McNally, Dennis (1979). *Desolate Angel: Jack Kerouac, the Beat Generation and America*. New York: McGraw-Hill.

McNeil, Helen (1996). "The Archaeology of Gender in the Beat Movement". In: *The Beat Generation Writers*. Ed. A. Robert Lee. London: Pluto Press. 199-223.

Meyer Spacks, Patricia. "Selves in Hiding". In: *Women's Autobiography: Essays in Criticism*. Ed. Estelle Jelinek. Bloomington: Indiana University Press. 112-132.

Meyerowitz, Joanne (1994). Beyond the Feminine Mystique. A Reassessment of Postwar Mass Culture, 1946-1958." In: *Not June Cleaver: Women and Gender in Postwar America, 1945-1960*. Ed. Joanne Meyerowitz. Philadelphia: Temple University Press. 229-262.

Miles, Barry (1989). *Ginsberg: A Biography*. New York: Simon and Schuster.

Miles, Barry (1998). *Jack Kerouac. King of the Beats*. New York: Henry Holt.

Miller, Nancy K. (2000). "But Enough About me, What do you Think of my Memoir?" *The Yale Journal of Criticism* 13.2: 421-436.

Miller, Nancy K. (1980). "Toward a Dialectics of Difference". In: *Women and Language in Literature and Society.* Ed. Sally McConnell-Ginet, Ruth Borker, and Nelly Furman. New York: Praeger. 258-273.

Millett, Kate (1977). *Sita.* London: Virago.

Misch, Georg (1950). *History of Autobiography.* London: Routledge and Kegan Paul.

Mitchell, Juliet (1986). "Reflections on Twenty Years of Feminism." In: *What is Feminism. A Re-Examination.* Ed. Juliet Mitchell and Ann Oakley. New York: Pantheon Books. 34-48.

Modell, Arnold H. (1993). *The Private Self.* Cambridge: Harvard University Press.

Moke, Susan (1998). "Desires of their Own. Twentieth-Century Women Novelists and Images of the Erotic". *Dissertation* Indiana University.

Morgan, Ted (1988). *Literary Outlaw: The Life and Times of William S. Burroughs.* New York: Holt.

Morris, Aldon D. (1984). *The Origins of the Civil Rights Movement.* New York: Free Press.

Nestle, Joan (1992). *The Persistent Desire: A Femme-Butch Reader.* Boston: Alyson.

Nicosia, Gerald (1994). *Memory Babe: A Critical Biography of Jack Kerouac.* Berkeley: University of California Press.

Oates, Joyce Carol (1991). *Because it is Bitter, and Because it is my Heart.* New York: Plume Books.

Offenbach, Judith (1998). *Sonja: Eine Melancholie für Fortgeschrittene.* Frankfurt am Main: Suhrkamp.

Olney, James (1980). "Autobiography and the Cultural Movement: a Thematic, Historical, and Bibliographical Introduction". In: *Autobiography, Essays Theoretical and Critical.* Ed. James Olney. Princeton: Princeton University Press. 3-27.

Olvera, Joe (1991). "A Review of Jack Kerouac's Tristessa". *Moody Street Irregulars. A Jack Kerouac Magazine.* 4: 12-13.

Orenstein, Gloria Feman (1979). "The Salon of Natalie Clifford Barney: An Interview with Berthe Cleyrergue". *SIGNS* 4.3: 484-496.

Peabody, Richard (1997). *A Different Beat: Writings by Women of the Beat Generation.* New York: High Risk.

Penn, Donna (1994). „The Sexualized Woman. The Lesbian, the Prostitute, and the Containment of Female Sexuality in Postwar America." In: *Not June Cleaver: Women and Gender in Postwar America, 1945-1960.* Ed. J. Meyerowitz. Philadelphia: Temple University Press. 358-381.

Perkins, Michael (1983). "Bonnie Bremser". In: *The Beats: Literary Bohemians in Postwar America. Dictionary of Literary Biography.* Vol. 16. Detroit: Bruccoli Clark Book. 33-35.

Perkins, Michael (1976). *The Secret Record: Modern Erotic Literature.* New York: Morrow.

Perry, Paul and Ken Babbs (1990). *On the Bus: The Complete Guide to the Legendary Trip of Ken Kesey and the Merry Pranksters.* New York: Thunder's Mouth Press.

Works Cited

Personal Narratives Group (1989). *Interpreting Women's Lives: Feminist Theory and Personal Narratives.* Bloomington: Indiana University Press.

Pinsker, Sanford (2003). "The Landscape of Contemporary American Memoir." *Sewanee Review* 111.1: 311–20.

Plath, Sylvia (1999). *The Bell Jar*. New York: Harper Collins.

Plimpton, George, ed. (1977). *Writers at Work: The "Paris Review Interviews"*. New York: Penguin.

Plummer, William (1981). *The Holy Goof: A Biography of Neal Cassady*. New York: Paragon House.

Polsky, Ned (1967). *Hustlers, Beats, and Others.* Chicago: Aldine Publishing Company.

Pomerleau, Cynthia S. (1980). "The Emergence of Women's Autobiography in England". In: *Women's Autobiography: Essays in Criticism.* Ed. Estelle C. Jelinek. Bloomington : Indiana University Press. 21-38.

Purvis June, ed. (1994). "Doing Feminist Women's History: Researching the Lives of Women in the Suffragette Movement in Edwardian England". In: *Researching Women's Lives from a Feminist Perspective*. London: Taylor & Francis. 166-189.

Quinn, Roseanne Giannini (2003). "'The Willingness to Speak': Diane di Prima and Italian American Feminist Body Politics." *MELUS* 28.3: 175-193.

Rainer, Gerald et. al. (2002). Stichwort Literatur. Geschichte der deutschsprachigen Literatur. Linz: Veritas.

Rawlings, Wendy (2005). "Just Beneath my Skin: Autobiography and Self-Discovery". *Fourth Genre: Explorations in Nonfiction* 7.1: 182-184.

Rosen, Marjorie (1973). *Popcorn Venus: Women, Movies, and the American Dream*. New York: Coward, McCann, and Geoghegan.

Ross, Andrew (1989). No Respect: Intellectuals and Popular Culture. New York: Routledge.

Rothman, Ellen K. (1984). Hands and Hearts: A History of Courtship in America. New York: Basic Books.

Rousseau, Jean Jaques (1953). *Confessions*. Harmondsworth: Penguin.

Rowbotham, Sheila (1992). *Women in Movement. Feminism and Social Action.* New York: Routledge.

Rowbotham, Sheila (1973). *Women's Consciousness, Men's World*. Baltimore: Penguin.

Ruzek, Sheryl (1986). "Feminist Visions of Health: An International Perspective". In: *What is Feminism? A Re-Examination.* Ed. Juliet Mitchell and Ann Oakley. New York: Pantheon Books. 184-207.

Sanders Valerie (1989). *The Private Lives of Victorian Women: Autobiography in Nineteenth-Century England*. Hertfordshire: Harvester Wheatsheaf.

Sandison, David (1999). *Jack Kerouac: An Illustrated Biography*. Chicago: Octopus Publishing Group.

Satin, Joseph (1960). *The 1950s: America's Placid Decade*. Boston: Houghton Mifflin.

Works Cited

Savran, David (1998). *Taking it like a Man. White Masculinity, Masochism, and Contemporary American Culture*. Princeton: Princeton University Press.

Schumacher, Michael (1992). *Dharma Lion: A Biography of Allen Ginsberg*. New York: St. Martin's Press.

Scott, Joan (1998). "Experience". In: *Women, Autobiography, Theory.* Ed. Sidonie Smith and Julia Watson. Madison: The University of Wisconsin Press. 42-63.

Sedgwick, Eve (1990). *Epistemology of the Closet.* Berkeley: University of California Press.

Sedgwick, Eve (1993). *Tendencies*. Durham: Duke University Press.

Shulman, Alix Kates (1990). *Burning Questions – My Life as a Rebel*. New York: Thunder's Mouth.

Shulman, Alix Kates (1997). *Memoirs of an Ex-Prom Queen*. New York: Penguin.

Shulman, Alix Kates (1989). "The Beat Queens. Boho Chicks Stand by their Men". *Village Voice Literary Supplement*. June 1989. 18+.

Siddons, Anne Rivers (1993). *Heartbreak Hotel*. New York: Harper Collins.

Slooten, Jessica Lyn van (2003). "Amen the Thunderbolt and the Dark Void: Spirituality and Gender in the Works of Male and Female Writers of the Beat Generation". *Dissertation* Auburn University.

Smith, Patrick (1998, July 27 – August 3). "What Memoir Forgets". *The Nation.* 30-33.

Smith, Sidonie (1987). A Poetics of Women's Autobiography: Marginality and the Fictions of Self-Representation. Bloomington: Indiana University Press.

Smith, Sidonie (1998). "Performativity, Autobiographical Practice, Resistance". In: *Women, Autobiography, Theory: A Reader*. Edited by Sidonie Smith and Julia Watson. Madison: University of Wisconsin Press. 108-115.

Smith, Sidonie and Julia Watson (1992). *De/Colonizing the Subject: The Politics of Gender in Women's Autobiography.* Minneapolis: University of Minnesota Press.

Smith, Sidonie and Julia Watson (1998). *Women, Autobiography, Theory. A Reader*. Madison: University of Wisconsin Press.

Solinger, Rickie (1994). "Extreme Danger: Women Abortionists and Their Clients before Roe v. Wade". In: *Not June Cleaver: Women and Gender in Postwar America, 1945-1960*. Ed. J. Meyerowitz. Philadelphia: Temple University Press. 335-357.

Solinger, Rickie (1998). "Pregnancy and Power before *Roe v. Wade*, 1950-1970". In: *Abortion Wars: A Half Century of Struggle, 1950-2000*. Ed. Rickie Solinger. Berkeley: University of California Press.

Solinger, Rickie (1992). *Wake Up Little Susie: Single Pregnancy and Race in the Pre-Roe v. Wade Era, A Cultural Study*. New York: Routledge.

Sorrell, Richard S. (1982). "Novelists and Ethnicity: Jack Kerouac and Grace Metalious as Franco-Americans". *MELUS* 9.1: 37-52.

Works Cited

Spengemann, William C. (1980). The Forms of Autobiography: Episodes in the History of a Literary Genre. New Haven: Yale UP.

Spengler, Oswald (1991). *The Decline of the West*. New York: Oxford University Press.

Stanton, Domna C. (1984). "Autogynography: Is the subject different?". In: *The Female Autograph*. Ed. Stanton. New York: New York Literary Forum. 3-20.

Stanton, Domna C., ed. (1984). *The Female Autograph*. New York: New York Literary Forum.

Struck, Karin (1982). *Kindheits Ende*. Frankfurt am Main: Suhrkamp.

Sturdevant, Saudra and Brenda Stoltzfuss (1995). "Why the Women do it: The Sale of Women's Sexual Labor". *Feminist Collections* 16.2: 81-86.

Sukenick, Ronald (1987). *Down and In: Life in the Underground*. New York: Beech Tree Books.

Suleiman, Susan (1994). *Risking who one is: Encounters with Contemporary Art and Literature*. Cambridge: Harvard University Press.

Theado, Matt, ed. (2001). *The Beats. A Documentary Volume*. Dictionary of Literary Biography 237. Detroit: The Gale Group.

Tomm, Winnie (1995). *Bodied Mindfulness: Women's Spirits, Bodies, and Places*. Waterloo: Wilfried Laurier University Press.

Tribe, Laurence H. (1992). *Abortion: The Clash of Absolutes*. New York: W.W. Norton.

Tyler May, Elaine (1988). *Homeward Bound: American Families in the Cold War Era*. New York: Basic Books.

Tyler May, Elaine (1994). *Pushing the Limits. American Women 1940 – 1961*. New York: Oxford University Press.

van Slooten, Jessica Lyn (2003). "Amen the Thunderbolt and the Dark Void: Spirituality and Gender in the Works of Female and Male Writers of the Beat Generation". *Dissertation* Auburn University.

Watson, Steven (1998). *The Birth of the Beat Generation: Visionaries, Rebels, and Hipsters, 1944-1960*. New York: Pantheon.

Watten, Barrett (2002). "What I See in *How I Became Hettie Jones*". In: *Girls Who Wore Black. Women Writing the Beat Generation*. Ed. Ronna C. Johnson and Nancy Grace. New Brunswick: Rutgers University Press. 96-118.

West, Robin (1987). "The Feminist-Conservative Anti-Pornography Alliance and the 1986 Attorney General's Commission on Pornography Report". *American Bar Foundation Research Journal* 12.4: 681-711.

Wilson, Elizabeth (2000). *Bohemians. The Glamorous Outcasts*. New York: I.B. Tauris & Co. Ltd.

Wilson, Elizabeth (1991). "Bohemian Love". *Theory, Culture & Society* 15.3: 37-57.

Wolfe, Tom (1968). *The Electric Kool-Aid Acid Test*. New York: Bantam.

Works Cited

Wong, Hertha D. Sweet (1998). "First-Person Plural: Subjectivity and Community in Native American Women's Autobiography". In: *Women, Autobiography, Theory: A Reader*. Ed. Sidonie Smith and Julia Watson. Madison: University of Wisconsin Press. 162-178.

Young, Iris (1990). "Humanism, Gynocentrism and Feminist Politics". In: *Throwing Like a Girl: and Other Essays in Feminist Philosophy and Social Theory*. Ed. Iris Young. Indianapolis: Indiana UP. 77-96.

"Buddhistisches Liebeslexikon". *Cosmopolitan.* May 2005: 64-66.

Der Brockhaus in Drei Bänden (2004). Band 3. Leipzig: F.A. Brockhaus GmbH.

Meyers Grosses Taschenlexikon (1999). Band 12. Mannheim: B.I. Taschenbuchverlag.

Webster's College Dictionary (2003). New York: Random House.

Internet Sources

"A Chronology: Key Moments in the Clinton-Lewinsky Saga". *CNN.* July 28, 2006.
http://www.cnn.com/ALLPOLITICS/1998/resources/lewinsky/timeline/

"Allison Landsberg". *Cultural Studies: University of Chicago*. February 12, 2007.
http://culturalstudies.gmu.edu/faculty/faculty_bios/landsberg.html

"Erotica and Pornography". An Encyclopaedia of Gay, Lesbian, Bisexual, Transgender & Queer Culture. September 7, 2006.
http://www.glbtq.com/literature/erotica_pornography.html

Broin, Valerie E. (2001). "Standing in the Way of Truth: Understanding Narratives of Domestic Violence". *International Journal of Philosophical Practice*. August 29, 2006.
http://web.csustan.edu/Philosophy/Data/Broin/Standing.html

di Prima, Diane (1981). "Cool". *The Shocking Tabloid Issues*. January 8, 2007.
http://www.researchpubs.com/books/tab2exc1.php

Frazer, Brenda (1997). "Poets and Oddfellows". *The Blacklisted Journalist*. August 14, 2006.
http://www.bigmagic.com/pages/blackj/column74d1.html

Frazer, Brenda (1997). "Do you Believe?". *The Blacklisted Journalist*. August 14, 2006.
http://www.bigmagic.com/pages/blackj/column74d2.html

Frazer, Brenda (1997). "Breaking out of D.C.". *The Blacklisted Journalist*. August 14, 2006.
http://www.bigmagic.com/pages/blackj/column74d3.html

Frazer, Brenda (1997). "Changes (May 1959)". *The Blacklisted Journalist*. August 14, 2006.
http://www.bigmagic.com/pages/blackj/column74d4.html

Frazer, Brenda (1997). "The Village Scene". *The Blacklisted Journalist*. August 14, 2006.
http://www.bigmagic.com/pages/blackj/column74d5.html

Frazer, Brenda (1997). "Triptych USA". *The Blacklisted Journalist.* August 14, 2006.
http://www.bigmagic.com/pages/blackj/column74d6.html

Works Cited

Frazer, Brenda (1997). "California Come-Down". *The Blacklisted Journalist.* August 14, 2006. http://www.bigmagic.com/pages/blackj/column74d7.html

Frazer, Brenda (1997). "How to be a Poet's Wife". *The Blacklisted Journalist.* August 14, 2006. http://www.bigmagic.com/pages/blackj/column74d8.html

Frazer, Brenda (1997). "Hoboken". *The Blacklisted Journalist.* August 14, 2006. http://www.bigmagic.com/pages/blackj/column74d9.html

Huffman, Emily. "Rhetorical Analysis – Maxine Hong Kingston's The Woman Warrior". September 15, 2006.
http://www.cwrl.utexas.edu/~waddington/web309/EMILY9.HTM

Jones, Hettie. "The Book that Changed my Life". *National Book Foundation. Presenter of the National Book Awards.* March 22, 2006. http://www.nationalbook.org/bookchanged_hjones_nbm.html

Morrisey, Brian. "An Interview with Diane di Prima". *POESY – An Anthology.* April 21, 2006. http://www.poesy.org/interviews.html

Solanas, Valerie "The SCUM Manifesto". *Gifts of Speech.* September 3, 2006. http://gos.sbc.edu/s/solanas.html

www.ingramcontent.com/pod-product-compliance
Lightning Source LLC
Chambersburg PA
CBHW080550230426
43663CB00015B/2783